The Diary *of a* Cricketer's Wife

Best Wishes

The Diary *of a* Cricketer's Wife

A Very UNUSUAL Memoir

PUJA PUJARA
WITH NAMITA KALA

HarperCollins *Publishers* India

First published in India by HarperCollins *Publishers* 2025
HarperCollins *Publishers* India, Cyber City,
Building 10-A, Gurugram, Haryana – 122002, India
www.harpercollins.co.in

2 4 6 8 10 9 7 5 3 1

Copyright © Puja Pujara 2025

P-ISBN: 978-93-6989-616-5
E-ISBN: 978-93-6569-907-4

The views and opinions expressed in this book are the author's own
and the facts are as reported by her, and the publishers
are not in any way liable for the same.

Puja Pujara asserts the moral right
to be identified as the author of this work.

All rights reserved. No part of this publication may be reproduced,
stored in a retrieval system, or transmitted, in any form or by any means,
electronic, mechanical, photocopying, recording or otherwise,
without the prior permission of the publishers.

Without limiting the exclusive rights of any author, contributor or the publisher
of this publication, any unauthorized use of this publication to train generative
artificial intelligence (AI) technologies is expressly prohibited. HarperCollins
also exercise their rights under Article 4(3) of the Digital Single Market
Directive 2019/790 and expressly reserve this publication from the
text and data-mining exception.

Typeset in 11.5/15 Adobe Garamond Pro
by HarperCollins *Publishers* India Pvt. Ltd

Printed and bound at
Thomson Press (India) Ltd

This book is produced from independently certified FSC® paper
to ensure responsible forest management.

HarperCollins *Publishers*, Macken House, 39/40 Mayor Street Upper, Dublin 1,
D01 C9W8, Ireland

To our parents

Contents

Author's Note   ix

PART ONE

1. A Game of Chance   3
2. Clean Bowled   13
3. Cheteshwar Comes a-Courting   24
4. A Whirlwind Betrothal, a Game of Cricket and Media Attention   36

PART TWO

5. In the Beginning   55
6. In the Maidans of Mumbai   70
7. My Friend Kuldeep   82
8. Mother o' Mine   95
9. The Anatomy of Pain and the Triumph of the Spirit   109
10. Déjà vu   124

PART THREE

11.	Jab We Wed	137
12.	A Short Vacation and Other Stories	149
13.	By Force of Habit	161
14.	The Fitness Revolution Comes to India	171
15.	Snakes and Ladders	187
16.	Miracles Do Happen	199
17.	Enceinte	209

PART FOUR

18.	Separate Rooms	225
19.	The Test	234
20.	The Year of the Pandemic	249
21.	The Ultimate Test Series	264
22.	Coping with Covid	275
23.	The Fight for Form	287
	Envoi	303
	Notes	313

Author's Note

Cheteshwar Pujara is a man of few words and fewer expressions. If a smile can do the job, he prefers not to speak. If a sentence can end in three words, he will make no attempt to add another. It is a complaint I have had against him for the longest time. My husband is stubborn, yet accommodating, secretive but with nothing to hide. He is spiritual without being sanctimonious and loves cracking silly jokes.

For someone who has travelled around the world, overcome incredible hardships and enjoyed unprecedented success, he is not very social. Yet, despite his reserve, he never says no to anyone, even if the request is made by a stranger; he will always go that extra mile, sometimes at great personal cost. He doesn't know how to relax, but is always at peace.

Cheteshwar has seen the worst of times—days of intense despair—yet, he does not know how to share his troubles or lighten his load. He keeps things bottled up, but has it in him to let go. He is not the greatest-ever batsman to play the game, but his journey is unique—one that I have had the privilege to be a part of and witness from close quarters. I truly believe that there is something for everyone in the Cheteshwar Pujara story and that is why I have taken time out to write this book.

Puja Pujara

PART ONE

CHAPTER ONE

A Game of Chance

Destiny sneaked in slyly without notice, in the guise of a phone call at around half past ten, on the night of 18 September 2012. My world, as I knew it, was about to change. Not immediately. But soon enough. The call was to herald the onset of a whirlwind of events that would eventually lead me willy-nilly into marriage with Saurashtra's latest batting sensation, Cheteshwar Pujara. Not that I knew who he was at the time.

My work phone, a much-used Blackberry, rang, rupturing my thoughts, annihilating my rest. I was lounging in my usual spot on the brown L-shaped sofa in the drawing room, still clad in my office gear—a formal shirt shrugged over a pair of smart-looking trousers—as I quietly reflected over my day.

My bua (paternal aunt/father's sister), whom I addressed as Geeta didi (or elder sister), for reasons now lost in time, was sprawled at the other end. She was unmarried; more like an older sibling than an aunt, except when she pulled rank on me now and then, as if to establish the exact nature of our relationship, just in case it ever slipped my mind.

I sighed as I groped for my phone which had slipped into a crevice in the sofa. I peered at the instrument. My fufaji's (bua's husband/uncle), name flashed on the screen. My eyes widened. Why was he calling me at this time of the night?

It must be important, I thought.

I sighed once more, not particularly keen to haul my now-relaxed body into a fresh spell of action just when I had managed to lull it into a comfortable state of inertia; the sofa was my sacred space; it was here that I shed my weariness and allowed myself to unwind, letting the various vagaries of my work day seep away.

Grudgingly, I got up, padding across the drawing room to step outside into the front porch; as the television was on at sufficiently high volume, it precluded all possibility of any lucid conversation indoors. I flopped onto the swing, a white wrought-iron three-seater thingamajig, completely oblivious to the pleasant post-monsoon breeze, the sweet scent of jasmines or the borsalis, tulsis, purple and butterfly peas that grew gaily amidst a few trees. I pressed the green button to accept the call. 'Hello,' I said.

'Get ready to travel,' fufaji boomed from the other end of the line.

'Haan, what?' I asked, startled. 'What are you saying?'

My brain switched modes and started racing at top speed, trying to make sense of fufaji's words. My family was not too happy about my current job at Vodafone; being a business family, the very idea of working for someone else was widely viewed as an outrage by my kin. They had been waging an incessant war to get me to chuck work and branch out on my own, ever since I had joined the company. 'I'll fund you,' my father would say enticingly. It was a promise made like clockwork, at regular intervals. But I held out, unmoved; my MBA training, always at war with the notion of plunging into business without a shred of experience. *Perhaps, fufaji has stumbled on to some exciting business prospect for me*, I thought, resignedly.

'Have you heard of Cheteshwar Pujara,' he asked, cutting into my thoughts.

'No,' I replied laconically. 'Who's he?'

'Oh,' he said, much saddened by this admission. 'He plays for the Indian cricket team. He's from the Lohana community like us, and he's from Rajkot itself. I've seen him play. He's wonderful!'

He waxed on eloquent. I heard him out, unimpressed. My knowledge of cricket would not fill out a postage stamp. But I could hardly tell him that. By now I had figured out what was coming and I braced myself for the impending grenade. I did not have to wait very long.

'We are trying to fix him up with you. His biodata will be coming to me soon, and I think both of you will be a good match.'

Really? I was not quite twenty-four years old, poised at the threshold of what looked like a promising management career; a serious employee who worked twelve-to-fourteen hours a day—and fufaji was holding forth on marriage as if it was the best thing since the discovery of fire in the old stone age? I couldn't believe it. Why was this cricketing hero amenable to the whole idea? Parental pressure?

I knew what was driving my family. In their eyes, I was now of marriageable age and they would be failing their duty by me if they did not get me 'settled' with some 'decent boy'. This was not the first time a member of my kith and kin had tried to 'fix' me up with some promising suitor, and I already had a fairly long history of deftly side-stepping all the snares that had been flung my way, despite my relative youth. I pondered on the problem at hand. What chance was there of a celeb-type being interested in someone ordinary like me? Minus ten on a scale of hundred, I concluded. I took heart from this happy fact and cheered up. Aloud, I said, 'Have you spoken to Dad?'

'I thought I'd speak to you first,' he answered. 'May I proceed?' I thought it politic to keep my views on the matter to myself. He was a wonderful man and I loved him dearly. Dampening his fervour seemed unkind. 'Okay. Speak to Dad.'

Pleased, he said, 'I'll talk to your dad right away.' He hung up, a happy man, and I returned to my sacred spot on the sofa, convinced that the cricketer would reject me summarily. I just was not glamourous enough. Having arranged the issue in this neat fashion in my head I decided to go with the flow. 'Why should I be the bad guy?' I thought to myself. On this decisive note I firmly dismissed the said cricketer from my very weary mind and resolutely headed to bed.

The next day was unremarkable except that it was a weekend. Fufaji, Dad and I congregated in our drawing room that evening for our weekly Pizza Night in the absence of my brother Jeet and sister Dhara who were away at Gandhinagar and Bombay, respectively, along with my cousin Mitali, my fufaji's daughter. The older women, my mother and two aunts, were never party to these feasts because as Pushti Margis, or adherents of the Pushti Marg—a Vaishnava sect founded by Acharya Vallabha in the sixteenth century—they were forbidden from eating food cooked by non-believers. Acharya Vallabha had propounded this sect on the principle of Shuddha Advaita or pure non-dualism. His followers worshipped Bala Krishna, or Lord Krishna as a child, and sought nirvana through seva or service offered to the deity.

It was a strait restricted life, both demanding and rigorous, requiring my mother and aunts to offer full-day seva to their adored Laddoo Gopal, day after day, week after week, year after year; yet they did it willingly. A large part of their time revolved around bathing the deity, clothing and preparing meals for him. Since food for the divine child had to be prepared in a sacred space, there were two kitchens in our house; the main kitchen, where prasad was prepared, served as a kind of sanctum sanctorum where only my mother and aunts entered; the outer kitchen was open to everyone. Their devotion was jaw-dropping and I admired them tremendously, seeing in them a purity of purpose that was markedly absent in my own makeup. I could not help recognize the degree of determination it took to attain this all-encompassing surrender to God so cheerfully. It was incomprehensible to me, but still laudable.

On that particular evening my aunts were upstairs with my mother, who was busy packing for a forty-day pilgrimage, colloquially referred to as Baithakji by Pushti Margis. My father had been roped in to escort her for the journey the following day and the house was more or less in sixes and sevens. The general mood at home was one of distraction and to my immense relief, the cricketing idol failed to crop up in the conversation in the drawing room where fufaji, Dad and I were busily attacking pizzas, supremely isolated from the flurry of activities that were taking place in the upper storey. Our discussions mainly revolved around business, current affairs, the work culture in different cities in Saurashtra and general chit-chat.

The dreaded topic did come up briefly, however, when the women entered.

'Have you heard anything from the boy's side?' my father asked.

Fufaji shook his head. 'I've sent Puja's biodata to the Pujaras and I am waiting for a response from them. They haven't sent us one as yet.'

'What arrogance!' I thought, irritably. He must be imagining that there's not a soul in the country who does not know him!'

Luckily, everyone else was too wrapped up to notice my face. I looked like I had swallowed a dozen lemons.

'I think we'll have to give them at least forty-eight hours before we follow up,' Fufaji continued.

'What do you know about the boy?' Dad asked.

'He plays cricket for India,' fufaji replied, as if this mere fact was a clincher.

The announcement did not make any noticeable impression on my father and Geeta didi, because, like me, they did not follow cricket.

'I've seen him play,' announced my mother, astounding us all.

'You have?' I asked, dumbfounded.

'Dada and I watched him when he played the IPL in 2010. He's good.' She was an avid cricket fan and I knew that she had often sat with my then-ailing and now-deceased grandfather to watch many a match. A momentary pall of grief descended upon me. He had not been long dead and I still missed him acutely.

My uncle looked approvingly at my mother. 'Yes, I agree he's good. I hope they send us his biodata soon.'

'I don't know why you are all getting so excited about a random biodata,' I burst out, unable to help myself. 'Right now, it's all in the air. They haven't even responded yet.'

The edge in my voice was palpable enough to alert them that I was unamused, and the subject was thankfully dropped. The women soon disappeared to tackle the last of the packing, while Dad, fufaji and I consumed the remaining pizza. We chilled for a bit and chatted generally, careful not to stray into touchy topics. That night, I went to bed, repeatedly telling myself, *This guy will reject me. He's a celeb. Why will he want to marry me. He won't be interested and then they'll all stop bugging me.*

The next day, my parents left and, to my intense horror, Cheteshwar's biodata arrived.

It was unique; a no-brainer, without parallel. A single-paged tour de force of non-information, minus the usual photograph, it read as follows:

Date of Birth: 25-01-1988. Place of Birth: Rajkot. Address: Plot No. … Height: Blank. Weight: 76 kgs. Education: HSC in commerce, currently doing BBA (first year). Work: Professional cricket player and employee of Indian Oil Corporation (grade-A officer). Father's name: Arvind Pujara. Mother's Name: (Late) Reena Pujara. Maternal surname: Kanani. Siblings: None.

What was I to infer? This particular one-pager had 'NOT INTERESTED' written all over it. Or perhaps he had assumed that he was such a huge poster boy that I already knew what he looked like. I thought of all the biodatas of prospective bridegrooms that I had seen in the past—they had listed their interests, hobbies, travels, favourite foods, allowing me a pretty in-depth peek into their lives and persons. Our cricketing icon clearly did not have the faintest clue of the purpose that résumés served.

I was undisturbed, certain that my father would back me up, whatever I decided.

A phone call from fufaji at around half-past twelve in the afternoon put paid to those notions the very next day. 'Cheteshwar's dad, mama and mami want to meet you today,' he announced, sounding very upbeat. 'Cheteshwar won't be there.'

What? I thought, poleaxed by this highly unexpected twist of fate.

I kept my head and tried to weasel out of the meeting with a touch of tact. 'But Dad's not there. Shouldn't we wait for him to come back? And, in any case, if the guy is not there, what will I go and do there?'

'This is just an initial meeting,' he explained.

I needed to get back to work. I did not want anyone in the office getting the slightest whiff of what was going on in my private life. 'I can't talk to you right now. Speak to Dad. I'll call you at lunch,' I said, and quickly got off the phone.

At lunchtime, instead of calling my uncle, I called my dad. 'Do you know what's happened?' I asked.

'Yes. They want to meet you,' my father replied.

'Is it okay for me to go ahead with this meeting when you're not there,' desperately willing him to say it was not.

He didn't. 'It's just the first meeting. What's the harm? Go, meet them.'

Obedient child that I was, I caved in. 'Okay,' I said. I always treated Dad's word as final because we were very alike. He was progressive, open-minded and, usually, in tune with me.

Routed, I rang fufaji. I knew he would be anxiously waiting for my call. He had put the 'boy's side' on hold while he waited for me to give him the go ahead.

'Why is the boy not coming? I asked, curious. I wanted to know why my nemesis was absenting himself.

'He's in Bombay, playing a match.'

Hah! I thought. Aloud, I warned, 'Don't schedule anything before eight, because I'll only get back home at half past seven.'

An hour later, my uncle informed me that the meeting had been arranged for half-past eight that night. At around 3 p.m., Geeta didi buzzed me. 'You come home early. We'll go dress-shopping.'

I rolled my eyes. 'Not possible. I can't just take off from work.'

'What will you wear?' she queried. 'You have to think about that.'

'I'll come home and decide. There are so many clothes. I'll put on something,' I responded, itching to get back to work.

'You're not taking this seriously,' she accused. 'They are coming to see you.'

'Please understand, I can't cancel my meetings. In any case, the guy is also not there. So, it doesn't really matter.'

She made a strange sort of sound and I almost giggled. Clearly, my aunt was furious!

She was even more annoyed when I reached home slightly later than usual, at about a quarter to eight, and had the temerity to demand food instead of worrying about the evening ahead. She had already harried me several times over the phone while I was driving home to know when I would reach. She regarded my entry home with a distinctly belligerent eye and immediately launched into a tirade.

'Don't scold me,' I said, halting her words, mid-flow. 'You can shout at me later. I'm sorry I'm late. There was a lot of traffic. Give me food, I'm hungry. I'll get dressed and go and meet them after I've eaten.'

'Don't you want to go to a salon for a blow dry?' she asked, as I was halfway through my meal.

'No. My hair is fine.' Inwardly, I thought, I'm sure the fellow is not serious. I'm only doing this for you guys.

She looked even more livid. I quickly gulped down my dinner and fled upstairs to escape her wrath. I grabbed the first thing I found in my cupboard, a pastel green silk kurti with gold borders on the sleeves, and donned it over a pair of beige corduroy trousers. I ran a comb through my hair, put some kajal and checked my watch. It was eight fifteen.

I dashed down with the car keys to find my aunt waiting for me, looking ready to explode. But she held her peace, obviously chary of rattling me just before we met the Pujaras.

We made it to fufaji's house, which was just half a kilometre away, in two minutes flat, well in time for our first encounter with the Pujaras. But this did not stop Geeta didi from muttering, 'we'll be late,' over and over again.

'Why are you complaining?' I said, somewhat triumphantly. 'We're ahead of time. Come on.'

What I left unsaid was the unspoken expectation that we shared, that the Pujaras would make us wait. Tardiness was an embedded tradition in Rajkot. Nobody was ever on time. The Lohana community to which we belonged was particularly notorious for unpunctuality. People were known to run an hour late, and both Geeta didi and I had resigned ourselves to our impending fate.

And then the tide turned.

The Pujaras were a pleasant surprise. At least Pujara senior was! The doorbell at fufaji's apartment, which was on the second floor, rang at 8.30 p.m., sharp. I had never come across a family that valued other people's time in Rajkot, except my own.

Fufaji ushered them across the wooden floor to the drawing room. It was a short convivial meeting that lasted for all of fifteen minutes. No mention was made of the batting maestro beyond the fact that he was busy playing matches in Bombay and therefore had been unable to come. His aunt took the opportunity to ask me the usual questions such as 'where have you studied?', 'what do you do?' and a few more queries along the same lines.

There was a small awkward pause as she fell silent.

It was breached by Cheteshwar's father in what was to be our first and only exchange that evening. 'Your uncle is sitting here. He runs a factory—you've done your masters in business administration. Who do you think is smarter—you or your uncle?'

I did not need to think. 'My uncle, of course,' I said at once.

'Why?'

'Because he has business experience, whereas I've only studied about it.'

He smiled beatifically.

I smiled back.

CHAPTER TWO

Clean Bowled

Peace reigned in my world for seven blissful days. No message, no phone call, no response, nothing. The Pujaras were maintaining strict radio silence, driving my family, the Pabaris, completely round the bend. My father had returned by this time, and speculation within the clan was endless. Were they inclined? Were they not inclined? Were they interested? Were they not interested. Nobody really had a clue. I found this never-ending guessing game tiresome, yet amusing.

I was not particularly interested in the outcome myself, having banished the Pujara family and their sporty scion firmly from my mind, quite convinced that Mr Cricketer would not bite bait.

I was wrong, and the calm—as it turned out—was just a short lull before the coming storm.

Fufaji buzzed me at work on 27 September. *This is becoming a habit*, I thought tetchily. He told me that 'the boy' wished to see me.

I kept my calm. 'Fair enough,' I said. 'We can meet after office hours.' I left the logistics of the whole tedious affair to my uncle.

When I reached home that evening, I learnt that Cheteshwar had insisted that we should meet at his mama's house.

Strange! I wondered why anyone would want to meet at an uncle's place in the twenty-first century. There were so many options—restaurants, coffeeshops—and this guy wanted to meet me at his mama's place? It did not make sense. And if he did not want an assignation at a public space, we could have easily congregated at his home or mine. Why did we have to gather at his uncle's house?

I decided to clarify a couple of things with my father when we sat down for dinner. 'I'm not going to say 'yes' to any guy just after one meeting,' I warned.

'I don't expect you to,' my father said, much to my relief.

'I need to talk to the person. Two-three meetings will not do. I need to get to know the guy,' I continued, belabouring the point.

'Don't think too much,' my father advised. 'Take it one day at a time. We'll start thinking about things when we get there.'

A look of perfect understanding passed between us. My father would not force me into anything. I felt reassured.

'Don't worry. I'll do what you say,' I assured him, much relieved.

The period post dinner was slightly more stressful. Geeta didi was fussing big time, like a seriously ruffled mother hen determined to keep her chick on the straight and narrow. A daughter of the house was about to meet a prospective bridegroom—she had to look perfect! My bua had barged into my room and was creating mayhem in my cupboard as she rifled through my clothes. 'Wear this, wear that,' she said, as she displayed various possible outfits.

'Chill!' I grinned at her. I had anticipated her meltdown and had already had the forethought to borrow one of my cousin's fancier duds. Mitali was currently studying in Mumbai and was blissfully unaware of this temporary raid on her wardrobe. Not that she would have minded if she had been privy to it. 'I've borrowed Mitali's clothes for the occasion.'

I raised the said attire for my aunt's inspection—a black and purple silk top that I had matched with a pair of jet-black formal trousers. Geeta didi calmed down several notches after she carefully cast a microscopic eye over the proposed apparel, and left me to titivate for the evening. I was soon rigged out in my borrowed feathers. The kohl lining my eyes and some balm glossing my lips were my only concession to the formality of the approaching occasion.

The drive to Cheteshwar's mama's flat, about one-and-a-half kilometres away from our house, was accomplished in barely seven minutes. I was accompanied by Dad, Fufaji and Varsha didi, his wife, so called because she had still been unmarried while I was growing up. Our bond had strengthened even more after her marriage; the doors of her home had always been open for me and I had spent several happy hours learning to skate and dance under her watch. Geeta didi had opted to stay behind.

We had to take the stairs, all three flights of them, because the elevator was not working. My Dad rang the bell and the door swung open. Cheteshwar's mama welcomed us with a beaming smile. My father and uncle stepped in first. Varsha didi and I followed.

When I entered the apartment, I had the first glimpse of my hotshot suitor, clad in denims and a striped polo shirt, looking nothing like a celebrity, whilst refusing to make eye-contact. Finding the situation awkward, I assumed it was going to be a very short meeting.

Cheteshwar had risen to greet us, and my initial impression of him was very hazy. All I could see was a shadowy figure about six feet tall. I would have had to turn my neck if I had wanted to examine him more closely. Under the circumstances, I naturally did not, so all I saw was a tall guy, about 74–75 kgs with the typical physique of a sportsman. The ceiling in the apartment was not very high, making him appear even larger. The average height of the rest of the men in the room ranged between five feet–six and five feet–seven inches. He towered over them.

I cast my eye about the flat and noticed that it was a small two-BHK apartment with an unpretentious living room where the seating had been furnished in the Indian style, or what was popularly referred to as a Bhartiya baithak in Gujarati, with two low short-legged diwans positioned against the walls. There was a tiny kitchen on the right side and two bedrooms adjacent to each other. A few Nilkamal chairs had been added to the mix to augment the shortfall in the normal seating arrangement. Cheteshwar and his mama sat on a diwan in one corner, my fufaji and Dad sat on the other and my bua and I occupied the chairs. There was another aunt present—his mama's cousin—who had apparently been instrumental in introducing the Pujaras to the Pabaris. His mami, who appeared to be a very good hostess, was scurrying back and forth from the kitchen trying to tend to her guests.

The first two-to-three minutes were spent in swapping 'Hi's' and 'Hellos'; once these had been dispensed with, fufaji cut the first turf with a comment that was directed at Cheteshwar. 'Oh, you came back. Last week you were in Mumbai.'

'I was playing some competitive matches for Indian Oil,' Cheteshwar offered by way of explanation.

'How did it go?' my uncle queried.

'It went well,' replied Cheteshwar, politely.

'I saw your century against New Zealand,' fufaji informed him benevolently.

Cheteshwar just smiled, nodded and turned the topic to the challenger trophy for which he had been selected. 'I'm now scheduled to take part in the Challenger Trophy, which will be taking place in Rajkot. In fact, all the matches I'll be playing over the next one week will be in Rajkot.'

They started discussing the upcoming tournament.

By this time five minutes had elapsed, and all my preconceived notions about Cheteshwar Pujara had crumbled to dust. He was definitely not a celeb-type. He had no airs, was extremely courteous and responded to questions that were put to him without a trace of arrogance. This was a young man who was serious and matured. His simplicity was apparent. His attitude towards clothes, at least, was exactly like mine: unfussy.

We had not yet exchanged a single word. His mami, through all her multiple forays into the kitchen, took the situation at a glance and decided it was time to intervene. She began to bundle us towards a room. 'Why don't you go into that room and chat. I'll get the chairs.'

Cheteshwar rose courteously, saying, 'No, you don't run around. I'll take the chairs.' He picked up two Nilkamal chairs and followed me into a room with blue walls and two diwans arranged in an L-shape against the walls. A small mandir stood in a corner, a typical feature in most Gujarati households.

As Cheteshwar and I took a chair each, his aunt came in to ask us what we would like to nibble. Seeing us tongue-tied, she left the room, only to return moments later with a tray laden with two bowls of rose-petal ice cream. She smiled at us, as Cheteshwar relieved her of her burden, and said, 'I won't disturb you now. You can chat in peace.'

I noticed that all the ladies had abandoned the men, who were busy chatting with each other and had made a general exodus to the other bedroom. Cheteshwar handed me a bowl of ice cream, which I immediately put aside. I am not too fond of sweets.

Cheteshwar spoke first. 'What do you do?' he asked.

'I work for Vodafone. I'm a relationship manager.'

'What does a relationship manager do?'

'I basically look after HNIs (high-network individuals) comprising factories and small-scale industries with forty-fifty employees. They're high-end customers. My job is to keep them happy, make sure they don't have any grievances and if they do, I send our teams to fix their problems asap.'

'Do you travel?' he quizzed, curiously.

'Day trips, mainly to Junagarh, Porbandar and Morbi. I love my work. It's challenging. We've just launched the 3G,' I told him.

'Have you?' he inquired interestedly. 'I love technology.' He looked a little self-deprecating. 'I'm something of a gizmo freak.'

A lively discussion ensued, as we dissected various aspects of telecom technology. We also discussed the merits of the iPhone.

He then divulged that he had bought a new house. 'I have to buy things for this new house I have constructed. I have already moved into it and I've just realized that we're having network issues.'

'I can get someone to check it up for you,' I offered tentatively.

He brushed the offer aside. I understood his unspoken logic at once and appreciated it deeply. At that point we were not sure we were ever going to meet again. I was beginning to like the guy.

We made no reference to his celebrity status, though I did say, 'I believe you have some matches coming up.'

'Yeah, I'll be playing some matches in Rajkot. I'll have to wake up early, you know—to practice.'

I felt that at this point that it was incumbent upon me to confess that his professional world was as alien to me as outer space. 'I don't know a thing about cricket, you know,' I told him resolutely.

He looked amused.

He then told me about his ACL (anterior cruciate ligament) injuries. The ACL is one of the two ligaments that cross in the middle of the knee and connect the thighbone to the shinbone. It is crucial for the stability of the knee joint. I was horrified.

An hour later, his aunt arrived with some rose-petal milkshake. By now, both our ice creams, largely untouched, had melted. I demurred. 'No please, I won't be able to have it.'

Cheteshwar also waved the milkshake away. His aunt didn't insist and left the room as swiftly as she had entered it.

'Do you have to count your calories,' I asked, wondering why he had refused the milkshake.

'Not really. It's just that I'm used to eating very basic food,' he said, by way of excuse.

'Which school did you go to?' he inquired, firmly switching the topic.

'Sophia High school in Mount Abu,' I revealed.

'How did you end up there?' he asked curiously.

'We are originally from Jamjodhpur in Jamnagar district.'

'My father is the only son, amongst five sisters …'

He raised his brow.

'He started helping out my Dadaji in business when he was barely fourteen.'

'What kind of business? Cheteshwar asked.

'Dadaji was a commodities merchant. My father took over the business after he finished high school at the age of sixteen.' I pulled a face. 'It was expected of him.'

I then chuckled. 'But in case you think we're very orthodox, let me tell you that nothing could be further from the truth. We're actually quite progressive, and gender has never been an issue in my family. You'll find this very amusing, but all my aunts have done their graduation and some of them even went on to do their post-graduation. Geeta didi, for instance...'

'Who's she?' he interrupted.

'My youngest aunt. She has an M. Com. degree.'

'Okay,' he said, smiling slightly. 'But how did you end up in Mount Abu?'

'I was eight, if you must know, and my mother was expecting my brother at that time.'

I laughed.

'I studied in a primary school in the village till then, you know, and I couldn't speak a word of English. My folks decided I needed to broaden my horizons, because clearly Jamjodhpur was not going to equip me with an adequate education. They started hunting around for a good school and picked Sophia.'

'How did you react to being shipped off?' he inquired.

'Oh, very well. I was an independent child and I didn't need my parents to fuss over me constantly. Actually, I joined late in my first term. And once I was there, I was quite happy because I had fallen in love with the swings. I remember my father, cousins and Gita didi crying when they were leaving me, and I kept thinking *why are they crying?*

'And your mother?' Cheteshwar asked.

'She wasn't there. She couldn't travel because she was expecting,' I said, matter-of-factly. 'I was there for eight years and I loved it. My sister joined the school during my last two years, but she didn't adapt too well, so they pulled her out.'

Suddenly his mobile rang. He looked at me apologetically and took the call. I sneaked a glance at my watch. It was around 10 o'clock. I could hear a male voice asking, 'You're still there?'

'Yes, said Cheteshwar briskly. 'We're still here.' He cut the conversation short. 'I'll call you in some time.'

'Sorry,' he said, putting his phone away. 'That was my dad. You were saying?'

'Not much more to say. I left Mount Abu and came to Rajkot for my eleventh and twelfth.'

'How did you guys land up in Rajkot?'

'Education!' I said, giggling.

He looked askance.

'No, seriously. My brother was growing up. He needed a proper education. Rajkot has good schools, so my parents decided to shift here.'

'And then you went to Ahmedabad for your graduation and did your PG in Navi Mumbai in retail and marketing at ITM (Institute for Technology and Management),' he stated, looking pleased with himself.

I chuckled.

He had obviously gone through my biodata with a fine-tooth comb.

There was a short pause before he asked, 'Didn't you ever think of starting your own business?'

'Not really,' I responded. 'It makes no sense to start a business without any experience. My family isn't too happy though. They want me to branch out on my own. They wouldn't even let me sit for placements at ITM.'

'Then how on earth did you land a job with Vodafone? he inquired, surprised.

'Through a watchman,' I answered, chortling.

'Through a watchman!' He looked at me disbelievingly.

'My Dad used to go to Shivalik 5. Vodafone has an office in the same building. I asked him to send up my CV to the company with a watchman. I was really surprised when I got a call a few days later. They grilled me for one hour and then told me, "We have no opening as of now but we'll keep you in mind". Apparently around 25 days later, somebody left abruptly and they called me and asked me if I'd like to join. My family was dead against it, but I pleaded, argued and finally managed to convince them to allow me to take the job. Now enough about me. Do you like movies?'

'Yes, I do,' he replied. 'And you?'

I confessed to a fondness for cinema.

'Have you seen *Barfi*?' he asked.

I nodded.

'I really liked it,' Cheteshwar said, enthusiastically.

'Me too!' I uttered.

It was a popular movie back then and had been released just a couple of weeks earlier. Everyone was raving about it. A romantic comedy, this Ranbir Kapoor–Priyanka Chopra starrer had strayed into rarefied territory, exploring the burgeoning love story between a deaf and mute young man and an autistic young woman. The plotline was still fresh in our minds and we launched into an animated discussion about the merits of the film, unaware of the passing time.

Outside, everyone had run out of steam and conversation. Talks had been limping along hopelessly for a while. At around 10.15

p.m. someone in the living room decided enough was enough. Cheteshwar and I had been huddled in our private corner for more than two hours. Surely that was more than enough time for an icebreaker?

'Are you through?' a voice called out from the living room.

We immediately got up.

'Yes, let's go,' I said at once.

Cheteshwar nodded, and we exited the room.

Once we got into the car and were on our way back, everyone chorused, 'What did you think? What did you think?'

How was I to answer that? I tried to gather my thoughts. 'I think,' I said slowly, 'he was very nice, very sensible, very grounded, very matured and very thoughtful.'

My reply seemed to please them, especially my uncle, who pronounced, 'He was very sweet. I also thought he was very well-mannered. He didn't seem to be in a hurry to talk to you. He was happy to talk to us.'

I hid a smile. What my uncle was trying to say was that Cheteshwar had not displayed any unseemly haste to engage me in conversation.

'Did you notice that he had green eyes?' my aunt inquired suddenly. 'I thought he was very good-looking. Sharp aquiline nose, pointed chin. Nice features.'

I did not reply. There was nothing to say. My aunt was perfectly aware that unlike most people in my generation, the outward casing did not impress me. It was only the spirit inside that counted. I wanted a good soul, an understanding spouse.

My father was more interested in my conversation with Cheteshwar. 'What did the two of you talk about?'

'Nothing much,' I said. 'It was just a random conversation. We discussed our interests. He asked me about my work—that sort of thing.'

What I failed to mention that night was the instant connection that I had felt with Cheteshwar, or that we shared the same wavelength. I had realized some time through the course of our conversation that he was a very serious kind of person. Up until this point, I had not even thought of finding out about him. I had not even bothered to search him on the internet. But now I would.

CHAPTER THREE

Cheteshwar Comes a-Courting

The Challenger trophy was in full swing, the Pujaras were incommunicado and Geeta didi was about to combust. This despite the fact that fufaji had run across Cheteshwar's father during a match that he had gone to watch. She may have been dispirited by the fact that they had merely exchanged smiles from a distance and had made no attempt to cozy up to each other, mainly because there were other people around.

We all knew that Cheteshwar was busy playing the domestic tournament from 29 September to 2 October, but it was pointless trying to reason with my aunt. She was constantly on tenterhooks and kept barraging me with her anxieties.

'Why is he not responding?' she nagged.

'How do I know?' I said, serenely.

'Did you sound very ambitious? Did you scare him away?' she asked uneasily. 'Did you sound too focused on your career?'

I controlled a strong urge to laugh. 'I told you everything that was said between us. How do I know?' I said, my tranquillity abating a mite.

'You must have said something,' she insisted.

'I didn't say anything apart from what I've already told you. If he's not interested, then fine. What can we do?' I responded evenly, praying for patience.

That quietened her for a short spell.

My father, meanwhile, remained calm during all the drama, a benefaction for which I was intensely grateful.

The Challenger trophy came to an end. Cheteshwar had had a great outing, emerging as the highest run scorer in the tournament. In fact, he had captained India B which had won the series against India A and Bengal. The newspapers were full of him.

On the fourth of October, Cheteshwar's mama called fufaji. 'Cheteshwar would like permission to start speaking to Puja over the phone for a while so that they can get to know each other,' he told him. 'He will be travelling and he wants to talk to her before he decides.'

Fufaji was in a dilemma. Such requests were hardly commonplace in arranged marriages and was not sure if allowing Cheteshwar such unfettered access to me was a particularly praiseworthy idea. 'I'll have to have a word with Puja's Dad. I'll get back to you after that.'

He hung up and got on the horn with my father, bringing up to speed with the latest request from the Pujaras. Dad was pleased, because it matched my own wishes to a tee. 'Puja wants the same thing,' Dad told fufaji. 'Let them talk over the phone. What harm can it do?'

But when he handed me Cheteshwar's phone number, he was far less blasé. 'Talk as much as you like. Take whatever time you need till you make up your mind. Be very frank and say whatever you want. But don't get emotionally attached to him, because if things don't work out, I don't want you feeling bad or becoming too emotionally invested in him.'

'Yeah, yeah you don't need to worry about that. I will not have that issue,' I assured him, breezily.

He gave me a penetrating look and then nodded, leaving me to tackle my future in my own way.

And that's when our tryst through telephony began.

It started with a message from Cheteshwar. "Whatever time you're free let's catch up. I'll be free in the evening after seven."

I called him on my way back home from work. 'We can talk now. In fact, it's a good time to talk for me. What about you?' I asked.

'It's a good time for me too,' he said.

By now I had made good my resolve and had googled him. I had also picked up something about cricket. I congratulated him for winning the Challenger Trophy. He brushed away my felicitations, almost as if he was embarrassed and told me that he was in Bombay for a match.

I felt a wave of nostalgia. I loved Bombay. I had studied there. 'Oh my God! You're in Bombay!' I exclaimed. 'It's such a lovely place. You should do something. There are such nice restaurants there.'

'I play all day,' he said somewhat diffidently. 'What can I do? In any case, I don't like eating out.'

I disagreed. 'I still think you should go out and have some fun.'

'It's only fun to go out if you have good company,' he commented flirtatiously in a very innocent way.

'Then find some company,' I retorted, trying to mask my embarrassment.

It was almost 8 o'clock, close to dinner time. 'Will you hold the call, while I order my dinner?' he asked diffidently.

'Yeah, sure. Please order your dinner. I'll stay on the line,' I said at once.

After he had placed his order, I asked, 'What do you usually eat while travelling?' I was curious.

'Either Indian or Italian.'

'What did you order just now?'

'Veg biryani and fresh lime soda,' he said.

'Fresh lime soda is not healthy,' I remarked disapprovingly.

'I know it's not healthy, but I need some liquid with my meal,' he said defensively and changed the subject. 'What time do you eat?'

'About the same time as you, I think,' I replied and then went on to quiz him about the game he had played in Bombay. 'How was the match?

'Good.'

I then confessed that I did not really know cricket. 'I don't even watch Cricket. I didn't even know who you were until fufaji mentioned your name.'

'I've been playing cricket all my life,' he confided, seemingly unoffended by my ignorance. 'Ever since I was a kid. My dad also used to play cricket. And my chacha.'

Every conversation we had—there were many over the next few days—flowed unstructured between us; easily and organically. We would just continue from where we had left off. It was almost as if we were friends and had known each other for a long time. There was a strange familiarity about him. I felt comfortable talking to him.

One evening, during one such a tête-à-tête, he shared that he was very religious. 'You know, I am a strong believer of God. I pray regularly.'

I was not particularly surprised. The raksha potli (protection pouch) on his wrist had not escaped my eye during our meeting. Somehow, I understood without Cheteshwar actually articulating it out aloud that he wanted his religious streak to be out in the open between us so that it did not become an issue later on. 'Yeah, okay, so does my mother. She's a Pushti Margi, you know.'

'You?'

'I'm not religious. But I can live with people who are,' I said with a laugh. He was intrigued, so I expanded. 'I'm a boarding-school kid, you know. Religion did not feature very large in my growing-up years.'

On 8 October, I mentioned in passing that the next day was my birthday. 'I'll be turning 24,' I informed him wryly.

'Should I stay awake and wish you at 12,' he asked hesitantly.

By now I had the measure of the man and this suggestion amused me greatly. I knew he slept early, and how hard put he would be if I actually took him up on his offer. I gently turned him down, treating the idea as something of a jest. 'No, no, don't put this kind of pressure on me,' I said instantly, extremely glad that he could not see my grin. 'You please sleep and stick to your routine. We're just getting to know each other. There's no need for you to stay awake.'

'I'm never awake at night,' he stated baldly. 'Actually, I don't believe in staying up and wishing people at midnight.'

Since I was a night bird, I naturally could not enter into his sentiments. 'I'm a night owl,' I declared flatly, not wanting him to harbour any misconceptions as far I was concerned. 'In my house, we wish each other and cut the cake at midnight.'

'But I sleep early,' he averred, holding his ground. 'And I don't think it's important to wish people at night. I can always wish them the next day when it's actually their birthday.' I could almost hear him saying 'So there!' in my head.

I wanted to laugh. Instead, I said, 'You please go to sleep. I don't expect you to stay awake.' We chatted desultorily for a bit longer and then hung up at around 11 o'clock.

Later, around midnight, as my family and I were getting into the birthday spirit, I heard my phone beep. I looked at the message box and saw a very sweet birthday wish from Cheteshwar. 'May you get everything you wish for. Happy birthday!'

Touched, I messaged back. 'Why are you still awake. Please go to sleep. You have an early day tomorrow.'

Cheteshwar continued to travel, but it did not stop us from talking nineteen to a dozen. A couple of times we tried to set up video calls, an endeavour that did not work. We finally decided that it did not really matter. Conversing on the phone was just as good. So what if we could not see each other?

One day, he casually mentioned that he was friends with an older couple who were having network problems. 'My friend is an orthopaedic surgeon and his wife is a dentist—'

'Okay,' I cut in. 'I'll get someone to check out the problem.'

'No, I'd like you to go personally,' he said.

There was a momentary silence as I realized that Cheteshwar was trying to pull a fast one on me. There was no network issue, he just wanted me to meet his friends. I got slightly irritated. 'If you want something, say so directly. There's no need to start playing games. Don't tell me there is a network issue when you actually just want me to meet these people.'

Not trusting myself any further, I ended the call.

A few hours later, Cheteshwar called me back. 'I'm sorry. You're right. They want to meet you. They're family friends. I've become even closer to them after my mother died. They look out for me and have always been there for me whenever I've needed them.'

'Fair enough,' I said, thawing a little. 'It's alright, I'll go and meet them.'

'Can you meet them tomorrow?' he asked.

'Sure,' I said. 'Send me their address. I'll go there straight from office.'

'Office? he asked confused. 'But tomorrow is Sunday.'

'Yes, but I have an important presentation, so I'll be working at office.'

The next day, I met the said couple at their hospital, casually dressed in a T-shirt and jeggings. Cheteshwar had already hopped on to a plane for his next destination, after calling me up for a very quick chat.

The hospital building was charming and had been beautifully done up with a swing et al. What caught my fancy was a lovely looking uruli, with flowers floating in the crystal-clear water within it. Cheteshwar's friends were very warm and welcoming, and soon put me at ease even if they did ask all kinds of penetrating questions about my interests and beliefs, which I was happy to answer.

By the time I reached home, Cheteshwar had landed. 'How did you like my friends?' he asked as soon as I answered his call.

'They were very nice,' I assured him.

He seemed to heave a sigh of relief. Much later, he told me that they had been just as complimentary about me.

Meanwhile, Cheteshwar was getting ribbed by his pals. A fanatic devotee of the game at all times, his teammates immediately noticed when Cheteshwar—always so dedicated to discipline—actually retained his mobile during one of the less important matches and appeared to be in constant conversation with someone while he was at the stands. He was talking to me at the time, but being tight-lipped at the best of times; he had kept me a closely guarded secret from all his cricketing buddies.

One friend in particular, Jaydev, was extremely suspicious. 'Who are you talking to?' he once asked.

'Nobody,' said Cheteshwar mendaciously. 'It's just a work-related call.'

Over time, I discovered just how cagey Cheteshwar could be about our phone calls. The minute somebody accidentally rolled up within hearing range, he would hang up. Even if it was his own father. When I found out, I teased him motherlessly and would not let him get off the phone, though he resisted my machinations vigorously.

We finally caught up in Rajkot during Navaratri. By now, Cheteshwar and I had become fast friends. I even felt that I had come to know his father, thanks to our various 'talk-a-thons'. Cheteshwar later told me that he had been more or less certain that he wished to marry me after I had met his family friends. But one issue remained: his Guruji's blessings.

I had learnt about his Guruji very early on. Cheteshwar was a staunch devotee of Haricharandasji Maharaj of Gondal.

'I worship him. I am an ardent follower,' he had once admitted, trying to explain his innermost beliefs. 'I'm a great believer of karma. I don't worship any human being or even deity lightly.' I had smiled thinking of my mother. I seemed destined to be surrounded by people with a deeply spiritual bent.

'Will you come with me to meet Guruji?' Cheteshwar asked when we finally met up during the Navaratri break. The festival is huge in Gujarat and celebrations during this time are intense. Most Gujaratis take their dancing and revelry very seriously. Not me—because of the Mount Abu effect—but almost everyone else.

'I don't mind. I'll come,' I told him, and promptly spoke to dad about the proposed trip. In fact, I had diligently kept him posted on all my conversations with Cheteshwar.

It turned out to be a family affair, with both clans determined to accompany us. It was not a long trip as Guruji normally left Gondal during Navaratri and spent it in his ashram in Rajkot.

Dad, fufaji, Geeta didi and I drove down to the ashram. We were to meet the Pujaras and Kananis there. It was an uncomfortable drive, primarily because fufaji was peeved. He though Cheteshwar and I had 'talked' long enough and just could not understand why we were not making up our minds. 'First, he wanted us to meet his uncle and aunt—we met them. Then, he wanted her to meet his friends—she met them as well. And now, he wants us to meet his Guruji! Why couldn't all this be carried out more quickly?' he grumbled.

My father did not add to my comfort either. Although, thankfully, he voiced his concerns in private. 'Are you okay?' he asked suspiciously. 'You haven't fallen in love or anything?'

I blushed. 'No, no. We're okay.'

Thing were to go even further downhill once we reached the ashram, when Gita didi met Cheteshwar for the first time. He had played the whole day and was clad in—horror of horrors—torn jeans of a light-blue hue; his darker blue T-shirt looked fairly respectable, but his beard was untrimmed, his hair long and unruly obviously long overdue for a haircut, and his face had tanned considerably, undoubtedly due to the long hours at the cricket field. He was looking as if he was ready to drop.

My aunt was so horrified by his appearance that she immediately whispered, 'Are sure you want to marry this guy? He doesn't look very good. Your mother may not like him even if he's very nice. (That was her way of saying: I'm not sure I like him). Are you really sure you want to marry him? You're so good-looking.'

I kept a straight-face and quickly hushed her, hoping that no one had overheard her remarks. I walked over to the Pujaras and Kananis, with my disgruntled kin flanking me on either side. There was a lady in a beige and white sari standing beside them. 'Meet my masi (mother's sister). She has taken sanyas (renunciation), said Cheteshwar.'

I smiled at her, finally understanding why Cheteshwar had asked me to come. Not so much to meet his Guruji, but to meet his masi to whom, I guessed, he was very close.

It was only then that I leisurely looked around to take in my surroundings. The Ram dhun was playing and I could see a big temple. Adjacent to it, on the right, was a small cottage. We had to walk past the temple to reach it. This was Guruji's pied-à-terre, consisting of a room, a kitchenette and a larger room where the satsang took place.

Guruji was seated on a wooden aasan. There were around twenty-five–thirty people in the room. His disciples thronged to him, bearing innumerable dabbas of mithai which he accepted, opened and distributed almost immediately. Cheteshwar told me that no pravachans (sermons) were held. People just came to pay obeisance, although there was a faction among them that flocked to consult Guruji about pressing matters such as the right mahurat for their children's weddings or problems related to property, and other issues that were critical to their lives.

Cheteshwar escorted us to his Guruji and made the following introduction. '*Gurudev, yeh Puja hai aur yeh unka parivar hai* (Gurudev, this is Puja and this is her family).'

I immediately folded my hands in the time-honoured fashion of reverence and said 'Namaste.'

The minute I made my salutations, he asked, '*Shaadi karogi issey* (Will you marry him)?'

Deeply embarrassed, I replied, '*Papa kahenge toh zaroor karungi* (If my father tells me to, I certainly will).'

I swiftly sped to the back of the room and sat on one of the durries on the floor. We were sitting in a triangle, in the same line, at different angles, when Guruji suddenly threw a peda at me and another at Cheteshwar. We both caught our respective sweetmeat and folded our hands in acceptance.

'You have to eat it,' Cheteshwar hissed, aware of my aversion to sweets. I heroically nibbled at it, determined not to offend sensibilities.

After Guruji had breezily bestowed his blessings for a match between us, Cheteshwar emerged from the ashram, even more convinced that he wished to spend the rest of his life with me. He expressed these sentiments to his father, who in turn duly conveyed them to mine—formally.

The ball was now well and truly in my court.

I thought very hard, chin on my palms. I liked him as a person. We got along fine, our thoughts matched, as did our values and beliefs but—and there was a big but—I did not want to be a housewife. I knew Cheteshwar would not be averse to a working wife, but I was not sure how his family would feel about it. If they felt that his spouse should stay home since there was no other woman in residence, I would be in a spot. Cheteshwar, from what I had discovered, was a self-made man, who was very confident of every decision he made. He was a no-fuss, no-frills person, who would be happy to accommodate me. But my worry was his family—if they had different expectations, there would be conflicts and he would be caught in the middle of the crossfire. He did not deserve that.

In my earlier avatar, I had dreamt of a life in a metropolis. But I was prepared to cast that dream aside if I could justify my existence as a useful, contributing member of society. Cheteshwar, I knew, would ask my opinions and respect them. This then was the crux. I would be happy to marry Cheteshwar provided I was not expected to be a Stepford wife. I had studied too hard to throw it all away. I wanted to do something meaningful.

That evening, I passed on my conclusions to my father. 'I like Cheteshwar, but I don't want to become a housewife.' I could see that he was listening to me intently. I took a deep breath and said, 'Go and speak to his uncle and ask him what the family expects from his wife. I don't want any conflict on the issue after we are married.'

Cheteshwar's uncle brushed aside all my fears. 'Of course, she should do something,' he told my father. 'They have sufficient staff—what will she do if she doesn't have some sort of occupation? Although, I do think that initially she should not take up a job so that she can travel with Cheteshwar and get to know him. But, of course, in the end, it's up to them.'

What about Cheteshwar's father? How would he feel? My father queried.

Cheteshwar's mama laughed. 'You need not worry about him. He does not have any thoughts beyond cricket!'

Finally, I expressed my concerns to Cheteshwar. He was equally encouraging. 'Why should you worry? You're so talented. You have so much to offer. Why shouldn't you work. Although…' he hesitated. 'Initially—that's if you don't mind—I have a request. I'd like you to travel with me. Make some memories with me. I haven't had anyone really close to me after my mother and, just for a while, I'd like to have you to myself.'

Phrased so lovingly, couched as a humble request, he cleverly backed me into a corner and I found myself saying, 'Yes!'

Later, at night, he called me up, 'I feel as if I have won a huge victory today. I felt such immense peace tonight. I suddenly realized how lucky I am. I have found just the kind of partner that I have been looking for.'

And barely a week later, our Roka ceremony happened. At his house. Most unexpectedly.

CHAPTER FOUR

A Whirlwind Betrothal, a Game of Cricket and Media Attention

Everyone in the know was aware that the Pujaras and the Pabaris had arrived at a de facto understanding that Cheteshwar and I would be tying the knot sometime in the future. We were only awaiting a formal stamp of approval from my mother, who was yet to meet him.

She returned from her pilgrimage on 1 November and from that moment on, it was all systems go! Cheteshwar was leaving for Bombay the following evening and his father thought that any further delay in setting up this final rendezvous would impose an excruciating strain on both clans. My mother, recipient of constant updates as our friendship progressed, was equally eager to get the first glimpse of her prospective son-in-law.

Telephone lines went berserk as both parties went back and forth trying to find a suitable time for the proposed tryst in the short window period that was available to us. Everyone was in a tizzy, starting with me.

'I'm sorry, I can't bunk work,' I announced firmly, an anxious look in my eye. 'What excuse will I give my office? So, before you decide anything, kindly remember it's a working day for me and that I have to be in office between 10 a.m. and 6 p.m.'

Eventually, an agreement was reached. We would all converge the next morning at the Pujara household.

Now that this particularly sticky issue was out of the way, by common consent, I decided to tackle problem number two—Cheteshwar's apparel—on the sly. Stung by my aunt's reaction to him at the ashram, I did not want any action-replay when he met my mother, which was certainly going to be the case if he showed up in torn jeans.

I was perfectly candid with him. 'Please clean up nicely because the elders will be looking at you … a lot of them will be judging you by your appearance,' I told him inflexibly over the phone. 'Please shave, so that we can see your face. Dress up smartly. Wear a nice shirt.'

By then, I knew he was not particularly fond of formal wear, that he did not own too many shirts and was happiest in a pair of shorts like most sporty individuals. It was not that he was shabby. It just would not occur to him that torn jeans which were admittedly 'in' and beards, which were also hugely popular amongst youngsters, did not hold the same appeal for the older generation.

To his credit, he did not take offense and meekly confessed, 'I have two shirts, one is white and the other blue—which one should I wear?'

'Wear the blue shirt,' I advised, silently vowing by way of atonement that I would never interfere in his choice of clothing hereafter—nor would I object to his bearded state if he preferred it. After all, everyone had the right to dress as they pleased and if Cheteshwar chose comfort over fashion, so be it!

There was quite an assemblage of people when we reached Cheteshwar's house the next morning. His paternal uncle and aunt, Bipin chacha and Sonal chachi, were there along with a few other guests. Given that we were meeting at breakfast time, samosas, chai and juice had been duly arranged for our delectation.

Cheteshwar's family greeted my mother warmly.

After pleasantries had been exchanged and snacks served, my parents wandered over to the terrace garden with my fufaji to ostensibly 'admire' it. In actuality, my uncle wanted to have a private tête-à-tête with my mother. 'Do you want to make a decision now or do you want to wait. The rest of us are happy with the match. We're now waiting for you to take a call.'

My mother looked thoughtful. 'I've been kept in the loop every step of the way,' she replied. 'I too am fine with this match. If the children are happy, why should I object? It's a yes from me too.'

At my mother's words, an ear-to-ear grin broke out on his face. He looked as pleased as punch at having wrung this final assent from the last and most important of the Pabaris.

People had scattered into small clusters across the house and I found myself chatting casually with Geeta didi, my mother and Cheteshwar in the immaculately maintained terrace garden.

Abruptly somebody called out to Cheteshwar. He looked at us apologetically and took off to discover why he was wanted. Geeta didi too wandered off inside. My mother and I remained where we were.

Suddenly, Geeta didi rushed over to us. 'They want to do the Roka right now!' she blurted out.

I was to discover later that Cheteshwar's mami, once she learnt that my mother had given her assent, had remarked, 'If everyone has said yes, then what are we waiting for? Puja has come to this house for the first time, she should not go home empty-handed. Let's do the Roka right now. Call Cheteshwar.'

And that's when Cheteshwar was summoned.

Ignorant of event's unfolding behind the scenes, I was flummoxed. And nervous. I immediately dispatched a frantic text to Cheteshwar from my phone. 'What's happening?'

No response.

I sent another panicky message. 'This is happening too quickly. I'm not up for it.'

I looked desperately at my screen hoping for some reassurance. It remained stubbornly blank.

I sent another agitated text. 'Why can't we wait and plan and then do this later.'

Radio silence.

By now I was really anxious. 'Why aren't you responding?'

This was to be my final message and it was already too late. Two white-coloured garden chairs had been fished out and placed in the living room by this time. I was firmly escorted to one. Cheteshwar was already seated on the other, with a slight smile hovering on his lips as he carefully avoided my eyes.

Before we knew it, we both bore vermillion streaks on our brows. The deed was done and we were being fed mithais by our loving relatives. My chagrin was acute, as I visualized unending bouts of mithai-eating looming ominously ahead of me. However, I forced down my rising hysteria. This was one of those times when discretion was definitely better than valour. Clearly, eating mithais was going to be one of the crosses I would have to bear in the short term.

I soon realized that the Roka, like everything else in my relationship with Cheteshwar so far, had simply sprouted wings and flown out of our control. Nothing had been planned. Everything had just happened spontaneously. Surrounded by a bevy of people, he had not seen my frenzied texts, I later discovered. In any case, there was not much he could have done even if he had.

Once the tilak ceremony and mithai-munching were over, I wondered what I would do about my office, which was due to start at 10. I figured out that I would be late by at least an hour. I voiced these apprehensions to my mother. She was unsympathetic.

'You're not going anywhere,' she decreed in an undervoice that brooked no arguments. 'Take leave. It would be rude to talk about office at a time like this.'

Firmly obstructed by my stern progenitor, I yielded and quietly dispatched the intelligence to my office that I would not be attending work that day. Pleased at this turn of events, Cheteshwar, who had been following the entire exchange with keen interest, immediately offered to take me on a lunch date. Until now, we had never had time alone together. We had always been carefully chaperoned. This luncheon à deux would be a first for us.

As soon as we left, Cheteshwar's relatives made avid attempts to uncover his schedule. Now that the Roka was out of the way, there was no reason to delay the engagement. Within minutes, they had discovered that he was participating in a camp in Mumbai on 9 November, that he would be busy with the President's X1 match on 2 November and would be, subsequently, playing a three-day match against England from 3 November to 5 November. Clearly, the only free dates he had fell between 6 November and 8 November. Another frenzied powwow took place until a consensus was reached that the matter should be put up to Guruji. Who better than him to decide on the right mahurat for an exchange of rings and a formal announcement of our upcoming nuptials?

A frenetic phone call was instantaneously made, requesting him to pick out a mahurat from the three dates. Guruji pronounced 6 November as ideal, a proclamation that was received with great rejoicing in the Pujara camp. My parents, apprised of Guruji's pronouncement, were equally enthusiastic and when the news trickled down to me, I was overtaken by a bizarre feeling of unreality. It was almost as if I was being sped full pelt on a roller-coaster ride, which was exciting, yet frightening, at the same time.

An hour later, Cheteshwar came to pick me up, looking equally bemused. We smiled at each other in tacit understanding, before I asked him where we were going.

'I thought I'd take you to Seasons,' he said, referring to a popular hotel in the outskirts of the city. At the time we had no idea that we would be celebrating our engagement there, just four days later.

After lunch, Cheteshwar asked me if I would go shopping with him. 'I have to pick up something for our engagement and I won't have much time to shop in Mumbai,' he explained. 'My mami and a cousin are meeting me at the Blue Club. Will you come? We'll only be meeting at the engagement after this.'

Blue Club was a popular one-stop multi-brand shopping centre where clothing, footwear and the like could be found with ease. Cheteshwar's mami and cousin were already there by the time we reached.

In deference to the newness of my status as Cheteshwar's fiancée, I took a step back and faded into the background. The salesman kept pulling out the most startling clothes into his arms, blinding the eye with their shine and shimmer, which he kept on trying without protest—sending my opinion of him rock-bottom.

'Have I done the right thing? Is this his taste?' I wondered gloomily. 'Will I be stuck for life with a man who looks like a Christmas tree?' It was a dreadful thought.

At one point, he looked at me and caught my expression. Cheteshwar demonstrated at this very early stage in our relationship that he could read my sentiments with frightening accuracy. He carefully turned his gaze away and continued to don all manner of repulsive clothing, almost hurtling my blood pressure off the charts. Finally, just when I thought I could bear no more, he gracefully brought the proceedings to a halt with a glance at his watch, announcing that he was running out of time. 'I'm going to Mumbai. I'll pick up something there,' he said decisively.

'Thank god!' I thought, much relieved. 'At least he would not stand next to me dressed in some blingy outfit during our engagement!'

Back in the car, I was far more candid. 'Thank god you didn't buy those clothes.'

'I didn't like them much either. But it would have been disrespectful to have said so,' he said, silencing me very thoroughly as I finally understood that he had behaved just as he ought. My respect for him mounted.

The next three days were hectic. By the time I returned home after my date with Cheteshwar, the two families had already finalized Seasons as the venue for our engagement. The responsibility to oversee the floral arrangements for the function fell on me. I was also entrusted with the all-important task of picking out rings for my intended and myself. I have been treated to legions of stories regarding the nightmarish nature of such undertakings that sometimes stretch to a harrowing fortnight or on extreme occasions, to even a month. For my own part, I neither had the luxury of time, nor the inclination to pore over endless gold bands. I simply chose the first two that appealed to me and moved on to other chores that needed my attention.

A car was then dispatched to Gandhi Nagar for my brother, Jeet. Special permission was sought from his school to allow him to attend the function. He was summoned to the office and told, 'You've been granted permission to go home because your sister is getting engaged.'

Jeet, unaware at the time that the engagement had become a reality, was mightily peeved. 'Why wasn't I informed earlier?' he sniped crabbily on arrival, sounding extremely displeased.

My sister, Dhara, was flown in from Mumbai on the fifth morning as she had to be appropriately outfitted for the occasion as befitted the sister of a fiancée. A great deal of collective thought and effort was expended on her costume, making her feel very grown-up.

Cheteshwar, in the meanwhile, also managed to address the hiatus in his wardrobe in between matches at the DY Patil Stadium, by virtue of dragging his cousin in Mumbai to a store in Church Gate, where he managed to find an attractive outfit. However, when I picked him up at 7 o'clock on the evening of the fifth, he was in something of a tizzy. He flew in earlier than expected as the match had wound up early, ending in a draw.

'I need to buy shoes,' he announced by way of greeting. 'I didn't have the time to go shoe-shopping in Mumbai.'

'Chill,' I said soothingly. 'We still have time. We'll go straight to some footwear store and pick up something.' I drove him straight to a shoe shop and dropped him home only after we had found a pair of nice formal shoes for him.

The next day was the engagement.

It went off smoothly, which was quite a feat, given the short time in which everything had been arranged. Cheteshwar looked resplendent in a black kurta with a leafy motif of light blue and brown. I wore a pastel-green lehnga with a floral motif in the chunni and an intricately embroidered blouse. We exchanged rings in the presence of over two-hundred guests in something of a daze. I cannot, for the life of me, recall what we sampled by way of food that day.

I was starting out with a clean slate. There had been no man in my life before this. Everything was new. I was quite naïve and did not understand much about life. But I was enjoying his company enormously and everything else seemed to get relegated to a second place in my head. I sleep-walked my way through the whole affair in a rose-tinted haze, barely registering what was going on around me.

At around four in the afternoon, after the engagement, I went to Cheteshwar's house for the pag phera, a short ritual in which the bride-to-be is welcomed with an arti into the house of her future groom by the women of his family; imprints of her feet are subsequently made, marking her formal entry into the home.

Once the ceremony was over, Cheteshwar and I snatched a quiet moment in the balcony. He had noticed in his unobtrusive way how I had tensed up after I saw my parents turning teary-eyed and emotional during the engagement. I have no idea how he knew that I could never bear to see my parents in distress. But, somehow, he did. His house was teeming with relatives, and he could see that I was struggling to maintain a calm façade. He discreetly guided me away from the crowd and, before I knew it, I was inhaling fresh air and feeling a whole lot better.

At first, we stood together, completely silent and yet somehow at absolute ease with each other. Then he said, 'Don't worry, we'll be staying in the same city.'

I smiled at him tremulously. Strange, how he could read my mind and what a blessing it was; there would be fewer misunderstandings in the future, I thought.

'Let's go out,' he said, suddenly shattering the silence, splintering my thoughts. 'I have only two days off. Let's make the most of it. We can go to Gondal to Guruji or we could go for a coffee. The choice is yours.'

I looked at my watch. It was only 5 p.m. I could do my own spot of mindreading and I was certain that Cheteshwar really wanted to meet his Guruji. 'I'm okay if you want to head to Gondal to see Guruji. I've eaten so much at the hotel—I'm not really in the mood for coffee, but we can always pick up some for you on the way to the ashram,' I said with a decisiveness that was in sharp contrast to the wayward emotions that had been so prominent just moments earlier.

Within an hour, we were at Gondal, where Cheteshwar sought Guruji's darshan. After that we spent some time with his masi, before whizzing back to his house, at break-neck speed. The youngsters in my family were expected at his place for dinner, and it would have looked very strange if Cheteshwar as their host was missing in action. As it turned out, the kids were already there, looking very much at home.

The next day, I had my first taste of press attention. The news of our engagement made it to both the print and television media, and our betrothal was widely being described as a 'simple ceremony' that had taken place in a 'posh hotel' at Rajkot.

Flustered, I called up Cheteshwar. I was a simple girl, who had hitherto lived a quiet life. How was I going to cope with the press?

'Don't worry about it,' he said, trying to calm me down.

Meanwhile, we tried our best to make the most of the two days we had. We did not have as much time as we would have liked but I comforted myself with the time-worn solace that something was better than nothing. We managed a dinner date on the first day but were barely able to snatch a coffee on the next. We were both busy till the evening—he with his morning and afternoon practice that would last from 7.30 to 9.00 a.m. and 3.00 to 5.00 p.m., respectively—and I with my office.

Cheteshwar picked Ishwarya Post as the site for our first formal date. Located on the Jamnagar Road at the outskirts of Rajkot near the Green Meadows golf course and Ishwarya Lake, this open-air vegetarian restaurant has been a hot favourite amongst locals for its authentic Kathiawadi cuisine. It spreads across four acres of beautifully manicured and elegantly landscaped gardens and boasts of a long walkway, lined with lush green trees, warm globular garden lamps and a host of green palms that seem to speak to the soul. Kids love the place because it has in-house magicians and a children's park; the musically inclined are attracted by the bevy of folk musicians that perform in its premises.

Cheteshwar had chosen the restaurant because of its walkway. He knew that he would have a hard time tethering me to one spot for three long hours just for a chitchat; the exercise offered by the pathway, he knew, would definitely keep me engaged!

Our two-day tryst came to an end and Cheteshwar left for Mumbai. My brother's school broke up for Diwali and we decided to head to Mumbai, ostensibly so that my siblings could chill with him. Our trip to Mumbai also wound up all too quickly when my fiancé left for Ahmedabad. The match was almost on his head and he needed to concentrate.

Diwali came that year and brought with it a huge culture shock. Gujaratis take the festival very seriously—certain foods are cooked, specific pujas performed—but not at the Pujara household. It turned out that in in their home, the only celebrations that took place revolved around cricket match victories. Festive seasons more or less passed them by like alien revels observed by extraterrestrials, as my late mother-in-law had been too long gone for festivals to matter very much.

My father-in-law's attitude towards Deepawali festivities verged on the casual. He was happy to consume boxes of sweets without engaging in the rituals that were so much part of the festival. Cheteshwar and he normally spent Diwali in a state of splendid isolation, but now—thanks to our betrothal—it was clear to the rest of the family that such a state of affairs could not possibly continue.

The extended family promptly stepped in and descended on them en masse, determined to steer the father–son through this particular year's celebrations. A nice Diwali lunch was duly ordered from outside in my honour. My fiancé was not around. He had left for a test series against England. I participated without comment, fully aware that I would have to take charge of these gaps in the future. I had realized by then that the Pujara attitude towards festivals was rooted in indolence. It was not that they had any deep-rooted objections to the revelries, it was just that there was nobody to take care of the nitty-gritty.

In the evening, when I spoke to my fiancé, I discovered that he had attended a net session and a gym session by way of celebration. He told me that a movie screening was scheduled for the team later. What a way to celebrate Diwali, I thought. It all sounded very tame to me.

On 15 November, the match was slated to start.

Cheteshwar's cousins, perhaps galvanized by the recent festivities, decided that a trip to Ahmedabad would be a fitting denouement to mark the end of the year's Diwali revels. The notion was immediately fine-tuned to include me in the excursion. 'Bhabi should also go,' someone suggested. This proposal once put to my family was met with animated approbation. Bhabhi would go, my folks decided, but so would her siblings! The general idea was to return to Rajkot that very evening—one that would go the way many a plan had gone before it.

On the appointed date, an enormous party comprising my siblings, Cheteshwar's cousins, mama, mami, chacha, chachi and me clambered on to a couple of cars for Ahmedabad, managing to reach the stadium at half-past-nine in the morning.

The Diwali vacations were not yet over. India had won the toss and chose to bat first. It was a grudge match for India—though I did not know it then—because we had lost 0-4 to England the previous year when it was regarded as the number one cricketing side in the world. This—I was to learn subsequently—was no longer the case.

At that stage, I was just soaking everything coming my way. It was very educational but I had ventured into completely unknown territory. Though my fiancé and I were in our courtship phase, I had not really had any meaningful glimpse of his professional career, mainly because he didn't talk about it too much and I did not like to probe.

When I look back, I marvel at the irony of it all; there was a copious amount of information available online about his cricketing career, and yet I never bothered to browse in-depth on the net to find out about it. Somehow, at the time, I had felt that it would be more natural to let that side of him unfold through his eyes instead of absorbing it impersonally through third-person narratives.

We settled down to watch the opening session. Gautam Gambhir and Virendra Sehwag opened the match. The former got out at 45 and Cheteshwar walked onto the crease—and that is when I had my second taste of media attention. It came as quite a shock. Our faces had been splashed in the newspapers extensively enough barely a week earlier, but the blissful anonymity that had ensued till this point had lulled me to believe that I was not interested enough to merit any further press coverage. Subsequent events soon put paid to this false piece of optimism.

Sehwag, from the little I understood of the game, played a scintillating innings, scoring 117 runs with a strike rate of 100 per cent. A loud cheer reverberated around the stadium when he was bowled by Graeme Swann. 'Why are they roaring when the poor guy has got out—that too after scoring a century?' I wondered.

I did not know then that the stadium had come alive, because Sachin Tendulkar, the demi-god of the cricketing world, was trotting in to replace Sehwag at the crease. He had debuted for India on the same date twenty-three years ago, as a sixteen-year-old. The crowd was ecstatic. Unfortunately, he got out at thirteen.

Cheteshwar stood his ground at the other end, and a couple of times when he hit a boundary, the cameras focused on me. Utterly self-conscious, I sported a constant smile on my face—good shot, bad shot, it did not matter—not that I knew much of what was happening in the game in any case. My facial muscles started aching. Valiantly, I persevered on, wondering if I would ever smile again.

This particular bout of media intrusion was just the harbinger of a string of seemingly never-ending woes. All of a sudden, I was inundated with a host of random messages. Matters did not improve. Soon people started approaching me; a patently peculiar experience that increased my sense of unease.

I stared at the steadily burgeoning crowd, with a spurious smile still pasted steadfastly on my face, wishing with all my might that I could turn into a latter-day Sita and invoke the earth to part and swallow me whole because, quintessentially, I was a very private person. I had never dealt with people in such large numbers before. If there had been an invisibility cloak[1] handy, I would have grabbed it.

At the close of day, Cheteshwar was batting at 98 and Yuvraj Singh at 24. The Pujara family was naturally disinclined to abandon its illustrious scion at such a critical stage of his innings, and decided to stay back at Ahmedabad for the night.

The decision was worth it. Cheteshwar, taught to put a premium on his bat, carried it through and remained not-out at 206, when India declared the innings after amassing 521 runs with only eight wickets down. Even I, a cricket-novice, understood the significance of the achievement.

Cheteshwar was on a high when I met him after the day's play. Caught up with the general sense of elation, I said: 'You have no idea how happy everyone is—and we're all thrilled to bits that you got your double hundred—it's truly amazing—'

He cut me short. 'This is truly amazing—what we have is truly amazing—this feels—' he paused, groping for the right word.

'This feels complete,' I said, finishing the sentence for him.

His eyes twinkled in response. I understood what he left unsaid. The fact that I had finished his sentence had just served to underline his point: this was complete; we were complete; we completed each other. It was a magical moment and his words never left me. Even today, when I look back, I can hear them loud and clear, as if he is still whispering them in my ears.

Team India declared and we left for Rajkot almost immediately after the declaration.

India would force a follow-on on England subsequently, and go on to rout it with an innings defeat. But for me the game stands out because it revealed an endearingly prudish side to Cheteshwar's personality.

~

Cheteshwar and I were having our customary nightly chat over the phone. He mentioned in passing that he was expecting to meet some acquaintances shortly. Soon afterwards, he took off and I thought no more of it.

Twenty minutes later, he called me up, shaken. His voice kept cracking because he was on the elevator and the signal was poor. I could not make out what he was trying to say, but it was clear that he was bursting to share some news with me.

'I can't hear you properly,' I complained.

'Just hold on, I'm about to reach my room. I need to tell you something,' he muttered, his voice suddenly loud and clear.

I heard him unlocking the door of his room and then latching it a few seconds later. By now I was brimming with curiosity.

He came back on the line. 'You remember I was telling you about these people I was going to meet?'

'Yes,' I admitted, cautiously.

Cheteshwar's story, the way he told it, bore close resemblance to a Grimm's fairy tale with a burlesque ending, in which he appeared to have starred as a somewhat naïve male version of Little Red Riding Hood. The big bad wolf in this instance turned out to be a young thirteen (maybe fourteen) year old girl.

In plain English, he met this family of four to five people who were friends of some friends. They asked for a photograph with him. He obliged. They wanted an autograph. He duly signed the bat produced by their son, who it appears was younger than his more intrepid sister. Just before they left, their young teenage daughter ventured to give him a quick hug and a chaste peck on the cheek to wish him good luck for his upcoming test match in Bombay, with her parents looking on benignly!

He ended his tale a tad disjointedly trying to soothe what he imagined would be my highly ruffled feathers by pointing out somewhat defensively, 'I couldn't do anything. It happened so quickly.'

I burst out laughing.

My amusement went unregistered and after a slight pause, avowedly determined to unburden himself, he continued in a stiff and embarrassed voice, 'I thought I should tell you.'

Still, in whoops, I chortled loudly and said, 'Cheteshwar she's only thirteen! Why are you even telling me about it? In fact, why are you even thinking about it?'

He grunted. His sense of humour had clearly gone abegging.

PART TWO

CHAPTER FIVE

In the Beginning

If cricket as a sport developed in the village greens of England, in India, it literally made its earliest splash in 1721 on the banks of the Dhadhar, slightly upriver from the Tankaria village, which served as a port in the then Jambusar district of Gujarat, courtesy some nostalgic English sailors of the East India Company. Desperately hankering to play the game, they decided to introduce some members of the Koli community to it.[1]

Cricket quickly became popular and percolated from the coasts to the rest of the Indian subcontinent and rapidly became the preferred sport not only amongst the white sahibs attempting to recreate a small piece of their mother country in an alien land but also among natives who were perhaps initially aping their colonial masters and later trying to best the British in their own game. During the 1930s, in a span of two short centuries, the bat and ball had not only become a national obsession but also the symbol of nationalism.[2] Around a decade later, by the time the Pujara clan became hooked to the game, it was well and truly entrenched in the country.

Cheteshwar is by no means the first of the Pujaras to play cricket seriously. His family's tryst with the game, described by *The Hindu* as part of the cricketing 'folklore of Kutch for more than half a century',[3] begins with his grandfather, Shiv Lal Pujara, in pre-Independence India. He played cricket for Dhrangadhra, a princely state in Gujarat, and passed on his love for the game to his two sons, Arvind, Cheteshwar's father, and Bipin, his uncle. Both went on to play Ranji for Saurashtra in the 1970s.

My father-in-law, born in 1950, played six Ranji matches as an opening batsman and has been described as an occasional wicket-keeper.[4] He still recalls how, as kids, he and his brother would tag along with Cheteshwar's grandfather to various matches and act as 'ball boys' on the boundaries. Cheteshwar's uncle, also an opening batsman and wicketkeeper, had a longer stint in first-class cricket and played around thirty-six matches. Cheteshwar's father bagged a job with the railways through the sports quota while his brother joined the Bank of India via the same route.

Sometime later, my father-in-law tied the nuptial knot with Cheteshwar's mother, Reena Kanani, the daughter of a cloth merchant. He was in his early thirties at the time and my mother-in-law, a few years younger. She hailed from a large family, comprising six siblings—four sisters and two brothers. Her dad was very strict, but her mother, very soft and sweet. Cheteshwar's mom took after her.

A tall, slim woman, with a fair complexion, longish face and an aquiline nose which she passed on to her son, my mother-in-law has been widely described as a deeply spiritual woman with a 'joyful nature' and an enormous capacity to spread happiness.

They quickly settled into connubial bliss in the regular small two-bedroom flat in the railway colony in Rajkot, popularly known as the 'Kothi compound'. Like most railway settlements, it was enormous, wildly verdant with dense clusters of neem, peepul and other native trees fringing every road and pathway within its precincts.

The place had a rich history and had once been the regional headquarters of the British East India company. The colonial hangover from the days of the Raj were still quite palpable in those days and the sahibs ruled the roost with a large battery of underlings from high-ceilinged offices overlooking large front gardens adorned with distinctly Victorian fountains. They lived in rarefied palatial homes that were referred to as bungalows while their minions lived in quarters. The officers and their families congregated to the club for a spot of recreation, whilst the rest made do with the institute, which was far more crowded and a lot less fancy. The officers did, it must be admitted, deign to venture into the institute with their kith and kin to watch the movies that ran on the 35 mm screen that had been mounted on the wall of the badminton court. They naturally sat on chairs in the viewing galley; everyone else meekly squatted on the wooden floor.

However, despite this palpable, in-your-face hierarchy, no one appeared to mind. Because the all-purpose railway ground was open to everyone and it was here that children converged each day to play tennis or cricket and volleyball. Everyone cycled around the grounds, flew kites and watched birds, most notably peacocks, that trod around fearlessly, quite indifferent to the humans that crossed their paths.

It was not a bad place for the newlyweds to begin their lives together. The money was not great, but neither minded, because even though my mother-in-law was only a matriculate, she had a good head for figures and knew how to hold the house on a shoe-string budget. She was an excellent cook, and a great housekeeper. They never ate outside and led a very satvik lifestyle.

In 1988, the couple were blessed with a son, to add to their joy. My mother-in-law, who consulted her guru on all important and not-so-important matters, requested him to name her newborn offspring, and draw up his birth chart. The neonate was initially named Amiraj, but when Guruji told her that the child's name should begin with the consonant 'ch', he was renamed Cheteshwar, which means 'long-lasting'. It is also one of Lord Shiva's names.

A noted Gujarati author once told the Pujaras that Cheteshwar meant 'the procurer of the soul', or someone who has attained mastery over his soul. Somebody else who studied Cheteshwar's astral chart pronounced that he would 'lead the life of a king'. At the time, neither of them dreamt that Cheteshwar would one day play cricket for the country.

Cheteshwar first held a bat in his hand when he was just three and that moment prove to be the turning point in his life. Ironically, he was introduced to the willow, not by the professional cricketers in the family, but by his maternal uncle, Bipin Kanani, the very same mama who played such an important role in getting the two of us hitched many years later.

The story, as I later learnt, is as follows. Bipin Mamaji had a friend, a professional shutterbug, who dedicated his weekends to capture life through the lens. On that particular day, the two chums decided to chivvy Cheteshwar and his cousin who were of an age, to a big field adjoining the Municipal Ground, the lone first-class cricketing turf in Rajkot that provided a half-way decent facility to practice the sport.

The intent was to click some action shots of the boys with the bat. Two toy bats were procured for the purpose. The shoot was successful and a composite of a photograph with Cheteshwar swinging the bat was duly presented to his dad by his uncle. Mamaji thought the picture was the perfect memento of Cheteshwar as a toddler and would be a joyful reminder of the moment for his parents in later years. It proved to be much more. It became an inflection point.

Cheteshwar returned home and took to playing with his bat as a duck takes to water. His father started studying the photograph. Something about the picture drew him to it time and again, almost as if he could not help himself. He did not just see a three-year-old with a toy bat. He saw a natural cricketer displaying a world of promise. He confided in his wife, who knew next to nothing about the game, but was quite willing to believe her husband's assessment—that the God's had favoured Cheteshwar with an innate cricketing talent.

'Why don't you concentrate on his gift and coach him?' she suggested.

My father-in-law laughed, accusing her of a mother's natural bias towards her son. 'You're overrating Cheteshwar because he's your son.'

However, he did not dismiss her counsel. Cheteshwar's father had learnt cricket under Velji Master, like his father before him, at the European Gymkhana, which had thrown up cricketing greats like Vinoo Mankad and Amar Singh. He had also worked as an assistant coach at Master's camp. His dad now resolved to put all the cricketing knowledge he had amassed at his son's disposal.

Thus began the saga of Cheteshwar's three-decades long and still-going-strong love affair with the game of cricket.

Growing up, Cheteshwar was probably a weird kid. His father comes across as even weirder. I say weird because from the moment my father-in-law decided to coach his son in cricket, there was no room for anything else in their lives.

Every morning, my father-in-law would accompany his young son to a huge neem tree just beyond their quarters to bowl under-arm throw-downs before dropping him to school.

In the late 1990s–early 2000s, Papa and Cheteshwar were a common sight in the corner of the railway grounds, under the neem tree, next to the volleyball court—my father-in-law rolling the ball along the ground, Cheteshwar methodically bringing his bat down and playing it straight back to him.

At this stage, my father-in-law refrained from the usual one-bounce throw-downs to the young Cheteshwar because at that age, he later explained, kids tend to swing their bat wildly at the ball and end up playing cross-batted shots. He didn't want Cheteshwar to develop the habit.

Cheteshwar never forgot his early lessons and continued to play with a straight bat throughout his cricketing career.

This strict regimen had a downside. He was not allowed to take part in any festive celebrations or co-curricular activities at school. My father-in-law thought they were an unnecessary distraction. The social life of the Pujaras became almost non-existent barring their rare expeditions to Bipin Mamaji's house. Cheteshwar tried to put things in perspective. 'In the initial years, we were barely able to make ends meet. The truth is we could not afford to socialize.'

Cheteshwar's schedule, growing up, had a set pattern. It involved waking up early in the morning, getting dressed to hit the nets, returning just in time to get ready for school, completing his homework post-school before his father came home from work, followed by another net session till sunset. Dinner was served at around 7.30-8.00 p.m., and lights in the Pujara household went off at 8.30 sharp and no visitors were encouraged beyond this hour. This was their standard routine. Day in and day out. Every single day. Throughout the year. His parents had only one collective vision: to make sure that Cheteshwar became a successful cricketer.

Not that Cheteshwar objected. Or rebelled. He loved cricket.

One of the first lessons he learnt from his father was that playing cricket was not enough; he had to play it correctly. Unlike a number of talented young cricketers who got burnt out or bored over time, Cheteshwar stayed the distance because he was in love the game.

The Pujaras became a permanent feature at the railway ground. Morning, afternoon, evening, summer, winter, monsoon—rain, hail or sunshine—nothing deterred them from the sport. My father-in-law ensured that Cheteshwar never played gully cricket and as a consequence, there were no instances of smashed window panes.

Cheteshwar's career path had been chosen even before he went to school!

By the time Cheteshwar was five years old, it was evident to his father that he had outgrown his modest playing field. Clearly, a larger ground was the need of the hour. This was duly found within the colony itself and their practice sessions shifted there, attracting a great deal of curiosity in the neighbourhood. Kids in the colony started gathering to watch them, initially to gawk, but this soon turned to enthusiasm for the game. Many of them now began approaching my father-in-law to coach them as well.

Amenable though he was to the idea, Cheteshwar's father thought that the ground would need an upgrade if he was to do justice to their request. He approached the Jagjivan Ram Railways Sports Institute requesting it to lay a cement pitch on the railway grounds, where he proposed to coach the kids for free.

The Pujaras could not afford house help, so Cheteshwar's mother took care of all the household chores, uncomplainingly. His father had a demanding job as a railway employee. However, it was a boon, as it allowed them to use the railway grounds and facilities for free—a silver lining they grabbed with gratitude.

Undaunted by their empty pockets, his parents took their meagre resources in their stride and went about their lives without wincing, staying focused on raising their only child with discipline; a key characteristic in the Pujara household, which remains to this day.

It was Cheteshwar's mother who helped him purchase his first bat on monthly installments from a sports store owner they knew. She stitched his initial cricket pads herself when she found out that finding a set for a kid of his age—he was seven at the time—was impossible.

Cheteshwar was barely eight when his father dressed him in 'dazzling' whites and home-made mini pads, and took him to the railway ground. I'm told, with his light eyes, he looked quite angelic. Everyone addressed him by his pet-name, Chintu.

In the meanwhile, despite the money crunch, my mother-in-law managed to ensure that Cheteshwar and his dad got top-quality food to refuel their energies for the next day. As Cheteshwar said wryly, 'In her mind, the fact that I was a vegetarian athlete meant that my diet needed extra attention.'

Cheteshwar's mother had uncovered the advantages of purchasing non-perishable products in bulk to benefit from the wholesale rate. She was an equally sensible shopper for clothes: she bought just a few things, but always of the best quality and her purchases were always driven by need and not want. 'She did not like to hoard stuff,' Cheteshwar once told me. 'She did not believe in unnecessary shopping.'

Overcoming challenges within their limited means, the Pujaras had made a small world of their own, one which revolved round Cheteshwar's progress in the game of cricket. My father-in-law knew making his son a renowned cricketer was not going to be an easy affair. It would take money and dedication and he sometimes wondered if he was overestimating his son's talent. He was also aware that no one he knew in Rajkot had the necessary knowledge to make an accurate judgement.

When Cheteshwar turned eight and had acquired enough experience in hitting the ball, his father decided to take him to Bombay to find out whether his son really possessed the qualities of a good batsman. To this end, he rang up his friend and former Saurashtra cricketer and India all-rounder, Karsan Ghavri, who was also from Rajkot and now coached for Bharat Petroleum Corporation Limited in Mumbai. He brought Ghavri up to speed with his dilemma and ended with the plea: 'Kadu bhai, please take a look at my son and tell me if he is actually any good.'

Once Ghavri had signalled his willingness to assess Cheteshwar's batting, without losing time, father and son hopped on to a train and reached Aziz Bagh, Chembur, in suburban Mumbai. It was his day off, but Ghavri was kind enough to oblige them with his time.

At the maidans, Karsan Ghavri watched Cheteshwar hawk-eyed, noting his batting, his shots and his stance. Several hours later, he pronounced: '*Jann mein dum toh hai* (he has strong possibilities). He is quite promising. You should work with him to develop his game.'

Much relieved, Ghavri's proclamation acted as a tremendous confidence-booster for both Cheteshwar and his father. At least they now knew they were on the right track. They returned home tired, but contented. The trip had definitely been worth it.

Cheteshwar's training leap-frogged to the next level.

This meant no off days. No Sundays. No festivals. Nothing. On the days he went to school, he would wake at 5 a.m., train at his father's camp, come back, finish his homework, attend school from 12.30 p.m. to 5 p.m. (the afternoon shift had been chosen because it allowed him to practise in the morning), rush back home and then head back to the camp to make the most of the remaining daylight.

He sometimes regrets not having been a normal Gujarati boy. Gujaratis love their festivals: flying kites on Sankranti, participating in garba pre-Diwali, and then of course, lighting diyas and bursting firecrackers on Diwali itself—a time of huge celebrations for everyone in Gujarat—everyone except Cheteshwar.

Even on Diwali day, he was not exempt from the game of cricket, even if they were due to visit relatives in the evening. He had to keep up with his practice session in the afternoon if he wanted to be allowed to take part in the fireworks and general festivities on Diwali night.

Cheteshwar's relationship with his father was somewhat uncommon because despite the discipline imposed by the former; it never engendered any dislike in the son for his dad or the game. Cheteshwar never resented being made to play cricket. If, once in a while, he told his father that 'he didn't feel all that normal, without holidays and friends', his dad would remind him that focus and dedication was de rigueur to succeed as an international cricketer and Cheteshwar, always sensible, would acknowledge his father's reasoning and pipe down.

If Cheteshwar's father was the moving force behind his career, his mother was the central figure in his life. She was his first friend. The only individual with whom he shared all his childlike thoughts and feelings. The one person around whom his world revolved. He would spend the best part of his days with her and she would allow him to do what he wanted—up to a point.

'She was very smart,' he recounts. 'She managed me in a very canny way, mostly allowing me to do as I pleased, while all the while ensuring that I didn't cross the line. I had my freedom, but there were limits.'

The next five years were hardwork, full of net sessions and endless days of perspiration. Cheteshwar's father had a vision and a roadmap very much in place for Pujara junior's career and his mother had a blueprint prepared for his spiritual journey. His parents thought the two objectives could easily coexist and from then on, they began to work towards these twin goals.

This meant living a hostel life at home with the family. At the age of eight, when most kids spent their free time playing gully cricket and building friendships, Cheteshwar followed his chosen career path with a seriousness that few adults can emulate.

If their domestic struggles were acute, their determination to chase their dreams was not all sunshine and roses either. Most people mocked them, often sneering at the impossible 'crazy dream' they pursued. This in an atmosphere where sports was 'big'! Everyone played some game or the other because it guaranteed a railway job through the sports quota.

Kothi compound, in short, offered the kind of refuge that very few wanted to abandon.

Not so my father-in-law. Even as a senior clerk in the engineering department. He was different. A quintessential outlier, his worst sin in the eyes of the sahibs was his forthright bluntness. He routinely clashed with them over his frequent absence from work, first as a player and later when he took to coaching his son.

Nowadays, he often snickers when he looks back at his days of office rebellion. He recalls getting a local MP to write a letter to the railway minister once when he failed to get a hike. On another occasion, he silenced an officer who called him a liability to the railways by reminding him of his 'corrupt ways' and told him that he was 'a bigger burden for the employers'.

'He didn't bother me after that,' my father-in-law chuckles.

'I was not looking for any favours from them, my dreams were much bigger.'

A kothi compound kid and later a sports editor of the *Indian Express*, Sandeep kept close tabs on Cheteshwar's rise in cricket and his family was instrumental in helping Sultan, a cricket enthusiast, who worked for them, to join the Pujara nets for coaching.

My father-in-law would throw the new ball to Sultan when Cheteshwar padded up. Sultan would update Sandeep about Cheteshwar's sturdy defence and joke '*Bhaiya bilkul Dravid jaisa khelta hai, out hi nahi hota*' (Bhaiya plays just like Dravid, he just doesn't get out).

In the meanwhile, blessed with a stoicism that can only be envied, the Pujaras accepted all the brickbats with a shrug and carried on, undeterred. An energetic planner, my father-in-law realized the importance of English-speaking skills in an international cricketer's career quite early and pressed the services of some able private tutors to coach him in the language when he was still a young boy. They were tasked to ensure that he learnt how to speak and write English fluently. It was a smart move, one that paid good dividends when Cheteshwar grew up.

Next, he focused on Cheteshwar's schooling. No school was going to impede his son's progress in cricket. In a span of five years, Cheteshwar changed three schools; each choice based on the institution's ability to offer maximum representation at tournaments.

This was the time when the only entertainment that Cheteshwar enjoyed were visits to his Mama's house on Sundays. It was his only recreational outlet and became something of getaway for him. It was the only place in his life where he did not have to practice cricket; in his uncle's abode, he could let his hair down and enjoy video games with his cousins. Cheteshwar's competitive spirit, omnipresent from a very early age, would manifest itself in the simplest games—physical or virtual. Right from the very beginning, he would only play to excel. He would lure those around him with his innocent face to play a game or sport which he knew he would win; more often than not, he would emerge victorious from these contests with a cheeky smile on his lips and a hint of glee in his eyes.

On one such evening, at his uncle's house, Cheteshwar spotted a football-shaped eraser that belonged to his cousin. It grabbed his eyeballs and seemed to shriek 'possess me'. It was love at first sight for the young lad and the beginning of a long-drawn battle with his mother.

'Ma,' said Cheteshwar, showing her his new-found passion. 'Look at this eraser. It's so cool. Will you also buy one like this for me?'

Never one to encourage the concept of 'keeping up with the Joneses', my mother-in-law flatly refused. Three hours went by and neither combatant backed down. What started as a request had slowly transformed into a clash of wills between mother and son.

His mom's stand was clear: if her child was demanding something out of a sense of competition with other kids, or because he felt disadvantaged, it would not be fulfilled. No amount of tantrums were going to work. To her, it was not about the eraser but a desire to inculcate the habit of being mindful of the purchases that one made and the understanding that one did not need everything that someone else owned.

The duel raged on. Cheteshwar's aunt tried to step into the breach to make peace—to no avail, with the two equally strong personalities standing their ground. Tired and angry, when Cheteshwar finally slept, his aunt had a word with my mother-in-law. 'Let him have the eraser. It's not that big a deal.'

Mamiji, by this time, had procured the coveted eraser and had it in her hand.

Cheteshwar's mother thawed slightly. 'Alright,' she said, resignedly. 'You may give it to him. But please wait for a day or two. Because I want him to learn the lesson I am trying to teach him. He can't just go around acting like a prince and demanding things just because he wants it. He must understand that it's not just about wanting something. The key question that he needs to ask himself is if he really needs it.'

Cheteshwar got his football eraser after a couple of days, but only after he had received his mother's message loud and clear. It was one that would stay with him for the rest of his life.

One aspect of Cheteshwar's life that his mother assumed iron control of was his spiritual education. Deeply religious herself, imbuing her son with a strong moral compass was almost a compulsion. She also tried to inculcate the habit of devoting fifteen minutes daily to his prayers when he was very young. Initially, she made deals with him. 'If you want to play your video games or play with your friend, you first finish your prayers,' she would say.

His mother would allow him 'video-game time' only after he completed his prayers. At every opportunity possible, she would take him to Gondal to visit the ashram and seek blessings from their guru. Birthdays were often celebrated with bhandaras that were organized to feed sadhus and the needier sections of society.

Cheteshwar's father too was against the idea of celebrating birthdays in the usual time-honoured way. He strongly disapproved of the entire cake-cutting ritual pronouncing it as a 'wasteful indulgence' and an 'unnecessary distraction'.

Did Cheteshwar ever feel deprived? He says not. As a young teen, he managed to draw every drop of enjoyment from his cousins' birthdays, treating these celebrations as if they were his own. On his tenth birthday, Cheteshwar's Mama and Mami insisted on visiting him, bearing a compass box which he had taken a shine to a few days earlier, as a gift.

As Cheteshwar tells it, his uncle returned from office at 8 p.m. and by the time he arrived at the Pujara household with his aunt, it was almost a quarter-to-nine, by which time he was fast asleep. My father-in-law was none too pleased to meet the two visitors who had dared to trespass past the witching hour of 8.30 p.m. But Cheteshwar's mother was unfazed. She was convinced that their presence would really lift up her son's spirits. So, she woke him up, and made some sheera, a sweet dish made of wheatflour, to strike a celebratory note to the whole proceeding. Cheteshwar remembers going to sleep hugging his precious compass box that night. His uncle and aunt had clearly made the right decision.

Over the next couple of years, my father-in-law realized that if Cheteshwar was to become an international cricketer, he would need to play a lot of competitive matches. It was also patently obvious to him that Rajkot was not going to provide him the kind of exposure to the game which he needed. At this point, he decided that for the next phase of Cheteshwar's training, the Pujaras would need to patronize the maidans of Mumbai.

CHAPTER SIX

In the Maidans of Mumbai

The maidans of Mumbai have a rich and varied history. The origins of the Indian love for cricket can be traced in their green expanse at the southern end of what was earlier known as the island of Bombay. Ringed by distinctive gothic colonial architecture—the High Court of Bombay, the University of Mumbai, St Xavier's college and the Victoria Terminus, these grounds which at one time fringed the fort—the city's earliest settlement—was razed by the British in 1777 to get a clear firing range when they feared an attack from the French. Over time, the threat waned and the grounds were put to peacetime use—exercise and recreation.[1]

The area known to the British Army as the Parade Ground, the English civilians as the Esplanade and the indigenous population as the Maidan,[2] in earlier times was the homing ground for small, mostly male, clusters looking for entertainment ranging from card games (badshai) to dice games (chopat) and board games like dam (draughts) and chess. Youngsters, in the meanwhile, spent hours here playing the old and most popular type of 'gilly danda' (a variant of tip cat) or 'asookh mahasookh (a form of physical exercise). By the 1850s, these traditional games had given way to cricket,[3,4] with the Parsis being the first to switch to the sport, followed by Hindus and finally the Mohammedans, each opening their own sporting clubs.

The early version of Indian cricket was played with 'chimney-pots serving as wickets and umbrellas as bats in hitting elliptical balls stuffed with old rags sewn by veritably useful cobblers.'[5] These initial attempts, at first, drew little notice, but later a Bombay journalist sneered at some Hindu players acidly commenting that 'their kilted garments interfered [when batting] with running, and they threw the ball when fielding in the same fashion as boarding school girls'.[6] The comments stung and the dhoti and dagli were duly discarded for cream-coloured flannels.

By the time Cheteshwar made his first foray into the maidans at the astonishingly young age of eleven, South Mumbai boasted of several grounds where young kids could train at camps during the week and play competitive cricket on the weekends.

Papa realized early on that match practice was the only answer if he was to imbue Cheteshwar with the confidence to survive in competitive matches. He figured that the only available option was to shift his son's training to the maidans in Mumbai. But how? Cashflow was a problem. If he took time off from work and moved his family to Mumbai during the summer vacations, he would have to forgo his salary once he had used up his quota of leave, and their money crunch would worsen even further. Then there was the problem of lodging. The Pujaras knew no one in Mumbai with whom they could kip, and there was no way they could afford to rent any accommodation. It was a daunting prospect.

Never willing to say die, my father-in-law put his mind to the problem and started exploring avenues for a way out. He had several dear friends to whom he sent out feelers, explaining his difficulty. A couple of them were generous enough to offer the Pujaras a pad free of cost, but they were usually in the suburbs.

'Needs must!' he thought, and quickly grabbed these offers with both hands, at least Cheteshwar would get the much-needed match practice!

The digs in Mumbai were by no means ideal. The Pujaras were sometimes lodged in flats awaiting new occupants, while at others, they boarded in buildings in the final stages of construction. But they faced these travails stoically. After all, as Papa had told his buddies, 'We don't need anything inside the flat—just electricity and water supply!'

Once their lodgings had been arranged, a different one every summer, the Pujaras were ready to tackle Mumbai. Every year, when schools broke up for the summer vacations, the Pujara family would pack up to head to the metropolis. Cheteshwar's mother would invariably carry a small bag of utensils, a stove and other items required to prepare meals. One year, they stayed at Panvel and during another at the outskirts of Thane.

While his parents took these temporary summer digs in their stride, to Cheteshwar it was 'the most irritating phase of his life' during which he had to hop on to local trains with his dad carrying heavy equipment and getting squished, and sometimes even hurt by inconsiderate commuters to whom he might as well have been invisible. The experience left him with a strong aversion to big cities.

When they first landed in Mumbai, Cheteshwar and his father would leave every morning with his kit and tiffin in hand. To get to a net, they had to reach the targeted maidan by 7 a.m., because every ground had to be vacated for matches by 8.30 a.m. But net practice was not what my father-in-law wanted for his son. He wanted Cheteshwar to get match practice. To this end, he turned to Ghavri for help once again.

Ever obliging, Ghavri put my father-in-law in touch with Ravi Thakkar, a former Mumbai player and selector who ran a camp in Mumbai. Papa met Thakkar and asked him to alert him whenever there was any vacancy in any team. Thakkar duly spread the word and soon after, the father–son duo began to head to various cricket grounds for the longed-for match practice, but without any assured guarantees.

There were times when Cheteshwar's mother would stay back in the borrowed flat to take care of the household chores and at others, she would accompany her menfolk. It was a touching tale of three dreamers with empty pockets and a bucketful of dreams. For them, retreat was not an option. They had come too far.

To grab a slot in the matches, they would have to reach the grounds by 9 a.m., which meant they had to leave their makeshift residence at least a couple of hours in advance. They would return to their billet only after the day's play, at around 7 p.m.

With these long journeys back and forth, if Cheteshwar failed to score runs, he started viewing it as a day's practice lost. He was taught to make the most of his opportunities and very early on, developed an obsession that prompted him to put a price on his wicket and play as if the life depended on it—which in his head, of course, it did—his entire future depended on his performances. It would shape him as a batsman. He not only started putting a heavy premium on his wicket, but also began to bat without the freedom displayed by other players. This was also in part his father's influence. Papa repeatedly told him that he needed to stay his ground if he wanted to attract attention.

In a fruitful summer, Cheteshwar managed three matches a week, totalling to about eighteen matches on different types of pitches.

'That was a lot more matches than we had in Rajkot in a year,' my father-in-law once told me. These vacations, the sacrifices that were made to get those matches and the discipline that it demanded, all went on to mould Cheteshwar into the player he is today.

My father-in-law still fondly and frequently remembers those days, and the people who helped him during his hour of need, purely out of affection for him and in recognition of the hard yards that Cheteshwar was making to clinch his future as a professional cricketer.

It must be remembered that this was a time when there was very little money in cricket—the big bucks started flowing into the game only in 2007 after India won the T20 world championship. Thanks to the ensuing hysteria in the country, a new idea materialized among the administrators and money managers of Indian cricket—T20 could be milked for more money than the sport had ever seen! The Indian Premier League, or IPL, was born on 18 April 2008 and the rest, as they say, is history. Indian cricket leapfrogged into a multi-billion–dollar industry! The Pujaras, however, it must be mentioned, were not driven by any craving for cash—there was none to be had at the time—their pursuit of the game was propelled by the sheer joy and passion for the sport coupled with a strong sense of purism.

These are tiny little tales of the miles they travelled to pursue a passion that had no guarantee of success. They brushed aside conventional views that education was paramount as a backup if one's dreams of cricket as a career went south. Cheteshwar's father did not have any inheritance to pass on to his son—all he had was his knowledge of cricket and this he passed on to his child in spades.

Cheteshwar began his foray into competitive cricket at the district level by representing Rajkot rural. He fared well enough to grab the notice of state selectors. His first big selection took place for an Under-13 team representing Saurashtra. This is exactly what he had been training for between the age of seven and twelve. All those years of sweat and sacrifice had finally paid off. But the biggest obstacle was still to be overcome—and it was Cheteshwar himself.

Most kids are euphoric when they are selected as state-level players. Not Cheteshwar. The match was in Pune, and Cheteshwar had a meltdown. What should have been a moment of celebration turned into endless hours of trial and tribulation. He was in a state of abject misery. Up till now, he had only represented the district, three-day matches that were played at places which were just half an hour from home and allowed him to come home at night.

But matters were different now that he had made it as a state player. The match venue was Pune, a long way off from Rajkot, which meant that he would no longer have the luxury of returning to his mother at night.

The crisis came to a head when he refused to travel with the team. He was ready to quit cricket, he declared, if it meant being away from his mother. A quintessential mamma's boy, the very thought was anathema to him. He had never been without his mother for a single day and now that the hour to fly from the nest was upon him, the very notion, terrified him.

Tension reigned in the house for the next twenty-four hours. Everything they had dreamt of—all that they had worked for was finally theirs for the taking and now when they were on the threshold of the door to success, Cheteshwar, the very fulcrum of their aspirations, was throwing a shindig and refusing to take the next leap forward.

Cheteshwar's mother pleaded with him. 'You've worked so hard for this—you've reached so far. You mustn't lose this opportunity.'

No reaction.

Then his father stepped in and tried to reason with his recalcitrant offspring. 'When you grow up, you'll have to travel. It's part of the profession. You might as well begin now. You know you love the game—this is just one of the sacrifices you have to make for it.'

Truculent silence.

The breakthrough ultimately occurred after a lot of persuasion, and only when Cheteshwar's parents promised to procure a mobile phone for him so that he could be in touch with them whenever he wanted. Much to their intense relief, he finally agreed to go to Pune. The separation anxiety still simmered beneath the surface, but he had now come to terms with the fact that travelling was a professional hazard he would have to get used to; it was going to be a constant feature in the career path he had chosen.

Today, Cheteshwar remembers the trip to Pune with a wry smile. 'We were all booked in a train and stuffed into one coach with a manager. We had to share rooms and none of us had any money. I think I was twelve years old at the time.'

There is an all-important fact that he fails to mention—that he broke down when the time came for him to leave for Pune. His father, however, is less circumspect and talks about it casually with a reminiscent grin. 'I think he cried at the thought of being separated from his mother.'

But all in all, they both agree that the said trip turned out to be a turning point in his life. He made his first set of friends, learned to cope outside his comfort zone, acquired an independent streak and managed to survive without the all-embracing love and security provided by his parents.

He fared well in the two one-day matches he played in Pune, and was picked for the three-day format shortly afterwards. His parents bought him the promised mobile, a second-hand devise. It was an expensive proposition because call charges were as high as Rs 20 for an outgoing call and Rs 16 for an incoming one. Once Cheteshwar got used to being away from home, they struck a compromise and he started using his mobile more like a pager, alerting his parents of his safety by sending them missed calls.

The highlight of this period was his first triple century. It happened in the very first year of his selection. Cheteshwar smashed a solid unbeaten 306 against Baroda in an Under-14 match. The year was 2002, he was just three days shy of his thirteenth birthday. He already had a couple of 70s and a 100 to his name. But my father-in-law, always a hard taskmaster, never let him rest on his laurels. He pushed him to score big each time. 'You must always ensure that your selection is never a matter of quandary for anyone.'

If Cheteshwar scored a 100, Papa would advise him to convert it to a double hundred. 'Stay put and don't get carried away, just because you've scored a century.' It was not that his father was not proud of his achievements. He just wanted to ensure that his son never became complacent about them.

Referring to Cheteshwar's first triple century, Papa's face takes on a strange reflective expression. 'These are the moments that make parents forget all the sacrifices they have made to see their child prosper,' my father-in-law tells me. 'But I had to make sure that he learnt how to put a price on his wicket. We did not have the luxury or the means to permit him to squander his opportunities and I made sure that he understood that.'

However, the triple-century did have three outcomes. The first two touched Cheteshwar.

When the team returned to Rajkot from Baroda, he had his maiden encounter with the media. His feat had made national headlines, his photograph was splashed in several local newspapers and the entire team was assembled at the coach's house where Zee news beamed a televised interview of the coach as well as of Cheteshwar.

Young as he was, Cheteshwar came across as very sensible, and matured in the interview. It was evident that he was not going to get carried away. My father-in-law's counsel had obviously fallen on receptive ears.

The second fallout was his maiden cricketing setback. He had just scored his triple century and the Under-15 Indian squad was due for selection. He was summoned for a camp in Bangalore.

His triple century had created a lot of hype around him and his peers at the camp were convinced that he would certainly get the captaincy. But when the team was announced, Cheteshwar discovered that he wasn't even in the squad. 'You're too slow' was the explanation. It was an early precursor of the strike-rate ghost that would haunt him throughout his career. He called up his father to share the bad news and boarded the train for the long trip back home via Mumbai.

En route, he got robbed. Someone walked away with his suitcase which was the repository of all his worldly goods—his whites, his money and his cell phone! He was just thirteen, but even at that age, he had developed a resilience that helped him keep his head. He borrowed someone's phone and made an SOS call to his dad. 'I've been robbed,' he informed apologetically. 'My suitcase is gone. I have no money.'

'Hang in there,' said his father, carefully concealing his concern. 'I'll meet you in Mumbai.'

My father-in-law rushed to Mumbai expecting to meet a crestfallen boy in need of a great deal of succour. Instead, he found his son undaunted, unperturbed and quite philosophical about the whole episode. 'He was absolutely unfazed,' said Papa. 'He didn't complain and he didn't blame anyone for what had happened to him. Since he seemed to take it in his stride, so did I. We just made small talk and moved on, leaving the whole incident behind us.'

In the meanwhile, another development occurred. While my father-in-law was at the railway station, he received a call informing him that Cheteshwar had to be in Baroda for an Under-16 game. 'I called my wife and asked her to hand over Chintu's whites to one of his Saurashtra teammates. We managed to reach on time. He scored a 100 in the game. When people talk about his ability to bounce back, trust me, I am not surprised.'

In the early 2000s, Cheteshwar scored 300 runs in an Under-16 game. At one time Papa actually feared that Cheteshwar might not be able to play the game. The reason: He didn't have the money to buy a new bat for him. To get round the problem, he went to Cheteshwar's school to borrow a team bat. The PE teacher was not in an obliging mood and the said willow was relinquished to the distraught father only after a bitter battle.

The tale of the borrowed bat has a riveting aftermath. More than a decade later, in 2017, when Sandeep arrived at Rajkot to cover the assembly elections, Papa caught up with him. Sandeep was accompanied by a friend who was part of his tennis group and a school teacher. My father was unusually silent and it was only later that evening that he told Sandeep over the telephone that his friend was the very same teacher who had tried to deny Cheteshwar the bat with which he later scored his triple century at the age of thirteen. The incident obviously stayed with Papa for a long time.

The third outcome affected Papa, who was so upset that Cheteshwar had been denied a place in the Under-15 Indian squad for the Asia cup that he immediately wanted to shift out of Rajkot and relocate his family to Bangalore. The move was shot down by his wife in her calm, quiet way. It was not the first time she would rein in her impetuous spouse during the course of their marriage.

'Why do you want to shift to Bangalore,' she asked tranquilly, when he first informed her of his intention.

'Rajkot is not good enough,' he said frustratedly. 'It's more or less a backwater as far as cricket is concerned. Bangalore has all the proper facilities for an up-and-coming cricketer.'

'You worry unnecessarily,' she stated serenely. 'Cheteshwar will go far. He will play for India.' Many years later, when he recounted the incident to me, he said, 'I don't know where Reena drew her confidence from. But she never wavered in her belief.' She even told her husband that nobody would be able to stop Cheteshwar's success. 'You may write this down in a paper. I'll even sign on it.'

Papa smiled self-deprecatingly when he finished his tale. 'It wasn't the first time that the mother–son duo ganged up and outvoted me.'

Once Cheteshwar managed to get more comfortable in his skin, he found ways and means to keep in touch with his parents telephonically every evening, either by using hotel phones or STD-PCOs, to keep them abreast of his day.

From what I have gathered from Cheteshwar, he made separate calls to his parents each evening. The first was reserved for his mother, who unfailingly reminded him to count his blessings, thank the almighty for the opportunities that he had been given and stay grounded. Their chat would then switch to his day, his food and his health.

His conversations with his dad ran on more predictable lines. It always veered around cricket. What kind of shots had he played? Had he played them along the ground? They would discuss the nitty-gritty of the game, his practice routine, and Cheteshwar would occasionally mention a change in technique suggested by the team coach of the moment. His father would then mull over it and relay his opinion on the subject the following evening.

Although my father-in-law had not had a very long innings in first-class cricket and did not have any major accomplishments to his name as a cricketer, he had always possessed a keen love for the sport. He knew Cheteshwar's game better than anyone else and would often push his son to discuss his game with the coaches, so that he could pick up some new ideas.

But he did not always trust their advice or think that it would work for his kid. Each advice, every suggestion was carefully scrutinized by him until he was convinced that it would actually add to Cheteshwar's game. There were no two ways about it—my father-in-law had the final word on his son's cricket. He was the one who obsessed about it and shaped the course for the future. Every one else was peripheral.

Balancing his education with cricket was no mean task. By the time Cheteshwar turned thirteen, his travels had begun and he would often miss school for days on end. When he returned home after outstation matches, he would find a mountain of school work awaiting him, because he had missed so much of it. Cheteshwar says he spent most of his growing years playing catch-up at school.

At a very early age, he became conscious of his diet when he was given literature on fitness and nutrition by the Zonal Cricket Academy and the National Cricket academy. Living in a small city in Saurashtra, where the concept of a well-balanced diet was practically non-existent, Cheteshwar struggled to eat healthy. He never ate outside food when was at home and tried very hard to consume freshly cooked meals. His mother, always ready to champion her son's needs, cooperated to the best of her ability although it must be mentioned here that typically Gujarati food is not particularly wholesome. My husband had acquired taste for a few deep-fried snacks and most of his meals were accompanied by a drink. There was no awareness at that stage that the said savouries which he was wolfing down with so much enjoyment were pure poison. Weening him away from them later in life would be a labour of Hercules.

CHAPTER SEVEN

My Friend Kuldeep

In every classroom, there are front-benchers and back-benchers: and a lot of pop psychology has been used to analyse their personality and behaviour. There is an oft-quoted line in the current politically correct era that claims frontbenchers are hard workers and backbenchers are smart workers. But back in the days when most people preferred to call a spade a shovel, frontbenchers were usually regarded as snollygosters and teachers' pets by their classmates; the more adventurous lot that occupied the last rows at the time and drew the unalloyed awe and admiration of their peers because all the interesting action took place there, far away from their eagle-eyed preceptors who conversely viewed the latter as 'troublemakers' with a capital 'T'.

No prizes for guessing where Cheteshwar sat—right under the teacher's nose in the first row. A typical frontbencher, he was a prim little soul, who had not yet learnt the art of being at ease with other children. He was not the kind of child who would join the other kids for a spot of mischief or fun or—horror of horrors—gang up with them to break some minor rule. If he cut a solitary figure in school, things were no different on the cricketing field. Never a pack animal, he kept to himself, always the lone wolf among a sea of players. As a result: growing up, he had practically no friends even among his teammates—this, despite shared journeys and communal digs that should have brough him closer to them through each cricketing event.

Why was Cheteshwar such a loner?

Perhaps because he was an only child and never had time away from cricket to come up for air to forge friendships. It could also be that he just did not know how, because he had never really learnt how to interact with people outside his house except at a minimal level. Whatever the reason, even as a teenager, Cheteshwar took life seriously and cricket even more so. He held the belief that team sports required neutrality and groupism was detrimental to the game. Even today, he believes that it is essential to maintain a neutral stance in all things related to cricket and one should speak up only when the need is absolute. It was an attitude that naturally did not earn him any cachet among his teammates, nor did it make him particularly popular with them.

This was exacerbated by Cheteshwar's failure to defend his team against players from other states of the same zone, even though his teammates made it a point of honour to take on the offenders from the 'other' side when they targeted Cheteshwar and teased him ceaselessly. Cheteshwar remembers them 'picking silly fights' and saw no reason to 'stoop down' and join the general melee. Annoyed by his lack of teamsmanship, the boys in his team, in turn, hit back at him by making fun of his game, his work ethics and his attitude. It did not matter. Cheteshwar just accepted all the brickbats with a shrug, turned a deaf ear to all the snide remarks that were hurled at him and simply plodded on.

His friend Kuldeep Sharma is a minefield of information about those long-ago days. They first met when they were fourteen years old. Kuldeep had ascended the various rungs of the game through sheer talent and, unlike Cheteshwar, he treated cricket more like a hobby; his family did not know much about the game and was disinclined to view it as a serious career option.

In the early years, the prospect of sharing a room with Cheteshwar was viewed by his teammates with extreme misgivings; he was regarded as 'rigid' and 'not very accommodating'. He had his 'routine' which he followed religiously and no one was allowed to hinder it. He would get up at six in the morning, never linger in bed and, even worse, any roommate who played loud music was asked to turn it down. He refused to adapt and expected his smarting co-lodger to make all the adjustments.

Under the circumstances, it was hardly surprising that his peers were baffled by him. They found him rude and selfish, and thought he was a self-absorbed boy who did not mingle and, worse still, refused to go the extra mile for them. His refusal to blend in extended outside the field and lodgings as well. While the other kids would head out to eat or shop, he would opt to stay behind.

If a teammate asked, 'We're eating pizza, why don't you join us?', he would invariably reply, 'You go ahead, I'll eat what I like.' His failure to run with the pack was greeted widely with askance. Everyone agreed he was 'difficult'.

Today, Cheteshwar ruefully confesses that as a teenager, he was the quintessential party pooper. 'But for me, cricket was a profession, not an excursion and there was no way I was going to get bogged down by peer pressure.'

He willingly admits that he just did not possess the teenage panache or enthusiasm to cut a dash, so common at that age. As a result, he became a misfit.

All the boys who spoke the same language hung out together and formed groups, but even over time, when Cheteshwar lost his rough edges, he would join in only occasionally, remaining consistently neutral, not caring what people thought of him. A lot of these traits exist even today and some of them maybe perceived as selfish. But there are layers to his personality, and it is only when someone has stayed with him long enough can these fortifications be penetrated to understand him.

Not even his best friends can call Cheteshwar a friendly person—at first sight, he appears rather remote. He holds on to his dignity rather doggedly and keeps his emotions in constant check. Even as a teenager, he was extremely slow to anger. It takes time to get under his skin, to gauge his emotions, and this can be irritating in the extreme to someone whom he has unconsciously aggravated without meaning to. But on the flip side, he doesn't hold grudges, he does not view any one as an enemy, not even those at whose hands he has suffered betrayal. He has an immense capacity for tolerance. When Cheteshwar makes friends, they are for life. He is also a giver. If he can help someone, he will—in every possible way, at great personal cost—this may be medical, financial, recommendatory or by way of a phone call.

Initially, Kuldeep did not want to hang out with him, but he too is an altruist at heart, always seeing good in others. When his teammates refused to kip with Cheteshwar, Kuldeep stepped forward and volunteered to share a room with him.

Kuldeep explains: 'If someone is praying or making that extra effort to spend thirty-forty minutes each day to stick to his routine, then it's fair to adjust to his bathing time or waking-up time. I could see that Cheteshwar was going that extra mile to chase his dream. What did it matter if I had to rise a little earlier or adjust to his ablutions. I didn't think it was that big a deal.'

The friendship between the two young lads started blossoming a little at a time when Kuldeep began noticing the small thoughtful gestures that Cheteshwar made towards him almost unobtrusively. Aware that Kuldeep was from Anjar in Kutch, the young teenager would ask his mother to pack some food for his friend as well. 'He's from Anjar,' he would explain. 'He can't carry food from so far. It will spoil.'

The upshot of this conversation with his mother was that whenever they travelled to Mumbai together, Cheteshwar would hop on to the train at Rajkot armed with food for Kuldeep as well. It was a long journey and he did not want his friend to go hungry. Kuldeep also started noticing his honesty and commitment to the sport. Clearly, there was more to his new buddy than met the eye. Their friendship started deepening and they began to hang out together.

One day, during a zonal camp in Mumbai, out of the blue, Cheteshwar made an announcement. 'I want to go shopping.'

By this time, his teammates had learnt to accept him as he was and were inclined to look at him with a more benign eye. His proclamation was greeted with a great deal of excitement, as such declarations were entirely uncharacteristic of him. Growing up, he had only possessed one pair of jeans which accompanied him wherever he went. Everyone in his team knew that he was not the kind to spend any money on fashionable items, if he could help it. He was more likely to don the zonal academy travel T-shirts when he stepped out. He would carefully save up his allowance from the cricket academy either to buy cricket gear on his return or to add the carefully conserved sums to his mother's judiciously accumulated hoard.

Kuldeep was suffering from inflamed sinuses that day, so the task of escorting Cheteshwar to Fashion Street fell upon Mohnish Parmar. When they left for the market at around 5.30 p.m., Mohnish looked positively jaunty. On their turn, some two-and-a-half hours later, he looked thoroughly disgruntled.

Kuldeep watched the two shoppers ambling back with amusement. After spending more than two hours there, all Cheteshwar came back with was a T-shirt worth Rs 60! Noticing Mohnish's peeved expression, Kuldeep burst out laughing. 'What's happened to you? Why are you looking so irritated?'

Thankful for an outlet for his grievance, Mohnish went on a loud and lengthy rant. 'How can anyone be so choosy? How can anyone be so calculative that he can find fault with all the 10,000-plus pieces that we saw?'

Cheteshwar as usual paid no heed and Mohnish's ire soon blew over. But the incident to my mind is Vintage Pujara! Even today, Cheteshwar is mindful of what he spends. He does not compromise on the things he needs, but when it comes to fashion trends, he will not purchase something just because his peers are.

His food habits at the time were equally peculiar. 'He had a specific way in which he would order and reorder the same thing with the same combination over and over again at the same place,' Kuldeep recalls. He also remembers Cheteshwar, true to his Rajkot roots, loved to spend his money on food, not just for himself, but for everyone around him.

However, their friendship was not without thorns. A particularly awkward incident took place one evening in Kolkata.

It began with an innocuous exclamation from Cheteshwar. 'I need to find an ATM! I'm almost out of cash!'

'I'll come with you,' Kuldeep offered, generously.

'Will you? Thanks!' said Cheteshwar, and the two boys headed out into the metropolis in search of an ATM outlet.

It was the year 2004, a time when there were not too many ATMs around. It took the two boys a good two kilometres to find one. As they had ambled across town rapt in an intense discussion—the substance of which neither can recall today—they finally reached their destination. Kuldeep was so engrossed in their conversation that he unthinkingly stepped into the ATM enclosure which Cheteshwar entered.

At this point, parietal training kicked in—one that decreed that the secrecy of his PIN must be preserved at all costs—and Cheteshwar became awkward and virtually froze. He pointedly stood in front of the machine without making any attempt to punch in his PIN.

Kuldeep, whose mind was still preoccupied with their conversation, failed to understand Cheteshwar's bumbling attempts to send his friend about his business in the clumsiest of fashions.

'What's wrong with you, why aren't you withdrawing any cash?' Kuldeep asked, puzzled.

'I'm waiting for you to go so that I can enter my PIN,' replied Cheteshwar, blunt to the point of rudeness.

The penny finally dropped. Kuldeep straightened up—all five feet ten inches of him—and glared at Cheteshwar icily. Deeply offended, he said, 'Friendship is all about trust. If we are friends, then you should have some faith in me.'

'It's not about trust. I'm just not comfortable entering my PIN with you looking on,' Cheteshwar informed him tactlessly.

'I was not looking at the keys,' said Kuldeep even more outraged.

Cheteshwar refused to budge. 'That may be so, but I'm still not comfortable.'

The argument went on for about ten minutes and in the end, Kuldeep swung around and stalked out of the booth. The minute he left, Cheteshwar punched in the PIN and withdrew the moolah which had been the cause of so much grief between the two buddies.

When he emerged from the enclosure, he found Kuldeep waiting outside with his back towards him, very much on his dignity. The walk back to their accommodation was a silent one, fraught with hurt and hostility on Kuldeep's part and a blind intransigence on Cheteshwar's.

Kuldeep gave Cheteshwar the silent treatment for the next few days, but he eventually cooled down. It was beginning to dawn on the former that his friend was not going to either justify his behaviour or offer any excuse and nor was he going to plead guilty, because to his mind, he had done nothing wrong. It took some time for normalcy to be restored between the two.

Kuldeep's conclusions were spot on. After several years of marriage I've learnt that Cheteshwar is a care-for-nobody, a Galileo-like creature, who will stand his ground against the world, to defend his belief, without caring for the consequences. Time and again, when something he's done has angered me, we have quickly reached an impasse, from which there's no way out. It is like banging my head against a wall. Once he's convinced he's in the right, there's no force on earth that can change his mind. Sometimes, it's sheer obstinacy and a determination to cling to his dogmas, and at others, it's because his judgement is actually sound.

In the meanwhile, time went by and Kuldeep progressed rapidly on the cricket field. His talent was swiftly spotted and he soon became one of two kids from Saurashtra groomed for the Zone. In the summer of 2004, a Zonal cricket academy organized inter-zonal matches for talented youngsters from each state at the National Cricket Academy (NCA), Bangalore. It was a month-long series, and the players boarded at the NCA clubhouse.

One evening, they learnt that a five-day conditional camp had been organized before the Asia Cup for the Indian Cricket Team at NCA, Bangalore. A frisson of excitement swept through the zonal players. By this time, Mohnish Parmar, Kuldeep and Cheteshwar had all reached the ripe old age of sixteen representing Saurashtra and Gujarat. They had also become fast friends.

When the trio learnt that the Indian players would be descending on the academy shortly, Mohnish managed to rent a camera and purchase a roll of film. Kuldeep and he could barely contain their elation at the thought of actually meeting the superstars of Indian cricket! This was the pre-social media age and the only access that kids had to their cricketing icons was through the odd articles or pictures they found in newspapers and periodicals.

'I barely slept that night out of sheer excitement,' Kuldeep recalls. Cheteshwar, as usual, maintained his customary sangfroid and seemed untouched by the general air of animation. Well-versed with his ways by now, his friends thought nothing of it.

The following morning, Mohnish and Kuldeep donned their Zonal Cricketing Academy (ZCA) T-shirts—their entry ticket to the stadium where the Indian team would be practicing. Once dressed, they turned to Cheteshwar.

'Get dressed and try and show some enthusiasm,' the duo told Cheteshwar, insouciantly.

'I'm not coming,' Cheteshwar announced, much to their surprise.

Kuldeep was shocked. 'Are you mad?' he asked. 'Don't you know what a memorable opportunity this is?'

Apparently not.

Cheteshwar remained unmoved. 'So, what! They're human beings just like us. Today, they are representing the nation, tomorrow, we will.'

'His statement gave me goosebumps,' Kuldeep later reminisced. What struck him at the time was that there was no arrogance in his assertion, just a strong sense of self-belief that he too would represent the nation someday.

Neither Kuldeep nor Mohnish were inclined to tease Cheteshwar that day; they were aware of his dedication to the game and somehow his avowal did not provoke any derision from them.

Kuldeep and Mohnish went on their own and managed to click lots of pictures with all the legends of the game. The following day, after a conversation with his father, Cheteshwar changed his mind and decided to accost the Indian team during a gym session. Papa had presumably told him that senior cricketers could be a source of learning and missing such a god-sent opportunity was pure folly.

To this end, Cheteshwar approached Rahul Dravid, affectionately known as 'The Wall' in cricketing circles and the one player whose staying power the young teenager wanted to emulate. He went armed with a book and a pen and took tips on batting from this seasoned international player, duly noting down every piece of advice that was proffered to him. But true to form, he did not ask for a photograph.

That evening in the course of a conversation with his two friends he casually asserted: 'If I do not play for India, I will quit cricket.' Such was his ambition that he was ready to sacrifice everything that seemed to be a hurdle to his goals and so deep-rooted was his self-confidence that no one doubted he would one day play with all the cricketing legends. His prediction as a sixteen-year-old would come true in just a few short years and unsurprisingly, Dravid had a hand in his rise.

Cheteshwar was playing a corporate tournament in Bangalore for the Indian Oil company which he had joined a short time earlier. He was piling up runs and had already scored a couple of hundreds. He was nearing his third when Rahul Dravid, then India captain, descended on the ground for a warm-up jog. The batsman at the centre square caught his eye and he approached the scorer to find out about him. The latter told him that the batsman was Cheteshwar Pujara who had recently been amassing a lot of runs.

Dravid then called up Niranjan Shah, longtime secretary of the Saurashtra Cricket Association. 'Take care of this boy,' he said. The Pujaras would have never found out about the exchange if Niranjan Bhai had not thought fit to repeat the conversation to my father-in-law.

Cheteshwar met Dravid again when the latter came to Rajkot for a Ranji match. Dravid stood at the slips and took a more prolonged look at the budding batsman's game. Cheteshwar was Saurashtra's no. 5 at the time. After the game, he called the Saurashtra captain and told him that Cheteshwar should be promoted up the batting order. 'This shows his class,' my father-in-law pronounces with a gleam of admiration. A few years later, Pujara junior would make his test debut and bat at No. 5, just below Dravid and Tendulkar

Meanwhile, Cheteshwar and Kuldeep went to Vizag (Vishakhapatnam) for a zonal match towards the end of 2004. They discovered a local dhaba they started patronizing for their dinner every day after training; both their pockets were to-let and they could not afford to eat at the hotel where they were residing. The dhaba was as unpretentious as Cheteshwar's meals which remained unvaried, consisting daily of paneer gravy, dal and roti coupled with sweet lassi.

When the Tsunami hit the east coast of India, Cheteshwar and Kuldeep were at a zonal camp in Vizag. Kuldeep saw Cheteshwar in panic for the first time. 'I could feel his fear by the speed with which he ran out with me.'

Frightened out of their wits, haunted by memories of the Gujarat earthquake in 2001 that were still fresh in their minds, they ran out bare foot on to the road. This was the moment when their friendship transformed from the ordinary to the extraordinary as the two teenagers clutched each other for comfort amidst the chaos around them. It forged an unbreakable bond between them—one that would last for the rest of their lives.

The year was almost at an end and despite all the runs, no call seemed forthcoming for Cheteshwar's selection into the Under-19 Indian team. Both Cheteshwar and Kuldeep were representing Saurashtra in Mumbai in the Under-22 matches for the Colonel CK Nayudu trophy against the Mumbai team, after which the squad was expected to sit out for the India Under-19 match.

Cheteshwar wanted to make the three-day Col. Nayudu trophy match count, even if they were up against the mighty Mumbai team and had been virtually written off by everyone as the underdogs. Everyone in the Saurashtra team knew that they faced certain defeat, but the point was to lose with dignity.

MY FRIEND KULDEEP

Cheteshwar was close to 150 runs when the ninth wicket fell and Kuldeep walked on to the crease.

Kuldeep was pumped up. 'Go for a double century,' he whispered as he crossed Cheteshwar.

'How?' responded Cheteshwar in despair, 'when we're nine wickets down.'

Kuldeep took Cheteshwar's desolation to heart and it motivated him to play an innings that was aimed at ensuring that the latter reached his double hundred. They played around thirty overs together that day and Kuldeep scored eighteen off eight-seven deliveries, allowing Cheteshwar to reach his double century, so that he could make a case for himself with the selectors.

Even more interesting was the conversation that was exchanged between the two during their partnership at the crease. For the first ten overs, Cheteshwar did not believe Kuldeep had the skill to stand and defend.

'Even when he reached around 165, Cheteshwar still did not want to take risks and kept defending full tosses. It was frustrating. I was getting restless at the non-strikers' end, but he just would not budge,' Kuldeep remembers wryly.

Slowly Cheteshwar relaxed and started trusting his partner. They built the partnership gradually, allowing Cheteshwar to reach his personal milestone of 200 not-out. After he had scoured his double century, Kuldeep kept urging Cheteshwar to go big.

Cheteshwar's response was a shock. 'Why don't you go big?'

This rejoinder infuriated Kuldeep who could not understand why Cheteshwar was still not willing to take any risk. When he spoke to him on the subject several years later, Cheteshwar barely remembered the match and had two possible explanations to offer, and this was only when Kuldeep showed him the score card. 'I may have acted that way either because of my obsession to remain not-out or maybe I thought we were heading for a draw in any case, so there was no sense in playing any rash shot.'

Immediately after the game, Cheteshwar was picked for the third youth test match for India Under-19. It was his debut match and he went on to hit a double century. India won the match. This triumph was especially sweet because it was Cheteshwar's only major achievement witnessed by his mother.

CHAPTER EIGHT

Mother o' Mine

'Your mother has cancer.'
Cheteshwar was fifteen at the time and no funerals buzzed in his brain when he heard the dreaded 'C' word. He tried to process the information and failed. 'At that time, I didn't know what cancer was,' he says. 'I didn't know there were diseases that are incurable or there are diseases for which chances of cure are very limited. I did not have any great grasp of science. I knew she had cancer because that's what I was told but I didn't know how dangerous it was. I always had the faith that since she hadn't done anything wrong, nothing horrible would happen to her.'

In fact, Cheteshwar, at that age, did not know very much about life. His world revolved around his parents—particularly his mother—and, of course, cricket. He never really overburdened himself with anything else. How then was he to comprehend that his days with his mother, who was his 'quiet home', were numbered? How could he possibly understand that the central figure in his childhood would vanish so completely and would live only in his memory within a short span of two years. He went on scoring runs, she kept on battling cancer, neither of them ready to let go of that special bond which entwined them.

His mother did try her best to prepare him for the inevitable, but never directly. She would sit him down and talk to him. She tried to explain the reality of the cosmos in simple words to give him a perspective. When he was home, she would fish out several spiritual books and read them out aloud to him. 'This is the reality, Chintu. Every person who is born will eventually die. But it is the deeds that one does that will matter' she would tell him over and over again.

Did he understand? Not really. In theory, it is easy to understand the phenomenon of death. But no one is ever really prepared for it, especially if it involves the passing of someone near and dear. Calm of demeanour, strongly spiritual, she quietly passed on this aspect of her personality to her son. His resilience, stubbornness, the will to stand up for what he felt was right, the spirit to fight against all odds and not allow anything to rout him were all traits that he inherited from her. But the books did help, especially one that pivoted round the physical journey of life and described the lives of sadhus. 'At that age, the content of the book surprised me and filled me with wonder. But in a funny way it also prepared me for the tragedy that lay ahead.'

On the face of it, his father was the moving force behind his cricket, but in reality, it was his mother who was the actual facilitator. Papa taught Cheteshwar the physical game of cricket, but the truth is that it is not just a physical sport, it is so much more. It requires mental strength; it needs synchronicity between mind and body and an ability to withstand acute and perpetual pressure. Most kids face these challenges, often lacking confidence and self-belief; but Cheteshwar was different; he had been blessed with his mother's obstinacy and could face the cricketing world in the eye, without blinking, as if to declare 'bring it all on—I will still stand my ground'.

My father-in-law may have been the one who trained him, but the nutrition to survive—both physically and spiritually—was provided ceaselessly by his mother. She was the one who made sure he had adequate sleep, the one who took care of every inch of the Pujara home and tended to all their social relationships. When she was not pinning a watchful eye on her husband and son's training schedule and rigorous routine, she kept up with their relatives—attending ceremonies, weddings and other family functions—as much as her busy time-table would permit.

She had a light touch and handled every aspect of their lives with tact and grace. It was on her sturdy shoulders that the framework of the house rested. My mother-in-law gave up her own life and interests so that Cheteshwar's training ran smoothly, never complaining, never expecting anything for herself; always content to subsume her own life to better his future. Her only outlets appeared to be the trips to Gondal on off-days or the odd visits to her brother's house.

According to family lore my mother-in-law was by no means an average, run-of-the-mill housewife. She was an unusual, enterprising woman who wanted to do her bit for the house. She began by stitching and selling petticoats to add to the meagre income on which her family subsisted. She subsequently graduated to making money by saving up cash from housekeeping funds and investing them in IPOs.

'She was extraordinary,' Cheteshwar says, his eyes alight with admiration. 'She used to fill a lot of IPO forms and apply for shares. No one advised her, she figured out everything on her own and she would sell them whenever money was needed at home.'

A quintessential giver, Cheteshwar's mother never sat back and allowed her husband bear the financial burdens alone. She was always by his side, ready to do battle, shoulder to shoulder, ever-willing to contribute to the family coffers actively. For instance, there was a time when my father-in-law took a loan from the railways and bought a plot. He also managed to find the money for construction. But there was none left for furnishings once the house was complete!

Unfazed, my mother-in-law did not turn a hair. She just dipped into her savings and furnished the place from top to bottom (in close consultation with her Guru over every purchase). She bought the fridge, beds, Tupperware—just about everything that went into turning an empty house into a home. But for her even this simple pleasure had a moral that needed to be passed on to her son. 'Don't splurge, Chintu. Always save up for a rainy day,' she would tell Cheteshwar. It was a lesson that would stay with him, even after she was gone.

'She was quite a character,' Cheteshwar states. 'When the house did not demand her savings, she would buy gold—and she always donated 20 per cent of her earnings to charity, no matter how low or high her income. I don't know how she did it. Her watchwords were honesty, truthfulness and simplicity.'

Even though she was not very well-educated, her approach to life was very evolved. She had a calmness, serenity and vision that was remarked upon by everyone who came within her periphery. She was always positive and managed to stay cheerful even when she underwent chemotherapy, which true to form, she insisted on funding out of her own money.

For Cheteshwar, his mother's chemotherapy was a nightmare. She had lost a lot of weight and although she bore it stoically, it was evident to the young teenager that she was in a lot of pain. 'It was tough to watch the process. There were times when they kept prodding her with needles, trying to find her veins—it was hard for me to witness it.' he says.

When she lost her hair, she remained unperturbed and joked, 'At least I don't have to waste my time washing my hair and oiling it!'

But for Cheteshwar, her hair-loss was distressing. She herself did not care and would brave public spaces with an air of panache and a lack of self-consciousness that was practically unheard of at the time. But her son was young enough to resent all the curious stares on his mother's behalf. 'These days, people are more open, but at that time, they would not only gape, but ask all kinds of nosey questions. A lot of kids would make fun of her and tease me—not my friends, but others. I don't know what drove them but they could be quite cruel. Imagine being told "Oh, your mother is bald." It used to bother me.'

However, it was also a big learning curve for him. 'She was so confident about herself and who she was, I learnt how to hold my head high in adversity.' But Cheteshwar does have a few regrets. 'I feel I could have spent more time with her instead of being so focused on my game.' But he is also philosophical about it. He knows that he is looking at things with the benefit of hindsight and that there is nothing he can do to change the past.

My mother-in-law was Cheteshwar's lodestar, and he coped by not dwelling too much on her cancer or the tiny pin pricks around him. As he said, he did not know that it could be fatal and he was never informed about the seriousness of her condition. Intrinsically private by nature, Cheteshwar clomped on, over the next couple of years, sporting a brave face, and never mentioning the situation at home to his friends. He did not even tell Kuldeep about the nature of his mother's illness.

The end, when it came on 5 October 2005, was devastating for Cheteshwar. He was seventeen years old; not quite a boy and yet not quite a man. The day she died, he lost his childhood and hurtled into adulthood, without noticing it. What would trouble him even more was that he was not with her during her final moments. Neither was Papa. He had stepped out to get some medicines for her and was at a sports store when he received a frantic phone call from his brother-in-law. 'She's in a bad way, you better come home quickly.' He rushed home but it was too late. His wife had already slipped away from life with the same quietness that had characterized her during her lifetime, with only her brother by her side.

My father-in-law's version of events that day is as follows: 'I'll never forget the day Reena left us. Her chemotherapy was over and she seemed to be recovering. I remember Chintu was in Bhavnagar for an Under-19 match. We were in the middle of moving house, so we were staying at my brother-in-law's place. It was my wife's idea. She thought she would at least be able to rest there.'

The Saurashtra team had lost early, and Cheteshwar called up his mother around 2 p.m. to inform her that he would be back in Rajkot that evening. Within a couple of hours, my mother-in-law suffered from a 'lightning heart attack'. 'It happened so fast that she couldn't even get up from the diwan and make it to the bed. By the time Chintu came home, we had been reduced to a family of two —his mother, my wife—the centre of our lives was gone. She had left us forever.'

It was evening time; dusk had fallen and Cheteshwar was on a bus with his teammates. They were on their way back to Rajkot from Bhavnagar after a match. Kuldeep was sitting next to him when his mobile rang. They were still about twenty minutes away from Rajkot. Cheteshwar took the call. It was from Bipin Mamaji. 'Don't get down at Hospital Chowk,' his uncle said tersely, alluding to the bus stand close to the Pujara home. 'Get down at the ST bus stand. Your parents as you know are here at our house.'

Bipin Mamaji's request did not set off any alarm bells in Cheteshwar. He knew his parents were at his uncle's house, because of his conversation with his mother earlier that afternoon. 'Your dad will come and pick you up at the bus stand and we'll go home together,' she had told him.

The first inkling that Cheteshwar had that all was not well was when he spotted Sunil Bhai, an elder cousin who was his senior by several years, at the bus stop instead of his father. He took one look at his grim face and white clothes and immediately knew that something terrible had happened. 'I knew that something was wrong. I knew it was connected with my mother. But I didn't want to think beyond that.'

His apprehensions turned to certainty when he reached his Mamaji's house. 'There were so many people and my conviction that all was not well grew stronger.' When he reached the third floor and entered his mamaji's apartment. He knew the worst had happened. 'There were so many people. Most of them were crying, all of them pitying the young boy who had just walked in. It was not hard to guess. Then I saw my mother and broke down. But not uncontrollably. Even at that age, I knew how to manage my emotions.'

It was only later that night at around 10.30 p.m. that Kuldeep learnt that Cheteshwar had lost his mother. He and a few others from their group decided to assemble at the cremation grounds for the last rites as a show of solidarity for their bereaved peer.

Kuldeep's first memory there is of a teary-eyed Cheteshwar descending from a van with his father, uncle and his deceased mother. However, as soon as he spotted his friends, he reassembled his face into a stoic mask and his tears evaporated, as if they had been wiped clean by an invisible hand. 'I've never been very good at showing my emotions. I've always been like that,' my husband now admits.

For Cheteshwar, life would never be the same again, but he could not and would not share the shadows that stirred within him, weaving a dark black cloud of immense isolation inside his head where he wanted to be alone with himself and the unbearable pain that wracked his heart. His anguish was his own and he clutched on to it with ferocity.

Kuldeep and the other boys wanted to look out for Cheteshwar. They were concerned about him and tried to show it. But he had gone quiet and withdrawn inwards. There was a stillness about him as if he was existing in some solitary fog that buffered him from the rest of the world. The future had arrived all too soon and yet he had still to come to terms with the past—that even now was all too alive and which he was not yet prepared to relinquish. There was also an immense anger within him against a god who had thought fit to make his mother suffer when she had been so good in both deed and words and had been so religious. Cheteshwar had several bones to pick with his maker and this he could only do when he was on his own.

He says, 'Initially I was in shock. I was still in denial mode. I was angry with god and was in the grip of a kind of hate against the universe which I could not control. I had never imagined that this could happen to us because we were so good as a family. At that age, I understood death, but I just could not accept what had happened to my mother because she was so spiritual. She was my role model, my perfect companion, and now she was gone. I lived in a state of caged isolation. My sense of alienation was intense—and there was no one I could talk to—certainly not my friends who were all from the cricketing world. Family was something we never discussed. Our conversations normally revolved around cricket or sports. Personal topics were off limits. So, there I was, sitting in my room—all alone—just trying to feel that sadness, always trying to speak to god—asking him, "why had this happened", questioning him. It was a terrible time.'

Five days later, Cheteshwar was back with his friends travelling to Mumbai, still lost, still silent. He went on to play two matches there and did not perform well. He then headed back to Rajkot for the rituals that Hindus offer on the twelfth day of the demise of a member of the family. These rites are traditionally performed by the son and heir, and this was the last task that Cheteshwar would be doing for his mother. He went through these ceremonies with the same impassivity that he had gone through everything else. After that he went to Guruji at Gondal for his blessings. He knew his mother would approve.

At one stage it seemed as if he would not be able to make it in time for the next match. The only way this could be achieved was if he travelled by air and that appeared to be a far cry. However, the Saurashtra Cricket Association, which had been keeping a close and compassionate eye on the grieving lad, stepped in and arranged for his flight tickets, a phenomenon that was practically unheard of at that level of cricket in those days. He was their top scorer and his absence from the forthcoming match was unthinkable.

In Mumbai, he hit a smacking century against Gujarat. The entire dressing room rose to cheer, emotions running high on behalf of the seventeen-year-old boy who had persevered and played even when the worst was upon him, epitomizing the very essence of the spirit of cricket.

Back home, the house was an empty shell. His mother was the glue that held them together. She was absent but her spirit seemed to linger in every room, every corner of their once-cheerful abode. Nothing was as it was; she had possessed joie de vivre that had brought the whole place alive; where once the place had brimmed with liveliness and merriment, there was now a constant gloom; the father and son found it difficult to bridge the chasm of grief that divided them to reach out and console each other.

They also approached their grief differently. For Cheteshwar, the material legacies that his mother had left behind were inconsequential; her soul and deeds were more important. Her clothes and jewellery meant nothing to him. His father, on the other hand, tended to clutch on to them, as if they would draw him closer to her.

Strangely enough, Cheteshwar bounced back to normalcy more quickly than his father. The process took place over a period of six months to a year and, as usual, it was cricket that helped him heal, and his Masi.

'I had my cricket,' he confesses. 'When I'd play, I would focus on the game—on the present—I would not think of anything else. On the field, I was normal. I wasn't grieving for my mother. Of course, once I was back in my room, I would return to my grief.

This kept happening in the initial days and the fact that I did not get picked for the Under-19 team even after my debut and my failure to selected for Ranji, strangely enough contributed to my healing process. There was a lot of politics at play and I had to work really hard to prove that I was worthy of being selected. This helped to divert me from everything else and helped me focus on my game. I was determined to show them that I was capable of playing Ranji and eventually, I did get picked. For my father, it was not so easy. He probably took around five years to come to terms with my mother's death.'

My mother-in-law's demise had also brought about a change in the father–son relationship. Hitherto, Papa had been an authoritarian figure in Cheteshwar's life. After his wife's death, he looked strangely helpless. For his son, he had been more like a coach and less like a father. It was his mother who had been the channel between them; she had been the filter through which they had communicated with each other. Now that she was gone, their link with each other seemed to have snapped and with each passing day, they realized how her passing had torn the very fabric of their lives.

Her loss was not merely physical, it had permeated their everyday lives as well. Once all their relatives left, the enormity of living in a house without a woman struck them. Suddenly they were faced with the onerous task of running a house, shopping for groceries, haggling with vegetable vendors—the chores were endless and the Pujara men were clearly out of their depths.

How had Cheteshwar's mother done it? How had she managed to provide them with nutritious food, fruits and nuts on a shoe-strig budget? How had she run the house on next to nothing? Even when she was sick? At that time, they had hired a maid for cleaning and swabbing. But my mother-in-law had not, however, relinquished the reins of the kitchen to the hired help. Over the years, Papa would invariably marvel over his wife's wizardry at housekeeping and her almost magical ability to eke out so much with so little. 'My salary was meagre and I don't know how she did it. But Chintu would have dry fruits before he left for training and coconut water when he came back.'

Several years later, after they had shifted into their spacious house with a garden on the first floor, he would still remember the meals she rustled up in the 'poky kitchen' in their tiny quarters in Kothi compound, with acute nostalgia. 'It was the best food, I ever had,' he would state tearfully.

While my mother-in-law was around, all the Pujara men had focused on was cricket, and adjusting to the new reality hit them hard. They engaged two maids, one for cooking, another for cleaning, but none of them could keep a sparkling house like Cheteshwar's mother, or rustle up the kind of scrumptious fare that she had produced day in and day out, so effortlessly.

Cheteshwar did not mind that he had to make his bed or pack his own bag because, as he says, he was old enough to do it. 'I did not miss my mother because of the chores I had to take care of—I just missed her.' But he did pine for her when he tried to figure out how many clothes he had to pack for his trips. This was one area where he had always depended on his mom.

For Papa, the biggest bête noir, after his wife's death, was grocery shopping. He would be haunted my memories of how she'd whizz in and out of the vegetable market, while he waited on his scooter impatiently, invariably grumbling at the time she had taken over a few vegetables. On those occasions, she had merely smiled and held her peace.

Now when the onus of shopping for vegetables fell on him, he realized what an onerous task it was and learnt to value her even more than he had whilst she was alive. At one point, not long after she had passed on, he broke down in the middle of the road. The maid had just informed him that they had run out of potatoes. 'How can you expect me to cook when you don't have the necessary ingredients?'

Overwhelmed, Papa hurried out of the house to fetch the requested tuber, but just as he caught sight of the vendor, the permanence of his wife's death struck him and he wept. 'Is this what my life is going to be like now?' he asked the almighty silently.

My mother-in-law's absence continued to niggle the Pujara men. Resigned, they learnt to make do and slowly started picking up the pieces of their tattered lives. Cheteshwar, as was his habit, concentrated on his game, and his father helped him, relieved to find that cricket—the one thing that had united them—remained an unhindered conduit of communication between them and was still very much alive as a bonding mechanism. Time passed and the Pujaras gradually came to terms with a life without her.

For Cheteshwar, the process was helped along by his masi who stepped into the transcendental void that his mother had left, and gradually began to fill out all the empty spaces in his heart. She became his mentor and guide and gradually, he started discussing all his metaphysical conundrums with her. She always had the right answers and, better still, she became the conduit between Cheteshwar and his guru. Any queries he had were put to his guru through her and slowly unnoticed, she slipped into his mother's place, replacing her as his best friend and spiritual companion.

Life took a new turn when Kuldeep moved to Rajkot to keep up with his cricket. Their friendship grew even deeper as the two friends began to practice cricket together. Kuldeep remembers Cheteshwar as an atypical teenager who, even though he had represented India in the Under-19 World Cup, did not have the usual adolescent penchant to flirt with girls, hit the fast life, party or swoop down to posh restaurants to foster the impression that he was au courant. All he liked to do during his time off was go on long drives with his friends, armed with sandwiches and some chai they would pick up at highway hotels or dhabas, and park at some solitary spot where they conversed about life in general or lightened the atmosphere with some silly jokes.

On one such evening, when they were on their own, Cheteshwar finally opened up to Kuldeep and admitted him into his inner world. He divulged the most intimate parts of himself, relating his deepest wishes and ultimate desires. His friend heard him out in silence, completely flummoxed.

Cheteshwar, eyes half-closed, declared: 'I wish to meet god one day and that is my ultimate quest.'

Kuldeep did not make the error of imagining that Cheteshwar was jesting. He knew that his friend was serious. What he felt at the time was an overarching sense of awe. He had never come across anyone else at that age who possessed such a strong moral compass or was blessed with such complete faith in the almighty despite losing his mother at such a young age. His profound, mostly arcane sense of spirituality was also extremely unusual. There were not too many teenagers around who were given to analysing the scriptures or on a quest to seek the maker.

When Kuldeep later told me about the incident, I was not particularly surprised. He had said the same thing to me several times after we were married. What touched me the most, however, was Kuldeep's summation. 'I hope he succeeds in his quest. I would like to believe that god has touched him in more ways than he realizes.

Over the years, Cheteshwar's group of friends expanded. I found it extraordinary that all of them had been part of the cricketing world at some stage or the other. But, despite his growing band of comrades, not much changed. Cheteshwar still avoided late nights like the plague and discipline remained his ruling deity. If he had an hour or so free in the evening, he would call his buddies to catch up with them. He, however, did not take breaks on holidays or festivals from his 'all-important' routine.

When he was convalescing after his ACL injury and could not train, he would usually meet up with his chums, catch up with their news, and they would generally 'be silly' together.

Today, Cheteshwar has a large group of friends—kids who have grown up and played cricket with him. There have been times in the past few years when they have even gone on a couple of trips together. They still have a lot of fun, but it never gets out of hand, because, as Kuldeep says, 'He has a habit of bringing out the best in everyone around him.'

But even after eighteen long years, still in some quiet recess of his soul, his mother's memories creak about making their own din, clanging reminders of that long-ago world when she would shake him out of his bed, hide behind doors to startle him and laugh with him endlessly at jokes that only the two of them understood. He is a father today, with an offspring of his own, but somewhere deep inside, the child that he was lives on hungering for that soothing calm that was symbolized by his own mother.

CHAPTER NINE

The Anatomy of Pain and the Triumph of the Spirit

Bloemfontein, South Africa, 2009. A grim March sky, dark and overcast, shrouded the Mangaung Oval where the Kolkata Knight Riders braved a light drizzle for a practice match just ahead of IPL 2. A few cricket enthusiasts ignored the elements and sat around in clusters on the grass banks at the periphery of the stadium to watch the game. The ground was muddy and sodden as a consequence of the incessant overnight showers, but none of the players paid heed to it. After all, it was part and parcel of the sport and they were all used to adverse weather conditions. What possible havoc could a little rain and wet earth cause? A lot—as it turned out shortly.

Saurav Ganguly was batting at the time and Cheteshwar was fielding at long off. Saurav hit the ball in the air and it arced towards Cheteshwar, who ran forward to make the catch. The ball fell short and became wedged in the ground after a short bounce.

Cheteshwar, racing full pelt, slid past the ball and tried to turn around to pick it up in a single fluid movement. His left foot got stuck in the mud and his knee twisted, accompanied by a crack that was loud enough to be heard by everyone nearby. He immediately crumpled to the ground and emitted a loud piercing scream: 'Aaaaiyeeee!'

'As soon as I fell, I knew my leg was gone. There was a big twist, a big noise. I felt as if I had lost my entire leg, and I was in terrible, terrible pain! I couldn't get up. I couldn't move. I heard a scream, it was only later that I realized that it was mine,' says Cheteshwar, a faraway look in his eyes as he relives the incident, his mind orbiting back to that fateful day.

Unnerved by sound, the physio and all the other players on the field rushed to him. By now, Cheteshwar was gripped by a host of unwelcome fears. 'This is what it feels like to be disabled,' he thought, desolate. Would he ever walk? Would he ever move?

As a sportsperson, Cheteshwar was used to injuries. Fractured fingers, getting hit by cricket balls on various body parts was par for the course. But this pain was new and quite different from anything he had ever experienced. He had always prided himself for his high threshold for tolerating physical pain. He had never ever screamed during previous injuries, and yet, here he was, howling like a banshee because the agony was just too overpowering. He felt as if someone had mangled his left leg with a stick.

His teammates gazed at him helpless and worried, as Andrew Leipus, the physio, got to work. It was completely obvious to every onlooker that his left leg was seriously out of alignment; his knee had swollen alarmingly and had taken on a deep purple hue.

Cheteshwar has no clear memories of succeeding events, but he does remember the physio trying to realign his leg. After that, he thinks, he was carried off the field on a stretcher to the dressing room upstairs, where a physio table occupied the pride of the place for just this kind of eventuality. He was shifted on to it carefully and icepacks were put on his knee to bring the swelling down. Later that day, he underwent a scan. The tidings were not good.

'I have bad news to share,' his physio said gravely. Cheteshwar's heart sank. 'Its an ACL rupture and you will have to go through a surgery.' Cheteshwar stared at him blankly, not quite registering what he was being told.

'But don't be disheartened. You'll still be able to play cricket. But only after six months. Because it's going take your leg that much time to get back to normal,' he was informed.

Six months! It was only then that the import of what was being said to him finally sank in. He stared at the man before him with acute horror. He had never been out of the game that long since he had started playing cricket at the age of seven. And now, at twenty-one, just when his cricketing career was on the verge of take-off, he was being told that he wouldn't be able to play cricket for six whole months. It might as well have been a lifetime!

Cheteshwar clung on to his threadbare poise by sheer dint of the same will that had seen him through all the other setbacks in his young life. He held back his tears and tried to concentrate on the physio's words, as the latter painstakingly explained the entire rehabilitation process to him.

'You will have to walk on crutches in the initial stages. It will be a bit of a struggle at first, but you will make progress. After that your rehab process will begin. For the first three or four weeks, you will have to be very sincere about it. After that you will be able to walk with a brace on your knee without crutches. After four months, you will be able to start your running sessions and after six or eight weeks, you can start cycling.'

By this time, Cheteshwar had tuned out. 'Nothing he said made any sense to me. It was all irrelevant,' Cheteshwar explains with an apologetic, half-embarrassed grin. 'The only thing that I registered was that I was going to be out of the game for six months. I couldn't think beyond that.'

Cheteshwar sat glued to his seat, disconsolate, wondering how he would cope. 'I was so overwhelmed with everything that was happening that I almost cried in front of the physio. It was hard for me to communicate with him. He just kept talking and I just kept nodding my head and saying "okay". At that moment, my entire focus was to somehow prevent myself from breaking down in front of him. I managed it, but with great difficulty.'

But it was a temporary calm that lasted only till he made it to the privacy of his room. Once there, he wept copiously, back in the same glass bubble that had encased him in the aftermath of his mother's death. He was in a foreign land, alone, far away from his father and the rest of his extended family, completely cut-off from the quiet support that was always on offer in Rajkot. Intensely private, he did not have the necessary tools to share his misery with anyone else. In public, he displayed a stoic mien, but in private, he succumbed to several crying jags, falling prey to a string of disquieting thoughts such as: Would he ever play again? Would he actually get back to normal in six months or would it take longer? Even if he recovered to pre-injury levels, would he ever be able to make a comeback?

To understand Cheteshwar's fears, one has to be au fait with his journey during the course of his cricketing career thus far. Just a year earlier, he had scored three triple centuries in a month followed by 189 and 176 in two Ranji matches; this at a time when he was a veteran of four first-class seasons and had an outstanding record in junior cricket with over 5000 runs in different age-group matches. But, in spite of this, whispers that he was a flat-track bully, whose shots struggled to reach the boundary and did not come up to par in big matches, dogged him persistently despite evidence to the contrary. Perhaps his father had been right and Rajkot was an impediment to Cheteshwar's progress in the game.

But then, in the same year, suddenly things changed and Kolkata Knight Riders (KKR) picked him even though India was still dragging its feet. All at once, Cheteshwar's prospects looked more promising.

In 2009, Cheteshwar had every reason to be upbeat. He had hit a purple patch with his bat in the domestic circuit the previous year, and the KKR management had promised that he would finally be part of the playing eleven in the coming IPL season. It was at this juncture, just when Cheteshwar thought that all his ducks were stacked in a row as far as his career was concerned, the ill-fated practice match took place.

Destiny impelled him to dash heedlessly to a fall for a catch that was never there; and the result: a ruptured anterior cruciate ligament, an impending surgery and a temporarily halted cricketing career—all without playing a single game for KKR. For the twenty-one-year-old, there could be no worse fate.

More bad news followed. His surgery, which was to take place in Cape Town, was pushed back. The doctors had decided to wait at least for a week for the inflammation in the knee to subside. But there were some positives as well. The KKR franchise was extremely supportive. It not only insisted on picking up the tab for the surgery but also convinced Cheteshwar to have it in South Africa as the 'doctors there were best for sports injuries'.

'We'll also fly down anyone you want for the surgery. We'll fly them here so that you have your own people around you,' a KKR representative assured him.

Papa did not even have a passport at the time and privately Cheteshwar wondered how KKR would get around the red tape to fly him to South Africa. But he had underestimated the KKR juggernaut, which efficiently bulldozed its way through officialdom and made all the necessary arrangements.

Back home, when the phone rang to inform my father-in-law about his son's fall and imminent surgery, he almost had a meltdown. At first, he dug in his heels and tried to cajole KKR co-owner Shah Rukh Khan to fly Cheteshwar back to Rajkot. After all, his good friend, Dr Nirbhay Shah, was an ace at operating sports injuries!

Besides, he was also worried about the lack of a support system in South Africa. Here, in Rajkot, any number of people could be roped in for any amount of assistance. Who would provide him the back-up in Cape Town?

Shah Rukh tried to reassure him, pointing out that since Rugby players were often injured during games, South African doctors were a whizz at performing sports surgeries. He offered to fly Dr Shah and anyone else he needed for the trip.

'What he said made sense,' says Papa, reminiscently. 'Shah Rukh also told me that Chintu had a great future ahead of him and should have the best-available medical treatment. When he realized I was worried about the absence of a support system in South Africa and my faith in Dr Shah's abilities, he offered to fly him and any family members I wanted with me.'

By now, my father-in-law was on a sticky wicket. 'I don't have a passport,' he said throwing his final trump card.

Shah Rukh was unfazed. He told Papa not to worry; everything would be taken care of. And it was—in record time, but not before my father-in-law had a quiet chat with Dr Shah. At that time, he didn't think KKR had the ability pull the rabbit out of the hat in time and had cautioned his friend of his lack of a passport. 'I don't think you should wait for me. You should travel alone.'

Dr Shah was unconvinced. 'You should also come. Chintu will need you.'

As it turned out, KKR not only managed to get Papa his passport in super quick time, but also managed to yank the required visas for the two friends in what appeared to be the blink of an eye. Once they reached Cape Town via Dubai, my father-in-law was glad he had made the trip.

In the meanwhile, things had not been easy for Cheteshwar in the week following his fall. Initially, it was not so bad because he travelled with the team to Cape Town. But after they left the city for subsequent games, he was completely alone, with too much time on his hands and not much to do. It was at this time that he succumbed to a strong sense of abandonment. 'I remember breaking down every other day for the first ten to twelve days.'

He underwent the same sense of ill-usage at the hands of the almighty that he had after his mother's death. 'Why me?' was a constant question that he hurled at god. He had also fallen prey to a host of uncertainties. 'At that age, the very fact that I had to sit out of the game for six months was challenging. I also kept wondering whether I would be able to make a comeback. I even wondered if I would ever be able to play professional cricket again. At that time, I didn't know how my recovery would pan out, how the surgery would go, how the rehab process would work. There were so many questions, and I was too scared to look for any answers.'

It was Cheteshwar's first major injury and he worried himself to death over his future. Somehow, his fall and his mother's death became inexorably linked together in his head. His emotions then, as now, were almost identical. Questions such as 'why has this happened to me' and 'why am I being punished' were constant companions. 'My career was going so well. I was on the verge of playing for the Indian team and yet, once again, god had put a hurdle in my way. I kept wondering why the universe was conspiring against me? I worked so hard and always tried to do the right thing and yet, here I was being made to pay for god knows what. How will I go through this? I wondered. How will my family go through this? How will I cope?'

Today, as Cheteshwar offers a microscopic view of his mind in that period, he says: 'I think it hit me more because I was alone. There was not much I could do. It was as if I was walled within my room. Everything had been arranged so that I did not have to move too much. The franchise had done it out of kindness so that I did not have to move and only suffer minimal discomfort. I was on crutches and going anywhere was a struggle. After a few days, I started watching some movies on television. It was a lonely phase. I was prey to too many thoughts, sulking a lot. I was dealing with enforced idleness, no exciting news and absolutely no routine—it was driving me mad. I think it was perhaps the hardest time of my life after my mother's death. I felt that the gods had been very unkind to me.'

For the injured batsman, the days limped on at an excruciatingly slow pace, till my father-in-law and Dr Shah arrived. 'I still remember the smile on Chintu's face when he saw me,' Papa later told me. 'He had been confined to his hotel room for days. He used to sound very low on the phone. But when he saw me, he smiled at me with such complete joy in his eyes that I was reminded of the little boy he had once been.'

Now that Papa and Dr Shah were there with him, Cheteshwar's anxieties vanished as if by magic. It was as if his mind had done a U-turn and rejigged itself becoming more open to the upcoming surgery.

The day of the surgery arrived and Cheteshwar finally went under the knife. Just before the operation he was informed by Dr P.J. Erasmus, the South African surgeon and head of the medical team that the procedure on his knee would take place under general anaesthesia.

'That was the first I had heard of it,' says Cheteshwar. 'I don't know why but I had automatically assumed that the surgery would take place under local anaesthesia and now the doctor was telling that I was mistaken and the procedure would take place under general anaesthesia.'

'You needn't worry, you will fall asleep and you won't feel a thing. You'll only wake up once the surgery is over,' Dr Erasmus explained painstakingly so that his patient was aware of the entire process.

In his new, positive frame of mind, Cheteshwar just nodded his head. 'I was more curious than scared at this point. I was also ready to treat the whole thing as a new experience; something to be savoured, not feared.'

The operation was duly performed and when he came, Cheteshwar felt as if he had gone through an out-of-body-experience. Instead of the usual disorientation, he felt as if he had been to another world while he was unconscious and was now waking up to a brand new one. 'It was almost as if I had left my body and had returned to find myself alive again.'

The first couple of days after the surgery were rough for Cheteshwar. The swelling was back with a vengeance and so was the pain. He had been plied with analgesics that were barely effective. Cheteshwar struggled to move. Initially, even turning to his side was onerous and moving his leg even an inch, a challenge. He was either lifting his leg with both hands when he wanted to move or asking someone else to help him lift it. In short, the tiniest tasks, like going for a shower or to the toilet, seemed like a trek to Mount Everest and back.

To top his woes, unused to drugs of any kinds, the medicines he ingested played havoc with his digestive system. Suddenly, it wasn't just about his knee. It was about his whole body. Everything seemed to have gone haywire. Aggrieved, dispirited and tormented by various aches and pains, Cheteshwar was convinced that he was no longer human. He was certain that he had been reduced to a subhuman mass of overstretched nerves, mangled muscles and tissues that were straining in different directions and functioning independently of his central nervous system.

As a sportsman, Cheteshwar also battled with the very natural dread of losing muscle mass. He had not used his left leg much even before surgery. 'I was not putting enough pressure on the left leg even before the surgery, though I was allowed to, because I was scared of damaging it further.' He also thought his left leg looked thinner than his right. His physio tried to explain to him that this was normal, and his left leg was by no means any thinner than his left hand. But his uneasiness persisted.

Eventually, as his condition improved, Cheteshwar started chaffing to get back home. 'I wanted to go home as quickly as possible, but I was told I had to wait. The doctors wanted to keep me under watch, just in case there was a blood clot.'

At last, he was pronounced fit to leave. On the flight back to Rajkot, Cheteshwar noticed that people looked at him differently because he was on crutches. He categorizes them into two—the patient empaths and the restless impatient sociopaths. The former were always accommodative and tolerant with him, whilst the latter were forever on tenterhooks, disgusted at being stuck behind a person who was negotiating his way forward inch by inch and holding them up in the queue. Inspired by his mother's example, Cheteshwar decided to ignore them.

Things became much easier for Cheteshwar once he was back home. He slowly began to pick up the threads of his life. He started meeting his friends; members of his family kept dropping by and his sense of loneliness disappeared. Emotionally too, he was a lot happier—now that he knew that he was making progress and that his situation was temporary.

His masi, especially, was a tower of strength. 'Be positive,' she prodded. 'You know you will emerge out of this. You will come back even stronger. Have faith in god. Control what you can instead of worrying about things that are not in your hands.'

It was during this phase of his life that Cheteshwar made most of his long-lasting relationships. 'I became close to my family, my friends. Because it's only in tough times that you recognize the people who are actually there for you and you learn to appreciate them.'

His rehabilitation process began. 'Every day, I was given a task, so there was something to look forward to. It began with small exercises. I worked hard during my physiotherapy. After a couple of weeks, once I got my knee brace, both KKR and BCCI arranged for the next part of my rehabilitation in Bangalore.

Cheteshwar started travelling frequently to Bangalore. He would be stationed there for a fortnight at a time before returning to Rajkot for ten-day intervals until he had to head back to Bangalore again. Gradually, the pain diminished and after a month, it all but disappeared along with the crutches. Around eight weeks after the surgery, even the limp vanished.

Six months later, as predicted, he was back in the game. More focused than ever. He started playing for Indian Oil, KKR, Ranji and even the India-A team. In 2010, he was retained by KKR and made the IPL debut in Bangalore. He even went to the UK with the India-A team, and came up with a stellar performance. Things were back to normal. He had recovered his rhythm and his injury had not noticeably hindered his cricketing abilities.

Then, at the end of 2010, he was picked for the Indian squad which would be playing against Australia for a two-match series. The first match was at Mohali Chandigarh and the second at Bangalore where he debuted unexpectedly.

This is how it happened.

On the morning of the first test, Cheteshwar was told that he would be making his test debut, as a replacement for cricket veteran V.V.S. Laxman, who was suffering from a back spasm from the previous match which had not yet healed. The news was broken to him just before the game after the team had reached the grounds after its warm-ups.

'You'll be batting at No. 5 in Laxman's spot,' he was informed.

His father had absolutely no idea that Cheteshwar would be debuting that day.

In the first innings, Cheteshwar faced three balls and struck a boundary before he was adjudged LBW to a ball by Mitchell Johnson. He was devastated. After preparing for this day since he was seven, he could not forgive himself for getting out so tamely. Sachin Tendulkar was at the non-striker's end at the time.

That evening, after the day's play Sachin paaji sat Cheteshwar down and told him not to get dejected. 'That ball had wicket written all over it. You could not have done anything else with it,' he consoled.

The cricketing legend's words went a long way in helping Cheteshwar to put his disastrous opening aside and concentrate instead on the innings to come.

In the second innings, the Indian captain M.S. Dhoni sent him to bat at one down in a tactical decision, a position he would occupy for about a decade.

Cheteshwar made 72 runs off 89 balls in the second innings before being bowled by Nathan Hauritz.

Coincidentally he had debuted on my birthday, although at that time we were unaware of each other's existence.

───

In hindsight, Cheteshwar looks back at his fall in Bloemfontein as a blip in his career. 'It was never about losing my place in the squad because I was already part of it. Okay, so I was actually about to play for the team, but it didn't happen that year. It eventually happened the following year. I lost six months of my career. But then injuries are a professional hazard that players have to deal with.

Cheteshwar spent the next couple of years making the most of the opportunities that came his way and overall, he was quite content with the way his career was progressing. In 2011, the Indian team travelled to South Africa for a test series. Cheteshwar played a couple of games.

Then, IPL 4 began. It was the month of April and this time, Cheteshwar was playing for Royal Challenge Bangalore (RCB). Just over two years after the first fall, disaster struck again—this time in Bangalore during a live match. Once again, Cheteshwar was fielding and once again, he twisted his knee—this time his right one.

Initially, Cheteshwar thought it was a minor injury. 'First of all, it wasn't too painful and I did not even think that it was another ACL rupture. I thought, I'll be fine in a few days' time.'

He went off the field and the physio tried to make an initial assessment. He too wasn't sure if it was an ACL injury. Anyway, to be on the safe side, he underwent a scan. As luck would have it, the results were not too clear and only a partial ACL tear showed up in the scan. He was advised to go through four weeks of rehabilitation. 'We'll figure out whether you need a surgery after that,' he was told.

Cheteshwar remained parked in Bangalore at the National Cricket Academy and diligently went through all the paces of rehab. But it didn't help. It finally dawned on everyone concerned that perhaps rehab alone wasn't the solution. That's when he was told to travel to London to consult Andrew Williams, surgeon at large, to find out whether he needed a surgery.

Cheteshwar flew to London to meet Mr Andrew Williams (surgeons in England are chary of being addressed as doctors). Regarded worldwide as top of the heap in his field, having performed a slew of surgeries on injured footballers, Williams' final pronouncement—after he had done a preliminary examination—was somewhat disconcerting. 'I'm not sure whether you actually need a surgery, and I won't know for sure until I open up your knee.'

Horrified, Cheteshwar stared at Williams, uncomprehendingly. 'You won't know whether I need a surgery until you've actually opened up my knee?' he asked, wondering whether his ears were playing tricks on him.

'That's right,' the surgeon informed him. 'We will prep you for a surgery and if it is not needed, I won't operate.'

So, Cheteshwar actually went into the operation theatre not knowing whether he actually needed the surgery. But this time around, there was no meltdown. By now, he felt like a pro at handling ACL ruptures. The process being the same, felt so familiar. He went under general anaesthesia and slowly slipped into unconsciousness.

But as soon as the effects of the anaesthesia wore off, Cheteshwar demanded to speak to Williams. 'I wanted to know whether the surgery had actually been performed or not,' he explains wryly.

'We did do the surgery,' Williams informed him. 'There actually was a rupture.'

Post-surgery, Cheteshwar went through another round of rehab. This time, it was a breeze. He was much more relaxed and confident. Mentally, there was no trauma, because he'd already gone through it once and triumphed. 'I was sure that I'd make a comeback. Besides, I had already debuted for the Indian team, which was the main goal at the time. Careerwise, I was more settled.'

Psychologically, he was more prepared for the rehab process and worked hard to get fit. The last time around, it had taken him six months to get back to the game. This time, it took five.

He wasn't particularly worried about the future either. He knew that if he scored sufficient runs in domestic cricket, he would get picked for the Indian team again. So that's what he did. He played domestic games, started stockpiling runs and was selected for the Indian team later that year.

The two injuries were a learning curve for Cheteshwar. They taught him how to live in the present instead of worrying about the past or the future. 'This was when I learnt to live from moment to moment. This was when I realized how important it was to be in the present. I began by telling myself, "just be in the present, do your own thing, don't be too emotional about the game". At first, it was a mantra I clung to but later, it became an essential part of the person I am today.'

As Cheteshwar says, injuries are a part of every sportsperson's life—sometimes major, sometimes minor—and sooner or later, they have to be dealt with. But if one trains well and follows advice, they can be minimized. But a cricketer's success is not only dependent on his physical well-being, his emotional balance is just as important. Success begets celebrity status and widens the gap between life's core realities and the game. To play at the highest level for a longer period of time, to hold on to that success, it is imperative to cushion it with both feet planted firmly in the ground.

CHAPTER TEN

Déjà vu

It was 30 July 2011 and Cheteshwar was in his room at the ITC Gardenia in Bengaluru. He had been parked there on and off for phase two of his rehabilitation over the last couple of months, after the ACL surgery on his right knee. He was still on crutches. Although he was a lot more ambulatory than he had been a few weeks ago, the afflicted joint was still painful.

His mobile phone pealed loudly, cutting through the night like a knife. Shrill, insistent and peremptory, its reverberations grated on Cheteshwar's nerves. He looked at his watch in exasperation. It was almost ten at night. Anyone who knew him well would not consider calling him at this hour. For a moment, he toyed with the idea of ignoring it. The ringing stopped momentarily and then began again. Whoever it was, was clearly not going to give up until he responded.

He grunted as he reached out for his cell phone. It was lying on the bedside table, quite close to him. He peered blearily at the screen in the darkness. The name that flashed against its white light astonished him.

Why on earth was Dr Nirbhay Shah, that busy Rajkot surgeon and a dear friend of the family, calling him at this time of the night?

Something is wrong! The thought darted through his mind unbidden.

He punched the green button and braced himself for some bad news.

'Hello, uncle!' he said softly.

'Cheteshwar?' murmured a gentle well-known voice on the other side of the line.

'Yes uncle, this is Cheteshwar. Is everything alright?' he asked tentatively.

'Well, no,' Dr Shah said, his voice calm. 'Your father has had a heart attack—'

Cheteshwar froze, hurtling back to that terrible day when his mother had died. There had been a phone call that day too, but nobody had told him the truth. They had just informed him that she was very serious, not that she was dead. He felt the old melancholy of impending loss tightening its strong serpentine bands across his chest. Not again, he thought bleakly. Surely, he would not have to live in that cold, lonely cage once again? The old anger stirred and with it the dark black cloud of immense isolation.

'Don't worry, he's fine,' Dr Shah's voice cut in from a distance, jerking him out of his desolation, almost as if he had sensed Cheteshwar's growing disquiet. 'There's no need to panic. We're at Sterling Hospital. Here, why don't you talk to him? I know you'll keep worrying until you've heard his voice.'

There was a moment's pause while the cell phone changed hands. A brief conversation ensued between father and son.

'How are you? Cheteshwar asked his dad, carefully concealing his panic from his parent.

'Don't worry, Chintu,' said his father in a surprisingly strong voice. 'I'm in the hospital. But I'm alright.'

Cheteshwar permitted himself to relax just a wee bit. Not fully; just a little. 'I'll try not to worry. But you must take care. I'll take the first flight out. You mustn't tax yourself. We can always talk when I reach Rajkot. Now let me speak to Uncle Nirbhay.'

'What happened? Cheteshwar asked once Dr Shah was back on the line.

It turned out that around half past nine, my father-in-law had called up Dr Shah. It was a Saturday night and Uncle Nirbhay was on his way for a late-night show with his wife and a couple of friends, who were also members of the medical fraternity.

Papa opened the exchange with an unnerving query. 'What happens during a heart attack?'

Dr Shah immediately went on the alert. 'Why?'

'I've been having a terrible pain in my arm and chest,' confessed Papa, his voice taut. 'First, I felt my heart beating vigorously. It was so loud that I could hear it pounding like a drum. Then the pain began in arm and chest. It hasn't stopped since.'

'Which arm?' asked Dr Shah, sharply.

There was a moment's pause.

'My right arm,' said my father-in-law, faintly.

'Where are you?' Dr Shah inquired.

'At home, in bed,' Papa answered, his voice growing more and more feeble.

Dr Shah immediately turned the car around. 'Hang in there! We'll be with you in a matter of minutes. We're not too far from you.'

Once they reached my father-in-law, Dr Shah took one look at his pallor and sweat-dampened shirt and knew that they had a crisis on their hands. He immediately bundled him into his car and drove straight to Sterling Hospital, which was just a couple of kilometres away from the Pujara home.

He and his wife, Aunt Saloni, had already decided to take him to the emergency at Sterling not only because it was one of the best private multi-specialty hospitals in Rajkot; but also, because it was the closest.

Once they were at Sterling, the attending doctors confirmed that he was having a cardiac event and immediately administered an injection to halt its progress. The ECG, they told Uncle Nirbhaya, showed 'some anterior wall changes'. It was only after Papa was safely tucked in a bed in the ICU that Dr Shah decided it was time to inform Cheteshwar.

Once he got off the call, Cheteshwar pushed his fears firmly aside and spent the next couple of hours on the phone that night. His first call was to the Royal Challengers Bangalore (RCB). He apprized the concerned authorities of the emergency at home. They were extremely supportive and put Cheteshwar in touch with well-known cardiac surgeon, Dr Devi Shetty, who was on the RCB panel of doctors, just in case he decided to place my father-in-law in his capable hands. Dr Shetty, he was informed, was one of the best cardiac surgeons in the country.

Cheteshwar then had a talk with Dr Shetty over the phone. He told him as much as he knew about his father's condition. Dr Shetty advised him to stay in touch and keep him updated. He assured Cheteshwar that he was willing to take his father's case if the need arose.

After his chat with Dr Shetty, Cheteshwar set about making arrangements for the first available flight out of Bangalore to Rajkot. He discovered the earliest flight was a long one and only flew out of Bengaluru at 1.00 p.m. the next day, and that too via Mumbai.

Though the flight was long, it was still the only one that could get him to his hometown by 6 p.m. the next evening. The others, he discovered, would land at Rajkot much later. With nothing else available, he decided to take it.

The next afternoon, he boarded the flight, still on crutches; a lonely figure among a sea of people. He was oblivious to his surroundings and spent the entire trip praying hard to keep his thoughts at bay. He was still not convinced that he would reach there on time to see his father alive.

He hobbled off the flight at around six in the evening and headed straight to the hospital. Family, friends, Dr Shah and his wife were all present.

'How is he?' he asked Dr Shah.

'He's holding his own,' Dr Shah said encouragingly. 'He'll feel even better once he sees you.'

Cheteshwar's first sight of his father came as something of a shock. Papa, a pallid shell of his former self, looked frail and achingly finite; he could have been a character straight out of some futuristic sci-fi movie, linked as he was by a network of tubes to some scary looking machines.

Taking a deep breath, Cheteshwar pasted a determined smile on his face.

'*Kem chho* (how are you)?' he asked, cheerfully.

'*Maja ma* (I'm fine),' replied his father, jauntily.

Unused to conversation beyond cricket, Cheteshwar just squeezed his father's hand gently; that solitary touch was enough communication between the two. Papa could see a wealth of love spilling out of those greenish brown eyes. He felt at peace.

Once Cheteshwar had reassured himself that his father was better than expected, he came out of the room to tackle all the practicalities that had been awaiting his arrival. One of his first decisions was to stay back at night despites protests from his relatives that he was on crutches.

He then spoke to the doctors for a proper appraisal of the condition of his father's heart. 'We'll only know once he's had an angiography,' they said.

'How soon can it be done?' Cheteshwar wanted to know. As quickly as he wanted was the reply. Papa's angiography was fixed for the following day.

Once the procedure was over, Dr Ajay Patil, a cardiothoracic surgeon, was called in for advice.

Dr Patil, who eventually became a family friend, later related the events of the time: 'I was first called in to give my advice on a coronary angiography of a patient in the Cardiac Catheterization

Lab by Dr Mridul Sharma who had carried out the procedure. This was routine practice. The patient had suffered from an acute myocardial infarction, or heart attack, and the angiography suggested the presence of very diffused diseased vessels. It was quite clear that the patient required immediate bypass surgery. I was also of the opinion that along with the bypass, an additional procedure to remove plaque from the vessels was required. It was a high-risk surgery.'

At the time, Dr Patil did not know the patient's identity. It was only after he met Cheteshwar to discuss Papa's case and warn him of the risks attached to the surgery that he realized that the infirm individual was his father.

The next couple of days went by in a whirlwind of activity. By now, it was clear to everyone concerned that my father-in-law would have to undergo a bypass surgery. The question was, where?

It was a heavy burden for Cheteshwar to bear on his young shoulders. He was completely unnerved. The fate of his father now rested on his judgement. What if he made the wrong decision? He spent the said time period discussing the issue with Dr Shah whilst seeking opinions from other cardiac surgeons in Mumbai and Bengaluru.

A conversation with Devi Shetty eventually helped him decide.

'Let me speak to Dr Patil,' he told Cheteshwar. 'We'll take a call whether your father should be moved out of Rajkot after that.'

Cheteshwar connected him with Dr Patil and they engaged in a lengthy medical discussion. At the end of the chat, Dr Shetty gave his verdict. 'Do not shift the patient! Let Dr Patil handle the case. I'm quite confident that he is capable of managing it.'

There was an immediate sigh of relief. Things were finally moving forward. At least a decision had finally been taken! Now all that remained was the actual surgery. Dr Patil set the date. Papa would go under the knife on 4 August.

The day of the surgery arrived in what seemed like a flash. Papa, outfitted in a standard patient's gown, was wheeled into the OT. Cheteshwar stood outside, flanked by friends and family, his eyes blank, his lips moving. He appeared to have withdrawn into a trance-like state. 'I was actually chanting some prayers,' he later confessed.

The doors of the OT opened seemingly after an aeon, and Dr Patil emerged, all smiles. 'The surgery was successful,' he announced. 'The patient is stable. We'll be wheeling him to the recovery room shortly.'

The tension outside the OT evaporated instantly, replaced by a collective sense of relief and jubilation. Dr Patil had pronounced my father-in-law stable. Nothing could go wrong now. Or could it?

In the meanwhile, the press had been loitering around the hospital premises seeking every nugget of information it could gather on my father-in-law's condition. As were Cheteshwar's fans. He decided to issue a press release to mollify them.

The press release issued the day after my father-in-law's operation stated:

'Arvind Pujara, ex-Ranji player, coach and father of test cricketer Cheteshwar Pujara, has undergone a successful bypass heart surgery after suffering a severe heart stroke on date 4 August 2011 at Sterling Hospital, Rajkot. Cheteshwar, who has been undergoing treatment for the knee surgery sustained during IPL 4, has rushed to Rajkot to take care of his father.

The health condition of Arvind Pujara is improving satisfactorily. Well-wishers, fans and relatives of the Pujara family are thronging to inquire about Arvind Pujara's health condition. Cheteshwar has expressed his gratitude towards them and requested them to extend their cooperation by avoiding personal visits and contact, and thereby help him recover speedily.

It was a premature pronouncement.

Just as Cheteshwar thought his father was out of the woods, calamity struck afresh—and within forty-eight hours of the surgery!

It was Saturday evening and Cheteshwar was sitting by his father, desultorily chatting with the Shahs. Aunt Saloni and Uncle Nirbhay had dropped in to ask after my father-in-law's health before taking off for Ahmedabad to catch up with their relatives there.

'We had just dropped in to see how Arvind was—it was a routine visit—we thought we'd say goodbye and leave for the station straight from the hospital—when suddenly Nirbhay noticed that the monitor showed Arvind's BP fluctuating. He pointed it out to me, and before we could react, it started dropping very quickly,' Aunt Saloni later recalled.

'We'd better call Dr Patil,' said Dr Shah grimly.

But before they could act, Dr Patil himself entered the room. He had become quite fond of the Pujaras and thought he'd check on his patient before heading home for the weekend.

He immediately figured out that something was terribly wrong. 'What is it?' he asked Dr Shah.

The latter pointed at the monitor.

Dr Patil took in the situation at a glance. He noticed that the blood pressure had started to drop on the monitor. The invasive pressure lines were flushed and yet Papa's blood pressure was dropping rapidly. 'Oh my God! It looks like a cardiac tamponade!'

Suddenly, without any warning, they were in the middle of an emergency!

'There's no time to take him to the ICU,' said Dr Patil urgently. 'I'm going to cut him open right here.' He picked up the phone and issued a string of orders. Within minutes, the room was overrun by members of the cardiology team and converted into a makeshift OT.

As Dr Patil would later explain, a cardiac tamponade is the excessive collection of fluids around the pericardium or the sac that covers the heart, impeding the heart from functioning properly. It usually happens within the first twenty-four hours of a cardiac surgery, but rarely after that. But here they were performing a re-exploration surgery in the recovery room for a patient who needed it urgently, right in front of his son!

And what of Cheteshwar?

He had been asked to step back when the procedure began. His face, leeched of all expression, was strangely still. Aunt Saloni stood next to him. They could both hear sentences like 'Oh my god, he's critical,' 'he's almost gone,' 'he's sinking,' being bandied about by the medical team with frightening regularity.

At this point, Aunt Saloni held his hand. 'I thought that this way, at least I could show him that he was not alone. That I was there with him.'

She noticed that his eyes were unblinking and lips were moving in silent prayer. He was somewhere else—in a private space where only he and his god existed.

The procedure lasted for about forty-five minutes. It had been a tricky situation and a stressful quarter of an hour. Finally, the crisis passed. The emergency was over. But for a time, it had been touch and go.

Dr Patil looked up and saw Cheteshwar standing like a wall, unmoved and unmoving without an iota of emotion on his face. He had witnessed the entire procedure, and yet he seemed untouched. How had he managed it?

In hindsight, there seems to be a certain inevitability about the way events played out that evening. The Shahs, who had just happened to be there, had deferred yet another trip in their life to stand by Cheteshwar and his father. Dr Patil's entry into the room, just when the medical emergency began, was serendipitous. Had he not arrived when he did, my father-in-law might not have survived.

It was almost as if destiny had already scripted a happy ending on that fateful evening.

Cheteshwar stayed with his father at the hospital till 21 August, the day Papa was discharged from Sterling. They moved back home until it was time for Cheteshwar to focus on his own rehab. He now looks at his ACL surgery as a blessing in disguise. 'If I hadn't been in rehab, I couldn't have spent so much time looking after my father.'

Cheteshwar left for Bangalore on 31 August. My father-in-law initially stayed with his brother. But after a few days, he staged a quiet rebellion. 'I'm fine,' he announced. 'I want to go back home.'

Initially, he faced some resistance, but eventually he had his way. Everyone knew how stubborn Papa could be. The extended family decided to amend their strategy. They withdrew their objections and instead inundated him with constant visits to maintain a benign surveillance over him. Moreover, there was a family in the house that had been retained as domestic staff, so there was plenty of house-help to keep a watchful eye on him.

Towards the end of September, the Pujaras moved houses, leaving all their old worries behind. When Dr Patil met them next, some three months later, at the cricket ground during a practice session, he knew that the bypass surgery had been a success. He saw Arvind Pujara, father, mentor and coach, bowling to his son and student, Cheteshwar!

The Pujaras were all set for the next phase of their lives.

PART THREE

CHAPTER ELEVEN

Jab We Wed

Cheteshwar and I tied the nuptial knot on 13 February 2013, just days ahead of the Border-Gavaskar trophy. India had just lost a series to England at home after a long time. I was still too ignorant about the game and did not really understand the nuances that prevailed in the cricketing world just before the onset of the four-match series with Australia. I was, however, aware that although M.S. Dhoni was still the captain, several star senior players like Saurav Ganguly, Anil Kumble, Rahul Dravid and V. V. S. Laxman had hung up their boots. India was now represented by a much younger side.

On a personal level, Cheteshwar had performed well in the first two matches against England, scoring a double century and a ton. But he had not done too well in the later games. Our wedding was to follow close on the heels of this rout and the team management had graciously given him the option to skip the training camp at Bengaluru and join straight for the matches.

In the context of India's recent defeat, the tournament with Australia was very important and the team was under a lot pressure. For Cheteshwar, who was just at the sunrise of his career, it was a big chance. But instead of taking a unilateral decision, he decided to consult me.

'What would you like to do?' he asked. 'We won't be able to get away for too long, because I have to be in Chennai on the eighteenth for the opening match. But we could go for a short honeymoon.'

I had been around him long enough to understand that what god had joined together—in this case Cheteshwar and cricket—let no man (or woman) put asunder. Who was I—a mere fiancée, soon to be wife—to come between him and his game? Privately, I was very touched that he had even bothered to ask. It was a promising sign for the future of our marriage.

Aloud, I said: 'It doesn't matter. We can always go for a holiday later.'

The look of undisguised relief and approval on his face told me I had made the right choice. I could see that he thought I was going to be an ideal cricketer's wife. I hid a smile.

Then the wedding was upon us.

The nuptials spanned three days and passed off in a blur.

The cricket team was busy training in Bengaluru for the upcoming series and his teammates had sent their regrets in advance.

We understood. Cheteshwar too had opted only for a two-day grace period to absent himself from the training camp, after the sorry-we-can't-take a-long break apologia my dutifully contrite better-half had treated me to while broaching the question of our honeymoon. The only concession that had been made to romance was that our wedding reception happened to coincide with Valentine's day.

Just before we headed out to the airport to fly out to Bengaluru, my father-in-law bearded me. Cheteshwar was still having a shower and I had descended down in search of a cup of tea. The room was jampacked with some fifteen odd people.

'Ah! You're looking for chai?' my father-in-law asked genially, nursing his own cup in his hand.

I nodded, tongue-tied.

'Sit,' he commanded, as he hollered for some tea.

I sat down next to him, feeling super nervous. He eyed me benignly, looking as if he wished to say something.

I waited.

'I want to tell you something,' he said at last.

'Yes?' I said, encouragingly.

'I know you are both newly married and want to spend a lot of time together,' he said gravely. 'But you must not think of this trip as a vacation. This series is very important for him, you know,' he paused as if was waiting for some kind of reaction from me.

I nodded dutifully.

'It's very important for his career,' my father-in-law persisted. 'Do you understand?'

I nodded again.

'You must make sure that he sticks to his routine,' he instructed.

'I will,' I assented softly, wondering what he meant by 'routine'. At that point, Cheteshwar's all-important routine was a foreign word to me.

He smiled approvingly. 'Now that you're going to the camp, try and keep out of his way. He needs to be dedicated.'

I kept nodding my head, completely at sea. I had no idea what he was trying to tell me. Thankfully, Cheteshwar turned up at that point and announced that it was time to go. Our relatives gave us a raucous sendoff boisterously reinforcing us with all manner of good wishes for a long and happy wedding life and the very best of luck for the forthcoming Border-Gavaskar series.

We reached the ITC Gardenia in Bengaluru at around nine at night and ordered room service, too tired to even venture out into the dining room. It had been a long day and an early night seemed vastly attractive. As soon as we consumed our meal, I flopped onto the bed in sheer exhaustion. I must have fallen asleep as soon as my head touched the pillow because I only woke up when Cheteshwar shook me gently the next morning and announced that it was time to rise and shine.

I met all the cricketing greats at breakfast. It was all very formal and I was completely unnerved. Cheteshwar grabbed my hand when he spotted his teammates and said: 'Come I'll introduce you to everyone.'

I was stumped. 'Do we really need to do this?' I wondered, feeling thoroughly awkward.

'It's expected of us,' said Cheteshwar, in an undervoice, as he dragged me forward.

Could he read my thoughts now—and we had only been married a day? I felt quite unsettled.

Suddenly, we were surrounded by the team. I stood there confused. What were the proper rules of etiquette governing greetings by cricketers' wives? Were we expected to shake hands, hug our husbands' teammates, say hello or namaste—one by one or individually? I had no idea how I was supposed to behave. I settled for a shy 'hello' that was meticulously directed at everyone.

In return, I was hailed with courteous congratulations and friendly smiles; then to my intense relief, Cheteshwar escorted me back to our table. Shortly afterwards he picked up his kit bag and joined the rest of the team, hopping on to the bus for his practice session. I headed back to the room.

On that note, our marriage began.

In the meantime, I tried to keep up with the vagaries brought about by my status as a newly married woman to a sports celebrity. Some of it was overpowering. For one, I was not used to staying in fancy hotels and forking out five thousand rupees for each meal. It was a culture shock!

Secondly, even though I had spent the last four months virtually living in his pocket, the reality of actually coexisting with him day in and day out was a whole new different deal. First of all, I discovered he was an extremely light sleeper—to the extent that he would be up if I so much as breathed loudly. It was quite disconcerting.

Next, I discovered that my husband was an extremely territorial creature. He was finicky about things like 'his side of the bed', 'his charger', 'his toiletry bag', 'his suitcase'—the list of items that fell into the 'keep-off-the-grass' category were endless. I was not permitted to share any of the said objects. Even more amusing was the utmost courtesy that couched his endeavours to mark his turf.

These attempts would inevitably begin with offers such as: 'pick your side of the bed, then I'll plug in your charger next to you' or 'I'll plug your charger next to you so you don't have to reach out for your mobile'. In plain English, what he really meant was: let's charge your phone next to you so that you don't wake me up when you grope for your phone in the dark.

Cheteshwar even tried to explain why such a degree of order was necessary to our lives. It did not make any sense to me, but I nodded, my understanding not quite up to the task of informing him that the workings of his minds were quite incomprehensible to me.

Aloud, I'd say 'okay'. Inwardly, I'd wonder: 'Why can't we share the charger if we have the same kind of phone?'

I suppose our contrasting attitudes were rooted in our childhoods. He had been an only child, to whom the notion of sharing was an alien concept whilst I had grown up with siblings and roommates and was quite used to sharing my possessions.

He was also very organized, unlike me.

Back in those days, I would dump my things anywhere, without worrying too much about the mess. Cheteshwar, on the other hand, would not only stack his own things neatly but would also stash mine in some sort of orderliness. His penchant for neatness even extended to used utensils. All dirty dishes would be piled tidily, with grubby forks and spoons placed painstakingly on one side. At that time I thought it was cute, it was only later that it dawned on me that there was a well thought-out method to his behaviour—it was driven by a need to avoid causing inconvenience to anyone else.

On 18 February, we travelled to Chennai for the opening match which was due to begin on 22 February. There were whispers that the pitch would soon turn into a ripper for spinners. India lost the toss and was asked to bowl. I knew nothing about the game, but I kept biting my nails in fear, wondering how this young Indian side would fare in the match.

The Indians held their nerves and soon put the Aussies on the backfoot. In the first innings, Cheteshwar got out at forty-four. M.S. Dhoni made a double century, Virat Kohli scored a century and Sachin netted eighty-one runs putting India firmly in the driver's seat. In the second innings, Cheteshwar remained not-out at eight and Sachin Tendulkar wrapped up the match by hitting two consecutive sixes to the immense delight of his fans. He too was undismissed.

We then moved to Hyderabad for the second test. I was told that this was Cheteshwar's lucky ground. The pronouncement turned out to be true and he scored a double century putting up a 370-run partnership with Murali Vijay who scored a ton. But for some reason, on the eve of the third day, when he was batting overnight at 162, I felt feverish and did not sleep very well. Perhaps, it was because I was not used to hotel-hopping.

Deeply worried about me, Cheteshwar did not sleep much either, and left the room stealthily the next morning to avoid disturbing me. Not that it would have made any difference had he beaten drums next to my ears—back then, I was a very deep sleeper and rarely knew when my husband slunk out of the room after whispering good-bye.

Aware that I was fond of my beauty sleep, he would usually put up the 'do-not-disturb' sign, so that I would not be troubled by housekeeping until I was ready to face the day. There were times when the wives of other cricketers would complain: 'We wanted to ask you to come with us for the match, but we couldn't get you on the mobile.'

I woke up late that day feeling much better. I looked at my watch and got a shock—it was 10 a.m.! The game had started at 9.30 a.m. and Cheteshwar had just been thirty-eight runs shy of his double hundred.

'Oh my god!' I thought in a panic. 'I'm going to miss his double century!'

I switched on the television to check his score. He was still batting at 175. I heaved a sigh of relief and quickly rolled out of bed. I dressed in double-quick time and was down at the foyer within half-an-hour hopping on to the first available cab.

When I reached the stadium, I heaved a sigh of relief. He had only added ten runs in the interim and was batting at 185. Thank god! I had not missed his double century! By this time, I had learnt that a century was good, but a double century was amazing!

Cheteshwar got out at 204 just before lunch and India declared the match sometime between lunch and tea after putting up a score of 503. The Australians had a tough task and were all out for 131 on day four of the match.

Cheteshwar, who became the second fastest Indian to score a thousand runs in test cricket in that match was declared player of the match. India was ahead in the series by 2-0. It was also Virender Sehwag's final test of his career.

The match wound up early and we realized that there was sufficient time to get back home to organize a bhandara, or free meal for the underprivileged, at the Gondal ashram as a thanksgiving for our recent nuptials. It went off smoothly, and immediately afterwards, we headed to Mohali for the third match.

～

It was at Mohali that I was introduced to the darker side of the game. It was here that I discovered that cricketers lived under constant threat of injuries; it was a risk that perpetually shadowed players, denting them not just physically, but putting them under enormous mental pressure, as well.

Australia had won the toss yet again and had elected to bat. But the weather was distinctly unfriendly on day one, and play was called off due to incessant rain.

It was on day two that Cheteshwar pulled his hamstring while running towards the ball to prevent a boundary. He left the ground for a bit. I was worried, but since I did not know exactly what had happened and did not really understand the nature of the injury, I was calm. I had not gone to the stadium that day and only discovered how awful it was when he came back to the hotel that evening.

'It's really bad,' he told me.

Cheteshwar had hobbled into the room with a strange machine full of ice. He kept pressing the button to cool the injury and seemed to be in quite a lot of pain. I was horrified when I discovered that he was expected to bat the next day.

'Why are you going to bat if your leg is paining so much?' I asked, perplexed. To me, it appeared completely senseless to aggravate an injury that already seemed to be quite bad.

'It doesn't work like that,' Cheteshwar replied, managing to wince and look amused simultaneously. He obviously thought my ignorance of the game was not only monumental but hugely entertaining to boot. I held my peace, realizing by this time that nothing I said would make any difference. Happily, thanks to a strong opening partnership between Shikhar Dhawan and Murli Vijay who scored centuries apiece, Cheteshwar's turn to bat came only on day four.

But, by then, the pain had become excruciating. He had been taking massages with icepacks all morning and he opted for a quick massage just before the match began. A few minutes into the match, the umpire ruled Cheteshwar out LBW. He had just scored one run.

Even before he got back to the pavilion, someone told me that the ball was missing leg stump. 'He was not really out, you know.'

'Then why is he walking back?' I asked, deeply puzzled. I was still to learn that the umpire's word was final.

'Because the umpire said he's out,' explained my informant. I felt like a somewhat backward child and nodded my head, acting as if I found his explanation enlightening.

Thank god! He was not really out! I thought, glad that he had been wrongly given an LBW. *At least he'll be able to rest his leg.* I was so naïve that I did not realize that wrongful dismissals were the ones that hurt players the most.

India did quite well and Australia lost this match quite decisively. We were now 3-0 in the series. But I was too worried about Cheteshwar to celebrate.

Both teams shifted to Delhi for the final test.

I was quite excited. We had a day off and planned to explore the city together after Cheteshwar returned from his anti-doping test. We thought it would take half-an-hour.

It took him three-and-a-half hours to return. The day had well and truly gone down the tube. He was apologetic, I was resigned. Exploring the city appeared to be an exercise in futility considering the time that was left in our hands. We decided to stay in and ended up watching some random movie on his laptop.

Exactly a month to the day, the final test match began at the Feroz Shah Kotla Stadium on 22 March. The pitch was a turner track and Australia won the toss and elected to bat. Cheteshwar managed to score a half-century despite an injured finger. A trip to the hospital revealed that he had fractured the afflicted digit.

By now, I was completely traumatized. He had barely recovered from his hamstring injury and now this! I almost had a meltdown.

'You cannot go to bat again with that finger,' I stated, firmly.

'I don't have a choice,' said Cheteshwar with a sigh. 'These things are part of the game and there's nothing anyone can do about it.'

I was unconvinced.

Determined to prevent my husband from batting with a fractured finger, I called up my father-in-law. Surely, he would support me? He did not. I should have remembered that he thought like a cricketer first and last.

'Don't worry, Puja, he's taken the injection, he'll be fine,' he told me kindly, imagining that he was soothing my fears.

I could not believe it!

'What's wrong with everyone?' I thought. 'Why is everyone treating the fracture so casually?'

In the end, empathizing with my uneasiness, Cheteshwar took pity on me and made me talk to Dr Nirbhay Shah, who had tasked himself with the job of keeping a benign eye on my husband's injuries for ages.

'How can anyone play with a fractured finger?' I asked Dr Shah, tearfully.

'I wouldn't worry too much if I were you, Puja,' said Dr Shah tranquilly. 'He'll be wearing a mould when he goes to bat in the second innings. It will provide sufficient protection to the finger.'

My exchange with Dr Shah soothed me somewhat, but I was still very scared. My apprehensions mounted when I learnt that he would be opening the second innings instead of coming at his usual slot at number three, because the original opener, Shikhar, had been ruled out of the game due to injury.

My nervousness skyrocketed as Cheteshwar walked to crease. To open on the last day to chase a team like Australia on a turning track was a daunting feat. My fears proved groundless. He ended up scoring eighty-two not-out and India went on to win the match and the series. In the given circumstances, my husband still rates it as one his top five innings.

India had done the unthinkable. It was a 4-0 whitewash—a first against the Aussies. I was ecstatic.

Then came the bad news.

We were ready to go home. IPL was round the corner, but we both knew that he would have to wait it out till his finger healed.

The same night, he got a call from the chief selector informing him that he was not in contention for the Champions Trophy which was part of the one-day format of the game. 'Given your fitness and your running, you have not been selected for the game,' he was told baldly.

It was a massive blow.

Cheteshwar had always wanted to play all three formats of the game. He was ambitious, he was doing really well and was working very hard to achieve his aspirations. Yet, slowly and systematically, he was being branded as a test player on the grounds that his fitness was not great and that he did not run so well. Thus began his long and torturous journey as a test specialist.

He had been a stand-out player in both the England and the Australia series, and it was hard for him to accept that he was unfit for the one-day game. It was painful to watch him struggle to accept the selectors' decision.

Till then, we had been living in a bubble. Cheteshwar had been having a dream run and for a brief spell, our days had seemed like a fairy tale. But, as a couple, we are both realists, and quickly realized that real life seldom follows the magical, mythical realms of make-believe. We decided to accept both the good and the bad with gratitude and count our blessings, of which we had many. We had each other, and success, as Cheteshwar often says, is only a temporary mistress to be treated with caution and humility.

CHAPTER TWELVE

A Short Vacation and Other Stories

Two months had passed since our wedding. The Indian Premier League (IPL) was almost upon us and Cheteshwar's broken finger had still not healed. We decided to go up north to Pandukeshwar, a small village in the Himalayas, where his Guruji had an ashram.

The village is the last hub with a year-round population, en route to Badrinath, one of the char dhams, or main pilgrimage centres, in the state of Uttarakhand. Both Guruji and Masi were there and my husband was chafing to meet them before he headed to Bengaluru for his rehabilitation.

Pandukeshwar is a quaint little hamlet by the banks of the Alaknanda River at an altitude of 6,300 feet above sea level. It is said to have been founded by Pandu, the king of the Kuru kingdom and father of the five Pandava brothers who famously fought their cousins—the Kauravas—according to the great Indian epic, the Mahabharata. Local lore says that Pandu was responsible for building the two famous temples in the village—the Yogadhyan Badri (one of the 'Sapta Badris' or seven Badris) and the Vasudeva temple, both dedicated to Lord Vishnu.

The ashram, a modest structure with very basic amenities, had some twelve odd rooms for overnight devotees. It also had a small Hanuman temple within its premises where artis were held each evening. Free food was offered to travellers as 'seva', or selfless-service, a vital part of karma yoga, extremely central to Guruji's teachings. Every morning, hot chole (chickpeas) and puris were prepared for pilgrims and passersby—which meant that devotees staying in the ashram were expected to rise by 5.30 a.m. and wash up, before heading down to help in the preparation and distribution of the said meal to yatris who were on their way to Badrinath.

Getting me out of bed soon became one of Cheteshwar's daily chores. I found it hard to wake up with the birds and Cheteshwar did not like to go down without me, worried that he would attract pitying looks from people who would judge me and think—this poor man is awake while his wife is still sleeping. He would leave me undisturbed in my slumberous state for as long as he deemed it politic, quietly getting ready himself while I napped. Once dressed, he would try to wake me.

Our days in the ashram invariably began with a loud announcement from Cheteshwar: 'Okay, wake up now. Time is short and we have to go and make puris.'

I would respond by digging deeper into my quilt.

'Umm two more minutes,' I would murmur sleepily.

His next attempt to rouse me would be met with the plea, 'Five minutes more'. While I slept, he would gallantly source hot water in an aluminum bucket for me, hefting it from the ground floor as the ashram functioned on the premise that god helped those who helped themselves. Then he would pace up and down the room till he figured that if he let me sleep any longer, we would be cutting things very fine indeed.

'Okay, now get up, we don't have time,' he would inform me firmly.

I would get out of bed very reluctantly, still half asleep.

Once he was sure I was up, Cheteshwar would venture forth to meet Guruji. 'Puja will be down in two minutes,' he would say

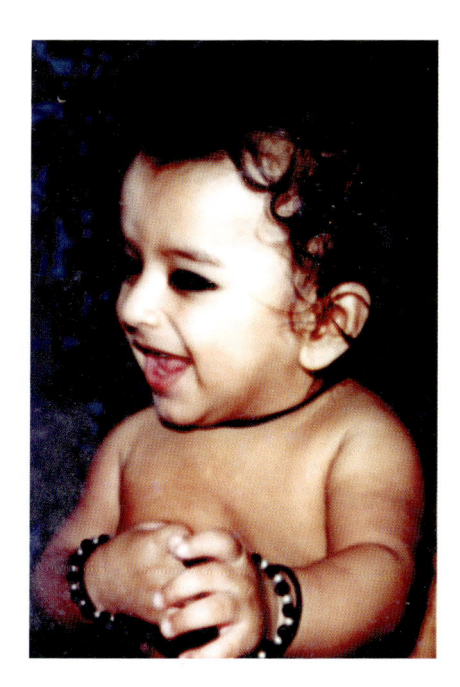

The Pujaras count their blessings: Baby Cheteshwar in a moment of joy, circa 1988.

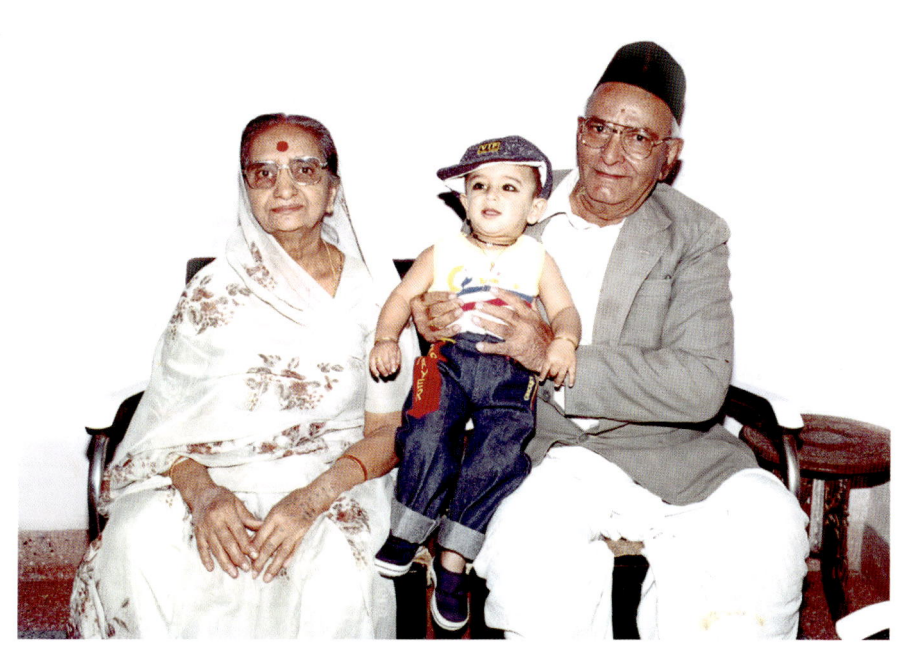

On the lap of his grandfather, Shiv Lal Pujara—the first cricketer of the clan who played for Dhrangadhra in pre-independence India, circa 1989.

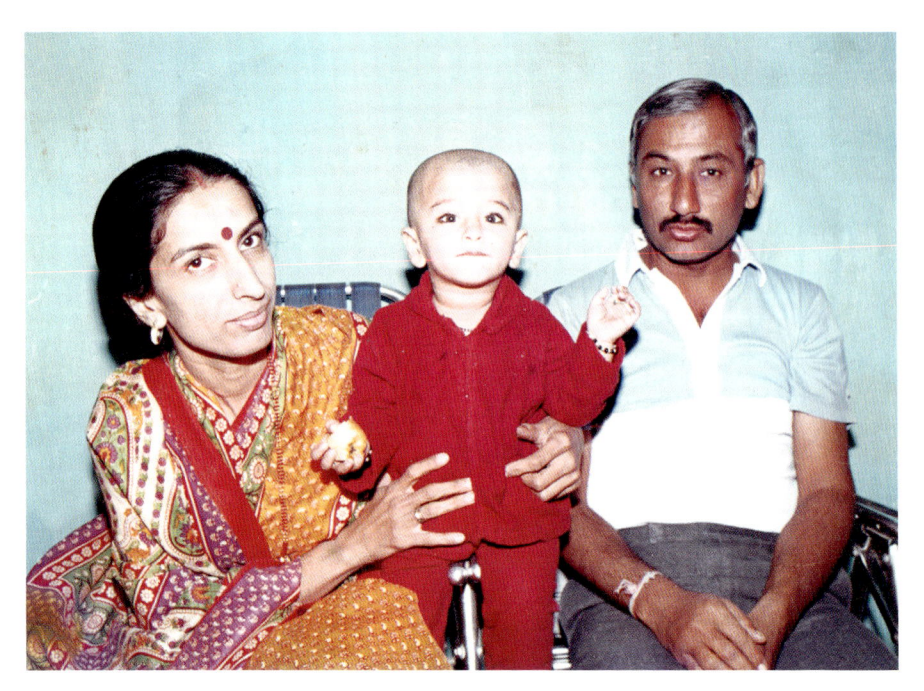

Off with his hair! Cheteshwar with his parents after his mundan ceremony, circa 1990.

Inflection point: The picture that convinced Arvind Pujara that his son was a natural cricketer. It marked the beginning of Cheteshwar's cricketing career at age three. The photograph was shot by Bipin Mamaji's friend, circa 1991.

A cup in hand: Preparing for the future with a cup that is not his, circa 1993.

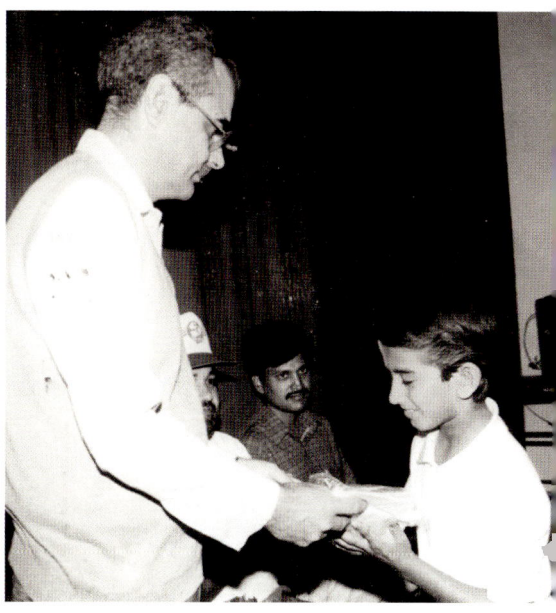

An early cricketing triumph! Circa 1994.

Cheteshwar earns a cap at the railway grounds in Kothi Compound, circa 1994. This was the time when Arvind Pujara had started coaching other railway kids in cricket along with son.

At the nets in pads handstitched by his mother, circa 1995. The sports shops did not have any in his size.

Big dreams in his eyes and family time: Cheteshwar as a teenager with his mother, father, Bipin Mamaji and his family—Mamaji always stood like a rock by him.

Cheteshwar raises his bat in his debut match after scoring 72 runs in the second innings at Bangalore, circa 2010.

Who's this girl! In the eye of the press, and a pasted smile! It was my second encounter with media attention in a week, this time during the first-ever cricket match I watched in Ahmedabad, circa November 2012. India was playing England and Cheteshwar was unbeaten at 206 not out. I knew it was an achievement, even though my knowledge of the game would not have filled a postage stamp!

Jab we wed! 13 February 2013. The wedding had to be squeezed between two series—one against England that India lost after a long time and an upcoming four-game series against Australia. Since it was an important series, we skipped our honeymoon so that Cheteshwar could join the training camp on time!

Posing in front of Tower Bridge, circa 2014. It was my first trip to England with Cheteshwar.

Masi's last bhandara, circa 2015, just a day before she died. She distributed food to the needy through sheer willpower even though she had been ill for a long time. Cheteshwar's mentor and spiritual guide, her passing was a huge loss for the family.

All smiles after the Border-Gavaskar Home Series 2017 (l-r: Cheteshwar, Ravichandran Ashwin, Basu Shankar (trainer) and Anil Kumble, then head coach).

When in England, do as the English do: Cheteshwar on a grocery run, circa 2017.

Eyes firmly shut: Cheteshwar meets his newborn daughter on 23 February 2018, several hours after she was born the previous day. He was away for the Vijay Hazare quarter finals in Delhi and rushed back to Rajkot in the wee hours of the morning. Aditi made him earn his parental privileges, making him wait before she deigned to open her eyes for him, almost as if she was punishing him for not being there when she was born.

Dressed to the nines: Cheteshwar, Aditi and I celebrate Aditi's first birthday early. As usual, cricket got in the way. Cheteshwar had to leave for the Syed Mushtaq Ali match trophy, 2019.

Doting grandparents: Aditi with my parents on her first-birthday revelries, circa 2019.

It takes a village: Celebrating Aditi's maiden birthday with family and friends! It was an unorthodox affair with a carnival theme. There was a Ferris-wheel, trampolines, balloon shooting, food vans and the works! Everyone was dressed casually and had a blast!

With Guruji during the Bhagwat Sapta to honour the memory of Cheteshwar's mum and masi. Circa 2019. His Guruji, Haricharandasji Maharaj of Gondal, played a pivotal role in Cheteshwar's life right since his childhood and guided him through his ups and downs, until Guruji passed on in 2024.

Cheteshwar's mancation in Goa, circa 2019. It was his second fun trip with no agenda!

On top of the world! Cheteshwar holds the Border-Gavaskar trophy as Man of the Series 2018-19, after India's first test series win on Aussie soil. It was a test of his personal resilience that he achieved this despite the various personal battles he was engaged in at the time.

Weight-training with his daughter: Cheteshwar baby-wraps a six-month-old Aditi, circa 2019.

A constant in our lives: Cheteshwar and me with Geeta Didi, circa 2019. Sometimes friend, sometimes aunt, she was quick to pull rank whenever she thought I was stepping out of line, especially during our courtship phase before our marriage was settled.

Sublimely glanced to the square leg boundary—a trademark Cheteshwar stroke that earned him countless runs all through his career.

Snatching the trophy from a draw: Saurashtra's first-ever Ranji Trophy win! Circa 2020. It was a hard-fought game at the start of Covid-19 against Bengal. The wicket slowed down considerably in a match that headed to a draw! Saurashtra emerged victorious because of its first-inning lead.

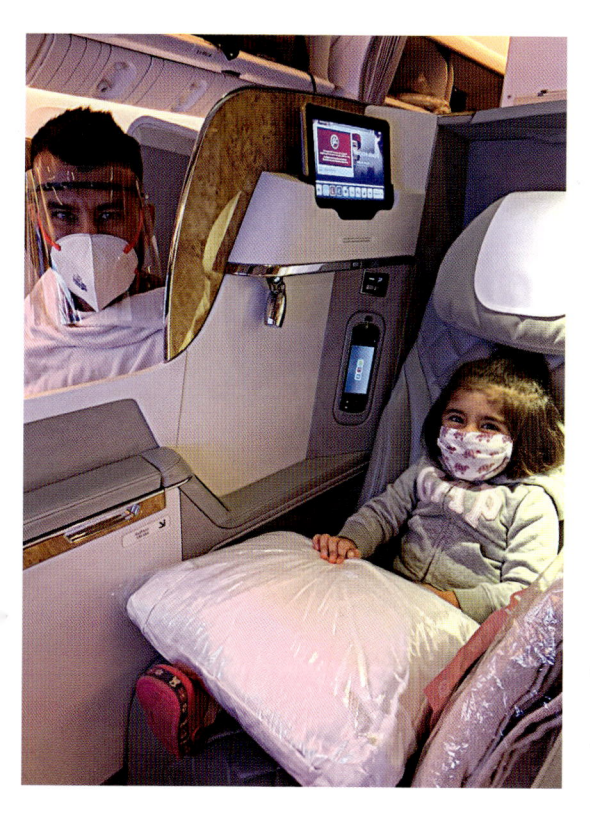

Travelling in Covid times. Cheteshwar and Aditi mask their way to Australia, circa 2020.

Playing a flick shot against the spinner in Border-Gavaskar Trophy—a shot Cheteshwar made his own.

Breaching the Gabbattoir! India's epic Border-Gavaskar Series Win in 2021. Dubbed the ultimate test series, it began with an Indian collapse, a stunning comeback, a draw, injuries galore—so much so that the Indian side had to draw on its reserve players! Despite the odds, the team triumphed in Gabba to create history!

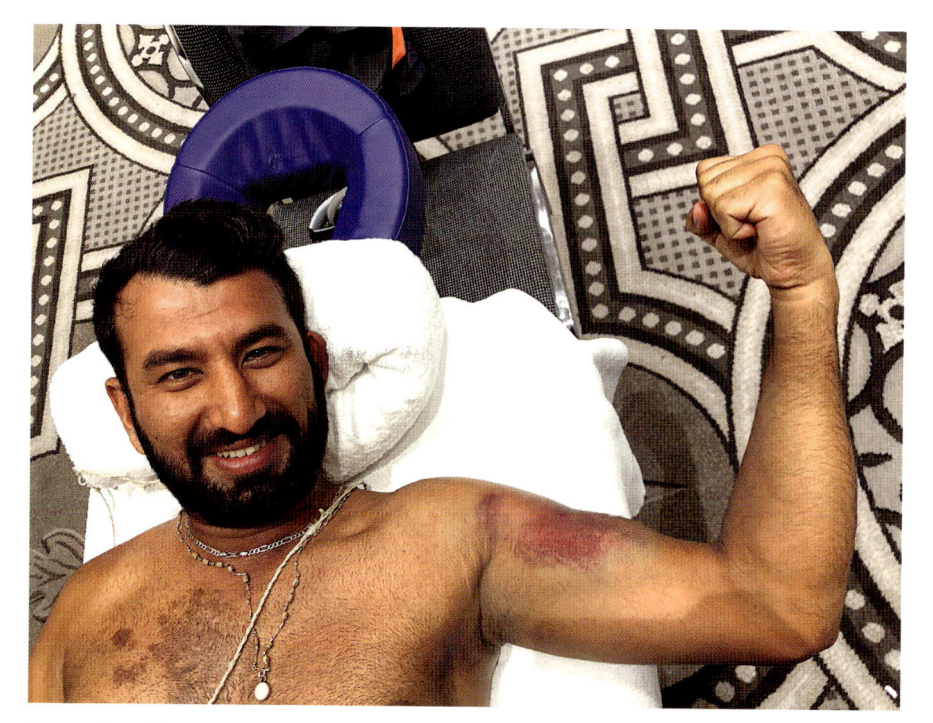

Battered and bruised but still grinning: He took thirteen visible body blows in the second innings of the last match during the Border-Gavaskar Trophy 2021. Despite the injuries, Cheteshwar was content, because to him this series symbolized the triumph of the spirt—a victory of the mind over the body!

Warm-ups at the Cheteshwar Arvind Bhai Pujara Cricket Academy, circa 2021, when the pandemic eased a little. The academy was established in 2014 to give back to cricket—the game which gave so much to Cheteshwar. It's a non-profit endeavour open free of cost to any talented individual looking for career in cricket.

Cheteshwar wins his Hundredth Test cap, circa 2023. The entire family attended the event.

Summer of '23: The Pujaras and Pabaris at Seven Sisters, East Sussex, England. This was the first time my parents travelled with us to England. For once, instead of just watching county matches, my father-in-law also willingly participated in the touristy stuff.

apologetically. Guruji would accept this blatant whopper with a twinkle in his eyes.

Our short vacation at Pandukeshwar, spanning a mere four to five days, provided us with a much-needed break. We drank water from a stream, went for long walks and chatted for hours. We also took off to Badrinath one day for darshan (a term widely used for the auspicious viewing of any deity) and organized a bhandara for numerous sadhus and yatris. I was quite downcast when it was time for us to leave the village. It spelt the end of a lovely interlude.

Immediately after our return, Cheteshwar left for Bengaluru and I stayed back at Rajkot. We were both miserable. He was dejected as he had to sit out several IPL matches and I was morose because I had nothing to do. The wedding fever had abated. I would wake up each day, early by my standards, at 7.30 a.m., and find myself twiddling my thumbs from morning to night. Things had been fine till March, because there had been bank statements that needed to be looked into. Both father and son looked upon it as an onerous task and were only too happy to hand over the dreaded chore to me.

It was at around this time that I started bonding with Papa, which was how I addressed my father-in-law; like everything else in my marriage, it happened organically and we quickly reached the ease and understanding commonly found in father-daughter relationships—much to the intense surprise of the extended family who held him in equal mixtures of awe and trepidation.

When I first married Cheteshwar, I had been given to understand that Papa was an angry man apt to fly off the handle at the drop of a hat. But I soon discovered that he was sorely misunderstood. My father-in-law did have a temper. But he was not unreasonable. He had strong opinions about anything and everything and loved the heady thrill of animated discussions and heated debates. Counter-expressions never annoyed him—he enjoyed arguing with people who stood up to him—it was frozen silences that unsettled him.

'Don't keep nodding your head if you don't agree with me,' he would instruct me during the early days of my marriage. 'If you don't agree with something, you don't have to say yes—say what you think.' He would keep at me till slowly our conversations became two-way channels and I started expressing my opinions as strongly as he; it was exhilarating.

As March came to a close that year, during Cheteshwar's cousin's wedding, I discovered just how fiercely protective my father-in-law was about me. Since Cheteshwar was in Bangalore, the task of representing the family at the nuptials fell on Papa and yours truly.

Just before we left for the function, he took me aside for a tete-a-tete. 'I want you to remember, you don't have to do anything you don't want to do.'

I was touched. This dictum was so unlike anything I had heard from my own parents who were quite clear that my siblings and I had to toe the line and rise to meet the social expectations of the extended family no matter how much we detested it. Papa, on the other hand, was giving me blanket clearance to do precisely as I liked.

'You don't have to be the ideal bahu (bride) as long as you are true to yourself and your beliefs,' he continued kindly.

Later that night, I thought how lucky I was to be part of a family that believed in the freedom of women. Cheteshwar too was a chip off the old block. Gujaratis have a tradition of inundating visitors with food. Cheteshwar always stepped in whenever he noticed that I was being force-fed by some of his over-eager aunts.

'Don't force her to eat. Her health will get spoilt,' he would protest bluntly.

If he saw me struggling to finish the food on my plate when we were on our own, he would tell me to leave it. 'You don't have to eat it if you don't want to … don't worry about wasting it.'

I would look at him in wonder. I came from a family which expected me to polish off every morsel on my plate and lived by the belief 'waste not, want not'. This was the first time in my life somebody was actually telling me it was okay to waste food if my stomach was not amenable. But I happily took his advice, though I did feel a twinge of guilt.

Over time, thanks to the tactics employed by Papa and Cheteshwar, hyper-hospitable relatives stopped using food as a device to demonstrate their affection. The Pujara men did not know how to offer me the usual conventional gifts, but the one benefaction they gave me in abundance was the freedom to be who I am—it surpassed every other boon I have received.

This was also the time when Papa told me about his early struggles, his wife and his life. We built an easy camaraderie. It helped us establish trust and laid a strong foundation for our future relationship.

———

March went and April arrived. The banking work was over and I was at a loose end. The house did not need my attention. It was a well-oiled machine run by an efficient battery of staff, comprising a cook, cleaners, a gardener, a driver—the works; there was no aspect of household management where I could pitch in. There was nothing for me to do.

I was used to working long hours that had mostly stretched ten to twelve hours. Suddenly, my days were empty and time a yawning abyss; without the slightest warning I was caught in an existential crisis, confronting a series of uncomfortable questions that kept exploding in my head.

'What am I doing?' I asked myself. This soon changed to—'What should I do? How do I pass my day?'

I started relaying my uncertainties to Cheteshwar over the phone. 'When you're there, there's still something to do, now that you're away, I don't know how to kill time. I'm bored!'

This was the crux of the problem: with no gainful occupation, I was in a state of constant ennui.

'I want to start something of my own,' I announced one day, during one of our many telephonic dialogues.

Cheteshwar was encouraging. 'Yeah, good, you should. What do you want to do?'

I was flummoxed. I had not reached that far yet.

Papa was equally supportive. 'You are so educated. You should definitely work. We need to keep talking. We need a strategy.'

My father-in-law was full of ideas and kept bombarding me with them. My husband was more circumspect. He gave the space to explore various options at my own pace. Even as I struggled for some answers during the excruciating monotony of those humdrum days, I felt a oneness with my new family. I faced no territorial issues (minus the unspoken 'stay away from my charger, suitcase and the like' from Cheteshwar). I was needed, I was heeded and every word I said was taken seriously. Very early on, the three of us had become a team.

Eventually, Cheteshwar was the one who was responsible for the final nudge towards my future profession—as his manager. He had just terminated his contract with the talent-management agency that had been representing him and needed an urgent replacement.

'Why don't you take over?' he asked. 'Nobody is representing me and we have two choices—either I look for a new agency or you can take over.'

All I knew about talent-management agencies at that point was that they had first originated in America and were generally involved in spotting and nurturing talent across diverse entertainment sectors including sports. The model first became popular in Indian cricket during the mid-nineties and gradually evolved over the years. Initially run by individual managers, professional firms gradually took over, their functions ranging from organizing meetings, securing contracts, client promotion, media management and logistics. I was also aware that connections were vital for the success of these agencies, and I had none.

'But I haven't the slightest clue how a talent-management agency works,' I objected flatly. 'I don't know anybody in the circuit. I don't know how they function. I'm bound to fail.'

'I'll guide you,' Cheteshwar offered.

'Let me think over it,' I replied, not very convinced.

I was just twenty-five years old. The only work experience I had was as an employee with a regular job. The long hours I had put in were undoubtedly mine, but none of the actual responsibility of the firm sinking or staying afloat had rested on my shoulders.

I had three options on my table at the time, excluding the one that Cheteshwar had just tossed at me. I thought long and hard.

I was nervous at the prospect of branching out on my own, well aware that any business I began would demand my full-fledged attention at least six days a week. It would also entail a certain amount of funds. What if I failed? The money we invested would then go down the tube. Even worse, since Cheteshwar was always on the go, a regular full-time business meant we would spend very little time together.

This was when the scales fell from my eyes.

In the end, it was this last realization that finally helped me decide. Besides, there was another advantage of taking over as Cheteshwar's talent manager. It required practically no investment—even better, it meant I could now travel with him constantly.

The first offer that came under my watch was from a soda water company. Cheteshwar was reluctant to endorse the product because its brand name was linked too closely to alcohol for his taste.

My father-in-law was even more vocal in his objections. 'Don't be greedy,' he thundered. 'Focus on cricket.'

Papa's hostility to the deal stemmed from an innate distrust of the talent-management industry.

I spared him a lecture on the ins and outs of the workings of the industry, but I was not prepared to cede ground.

'There needs to be a shift in the mindset in this family,' I averred, sticking to my guns. 'You should keep an open mind. Hear them out, try and talk to them and then decide.

Eventually, Cheteshwar's masi stepped into the breach. 'You should not be rigid,' she advised. 'If you don't like what you are endorsing, you can always donate the money to charity.

It was sage advice and went a long way in dispelling the initial resistance to the idea. The deal with the soda water company did not materialize, but later, when we did agree to endorse a couple of products that went against our grain, we donated the proceeds to some deserving charities.

I made another discovery when I went to visit my husband whilst he was in rehabilitation. His finger had not yet healed fully so he still could not play any matches. Cheteshwar was seeing Dr Prashant Shah, a homeopath, to see if this line of medicine could accelerate his recovery process.

'Since when have you been seeing Dr Shah,' I asked, my interest aroused. This was the first time his name had cropped up.

Cheteshwar told me that he had been consulting Dr Shah regularly since he was twenty-three. I kept quiet, as I did not want to appear nosy. But I volunteered to accompany him during his upcoming visit—and this was when I uncovered the mystery behind his uneasy slumber.

Dr Shah told me it was caused by fear.

I found out that Cheteshwar had struggled to sleep since the age of nineteen after he had a panic attack during a first-class game. 'I can't breathe', he had announced during the episode. 'I need to be admitted.'

At that time, the doctors had pronounced that the panic attack was idiopathic, caused by reasons unknown. A series of medical tests ensued and he was diagnosed with a deviated nasal septum for which he underwent surgery at the age of twenty-one.

Cheteshwar thought it was a corporeal problem, but Dr Shah disagreed. So did his relatives, as I would later find out. According to the homeopath, his mother's death had created an unconscious fear within him—of injury and loss. His anxieties did not allow his body to switch off and rest, and it was this distress that prevented him from sleeping.

'It's psychological,' explained Dr Shah. 'It has been triggered by his mother's void. He keeps inviting fear and that's why he attracts injuries.'

Even though Cheteshwar did not agree with Dr Shah's diagnosis, he nevertheless tried a whole host of remedies to unblock his sinuses, ranging from steam, jal niti and vapourizers. After this visit, I insisted on accompanying him to Dr Shah regularly. We tried to map his schedule. If he forgot a symptom during a consultation, I would chip in, and I slowly inveigled my way and became an integral part of his health management. He is still a light sleeper, but things have improved over time, although even now he struggles with air-conditioning.

A few months into our marriage, I woke up in the middle of the night only to discover that Cheteshwar was awake. I turned on my side and cracked some dumb joke, which I can no longer recall. We both burst out laughing.

'My mother also had the same ability to make people laugh at the drop of a hat,' he said reminiscently, with a faraway look in his eyes.

I held my breath. This was the first time he had mentioned his mother in my presence. It was a precious moment.

Cheteshwar did not like talking about the past, and rarely spoke about his mother. I tried not to push him, especially during the nascent days of our marriage. I was frightened that I would accidently open some pandora's box or rip open old wounds by asking the wrong questions. Whenever he did mention her, I would listen intently, hanging on to every word. I treasured every story, holding back my emotions resolutely, scared that his tales would dry up and I would miss a piece of the picture of the woman I was truly coming to admire. 'She has given him so much joy, if I could give him even a tenth of that happiness, I will feel fulfilled,' I thought

It was moments like these—raw and organic—that stitched our marriage into the rich tapestry it would become. Infinitely precious, they would help tide us through periods of difficulty, mooring us in choppy waters when times were tough.

When I came into Cheteshwar's life, I entered a house that had been missing a woman's touch for several years. The two men in it were like chalk and cheese. If Papa was fire, Cheteshwar was ice—although they did share certain traits: obstinacy, determination and resilience.

They would clash regularly. Mostly about cricket. When it comes to his performance, Cheteshwar is always at war with himself, and by extension, with his father and lifelong coach. For instance, after hitting a double hundred in Hyderabad against Australia, Papa's first reaction was, 'Why did you play the hook shot?'

Cheteshwar's first instinct after the game was to take a step back to seek the quiet spaces in his head. My father-in-law's natural impulse was to discuss the game to death.

This would inevitably lead to an explosion.

Cheteshwar, blessed with the ability to detach himself from any situation, would immediately hide behind an icy silence. My father-in-law, in stark contrast, would scream and shout to make his point, and push for a conclusion.

They are both strong-willed and unwilling to cede ground. I quickly figured the crux of the problem was not their inability to find common ground, but the manner in which they expressed their differences. I found myself increasingly taking on the task of peacemaker.

The two men have been each other's pillars of support for so long that these rows usually blow over quite swiftly. For years, they silently worried about each other, too reserved to voice their anxieties; but now that I was there, it was almost as if the atmosphere had lightened.

My presence brought a sense of harmony into their lives in several ways. For one, they were only too happy to offload their domestic responsibilities to me. But one area that Papa found difficult to delegate to me was serving Cheteshwar his food. He still tends to lay his son's plate and cutlery at the table just to make sure that he has a hearty meal.

'What about me?' I sometimes joke. 'I also eat at this table. Don't I count. Where's my plate?

Papa usually ends up looking sheepish, and I generally changed the subject to spare him further embarrassment.

When a family has emerged out of tragic times, they appreciate every small gesture, even if it is mundane, and there is nothing extraordinary about it. I was touched when I discovered just how much Cheteshwar and Papa valued the tiniest things I did for them. Even something as simple as keeping tabs on my father-in-law's medical needs.

When I learnt that Papa had undergone a bypass surgery in 2011 and tended to skip his medicines through sheer absentmindedness, I volunteered to take over his medical file and accompany him for his doctors' appointments. Their reaction surprised me. They acted as if I was handing them the moon. It was then that it dawned on me how much they had missed the warmth of a woman's presence in their lives.

My entry into the Pujara household seemed to fill that void.

CHAPTER THIRTEEN

By Force of Habit

Within a few months of our marriage, I discovered an annoying thing about Cheteshwar: his inability to take a back step and enjoy himself. My mind boggled at the realization that he had not taken a single holiday in his whole life to unwind and snatch a few moments for himself away from cricket. There had been no rapturous care-free, fun-filled trips with his friends, no snatched vacations to relax; his entire existence rotated within the extremely narrow perimeters of his game, unlaced by unworthy mood-lifters like rest and recreation.

No matter where he was, he would be back home by 10 p.m. sharp. He immersed all his energies in his profession; non-playing days were uncomfortable periods of protracted vacuum, notable only for their emptiness, because neither Cheteshwar nor his father could ever contemplate a life beyond cricket.

Theoretically, I understood what drove them: after the loss of Cheteshwar's mother, the duo had survived only because of cricket. But, from a practical angle, I could see quite clearly that this unidimensional approach, determined by a tunnel vision, would extract a heavy cost from them if they did not learn how to lighten up.

I said as much to my husband. He took no notice.

Cheteshwar was equally closed about his game. When it came to cricket, each performance was a thorough analysis of the areas of his game that needed improvement and the answer was always: more hard work, more practice. This was the mantra with which he had tasted success and they knew no other way.

And they had never paused to celebrate.

Victories were accepted stoically, losses battled ferociously. Cheteshwar dealt with the latter by internalizing his feelings and suppressing them. He would grow quiet and turn to God for strength. His faith in the Almighty was boundless, meticulously instilled in him since he was a child, his spiritual beliefs were an innate part of who he was as a man.

The endless hours he spent praying and chanting played a large role in shaping his personality and became an inextricable part of every facet of his life. Very soon after our marriage, I discovered that he often chanted chaupais or quatrains from the *Hanuman Chalisa* while he was at the non-striker's end; there was a guru mantra which he recited as part of his daily devotional routine, but most especially, when the going got tough, either on or off the field.

Prayers were an intrinsic part of Cheteshwar's coping mechanism. They had helped him handle his mother's death, his father's surgeries, his own medical procedures, and every difficulty and loss he had faced in his young life. Once, when I had a bad migraine attack not too long after our wedding, he held my hand and started chanting, because the episode was very severe and I could not bear the pain. He was trying to help me through my pain in the only way he knew—through prayers!

But his constant withdrawal inwards into his spiritual world was frustrating for me as his partner. It was not easy as his wife to watch him shuttering down and withdrawing into some deep recesses within himself, pointedly refusing to share his feelings. Often, there were times when he would fail to mention his professional anxieties and I would inadvertently learn about them from someone else.

I felt that one of the main reasons that prevented him from exploiting his full potential were the myriad theories and assumptions that were floating around about his game. His inability to express himself had not helped his situation. He had been so busy suppressing his feelings that he could not come to terms with emerging circumstances on most occasions or recognize that there was an issue that needed to be addressed. Cheteshwar's solution to all his problems was to pray even harder.

In hindsight, his refusal to perceive his triumphs and minor achievements as a cause for celebration was a mistake. It predisposed us to view the glass as half empty instead of half full, till recently, and that should be a matter of regret. I have come to the conclusion that one can be twenty-five years of age only once. It is important to unwind and enjoy one's youth. Since he was scared, we did not grab life with both hands and wring every drop of pleasure from it.

At the time, I supported him. I could see, how much more relaxed he was on the field when he had finished his full quota of prayers. It helped him to relax. We reached a stage when I was the one who would nudge him to complete his prayers and stick to his routine.

I became so much a part of the same belief system that without realizing it, I also took to chanting in the stands or in front of the television. The change within me happened organically. I absorbed his philosophy: 'If this is what works for him, it must be the right way, because he's been following this path forever.

Initially, my thoughts had been different. I would say, 'If you've won, celebrate.'

But now, late nights, which had been such an intrinsic part of my life when I was single, were steadfastly shunned. Whenever such a prospect loomed in our horizon, I would step in. 'We need to sleep on time' was a common reminder I dutifully trotted out during this period.

Any suggestions of a break were firmly dismissed. 'We need not take a vacation right now,' I would state firmly.

I was now an ardent advocate of the same philosophy he espoused which, in a nutshell, hinged on three notions: pause, reflect and feel grateful. The last we expressed by organizing endless bhandaras.

But a belief-system is only right till it works. Small issues started cropping up—not being picked for matches, injuries, getting stereotyped as a test specialist. The irritants were multiple, our solutions singular: work harder, pray harder. Celebrations were still eschewed, recreation for pleasure continued to be side-stepped and getaways long or short remained a far cry. We neglected the outer world and continued to exist within those narrow limits which had defined his existence when I entered it.

But, as a result, our marriage became rock solid.

We concentrated on building our roots—the family structure, our home—and used this period to spend as much time as we could with each other's families, and began to bond with them. The relationship between our kins grew seamlessly, and by and large, we were content. At least we had each other, and this alone counted for a lot in our relationship.

In August 2013, Cheteshwar was named captain of the India A team which was slated to tour South Africa and Zimbabwe. Several senior players had been selected as part of the playing eleven. I did not accompany him on the trip.

Life at Rajkot was very different after Cheteshwar left. When he was around, our days revolved around his routine, which in turn rotated round his match schedule. He was away for six weeks and my education in cricket began in earnest during this time. I had decided that if I was to become his manager, I needed to know the game inside-out. My father-in-law was only too happy to hold forth on his favourite topic. I lapped up every word he uttered and pleased him no end with my acute attention.

In the meanwhile, all was not hunky dory at Cheteshwar's end. A senior player had his eye on the captaincy and managed to convince the coach to ask Cheteshwar to 'rest' for one match.

It was a tricky moment. Cheteshwar did not want to get into a conflict with his coach. His scores had not been too great in the last couple of games and he did not want to sit out for the coming matches. He decided to be assertive without being offensive, and sent the venerable gentleman a text message stating: I'm the captain. I'm match-fit and fully ready to play.

The matter went no further and Cheteshwar continued to play and captain the side. It had been a delicate situation, but he had managed to defuse it gracefully without causing umbrage. He then let his bat do the talking for him and scored a century in the match he had been asked to sit out.

I only learnt of this incident much later, and it was only then that I realized that like every other profession, there was backroom politics in cricket as well. It was the first of many such delicate episodes. Cheteshwar would try and survive them all with the same combination of discretion and savoir-faire.

All too soon, Cheteshwar was in the thick of a pre-series tour against the West Indies, captaining a side peppered with a number of cricketing greats who were not part of the ODIs and T20s. All the games were played in Karnataka. The first two were nothing much to write home about as far as India was concerned, as we lost one and drew the other.

The third match was in Hubli and was slated to begin on 9 October, my birthday. We decided to spend it together.

I reached on 6 October, anticipating a glorious celebration to mark the occasion, as it was my first birthday after our wedding. But since he was in the middle of the series and his entire effort was devoted to winning the match, he stuck to his routine and we agreed to travel to Goa after the game for a quick getaway.

The match started on 9 October. We won the toss and chose to field first. Towards the end of the day, India came in to bat, which meant that Cheteshwar would be batting on the tenth. He had arranged a private dinner for us at the hotel but under the changed circumstances, he shifted the timings and requested an early dinner so that he would be match-ready the following day.

It was then that I realized that he had no present for me!

'I'm sorry,' he said apologetically. 'I did not have the time to pick up a gift for you as I was travelling.'

I gaped at him.

I knew he did not believe in grand gestures to commemorate memorable occasions, either for himself or anyone else. Cheteshwar had made this very clear to me right at the beginning of our courtship. He had warned me that I would be doomed to disappointment if I harboured such expectations.

But I was disappointed all the same.

Everyone has a romantic and loving side. Cheteshwar exhibits his by empowering me, offering me respect and independence in our daily lives. He is not your garden-variety romantic, given to grandiose gestures; he expresses his love in small, thoughtful ways on a day-to-day basis, and makes every effort to make me feel special in a thousand different ways.

But this was one of the complaints I had against him for a long time and maybe that is the reason he wanted me to write this book and talk about his life. He was never blessed with the gift of the gab. If a smile can do the job, he will not speak. If a sentence can end in three words, he will not add another. It is a two-edged sword, which can be very frustrating for me as his wife. But over the years, I have learnt to accept him, just the way he is, warts and all.

On that birthday, we had a low-key dinner à deux, with dessert being the only departure from our normal meal. The following day turned out to be a belated gift—he scored a 100 not-out. The team too was in a strong position. The cherry on the cake followed—he went on to score 306 not-out!

We ended up going to Mumbai instead of Goa for an IOCL match which cropped up out of the blue. He was reluctant to abandon our getaway despite the time crunch.

'But what about the birthday trip to Goa?' he asked, when I suggested we head to Mumbai.

'Forget it. Let's just go to Mumbai. We can have a good time there.'

By now, I had understood that it was not that he did not want to do something for me by way of birthday celebrations, it was just that the situation was such. We needed to be practical and at that stage of his career, he could not afford to take too many off days. He needed to play as much cricket as he could.

The Mumbai trip was hectic and we got home just in time for the Diwali festivities.

The next series was Sachin Tendulkar's 200th match against West Indies, after which he had announced retirement from international cricket. The buildup to the game was humongous given what Sachin Tendulkar meant to the nation.

I tagged along with Cheteshwar for the series.

At this time I was struck by an epiphany: retirement was a reality from which no one could ever escape. Everyone retired at some point, no matter how great they were. It was a sad thought. But I tried not to dwell on it because Cheteshwar was in a good headspace and I wanted nothing to disturb his serenity.

Emotions ran high during Sachin's last match in Mumbai. India had won the first match in Kolkata and after that the team had attended the MAK Pataudi lecture. At the start of the Mumbai match, Cheteshwar had not imagined the role he would be expected to take on by the crowds.

After the day's play, we were hanging out together, sipping coffee.

'You have no idea how difficult it was for me to concentrate with the crowds constantly chanting 'Sachin-Sachin'.'

I nodded my head sympathetically. The crowds usually went berserk when Sachin was on the crease, but during this match they'd gone completely insane.

'Sachin paaji knew I was finding it difficult to concentrate and he kept telling me to focus on the match and cancel the noise.'

I could relate to his comment, remembering how Cheteshwar's singles were cheered louder than his boundaries. It had been a spectacle to watch. I must have been the only person in the stadium who rejoiced when he hit a four. The crowd just wanted Cheteshwar to take singles so that they could watch Sachin bat.

When Sachin got out on seventy-four, the entire stadium went quiet; there was pin-drop silence for a moment and then a thunderous applause broke out; it went on and on, non-stop, for seemingly an aeon. I get goosebumps when I recall the moment to this day.

Cheteshwar went on to hit a century during the match. It turned out to be one of Cheteshwar's most talked-about innings. He was the only one who had a partnership with Sachin that day and his game was discussed threadbare: how he had remained focused on the job at hand; how Sachin paaji, as his senior partner, had encouraged him to block the din; and how he had kept his head throughout the partnership.

After the match, Cheteshwar and I were snatching a quiet moment together.

'What was the dressing room like?' I asked, curiously.

'Very emotional. Everyone was teary-eyed,' replied Cheteshwar before changing the subject abruptly. 'Sachin paaji is hosting a party after the game.'

'When?' I inquired.

'The day after tomorrow,' he responded. 'Everyone thought the match would finish tomorrow. But since it's ended early, it's not a possible to attend the party.'

'Why not?' I queried.

'Because it means we'll have to hang around in Bombay needlessly for an extra day. I want to go home.'

'I think we should stay for the party,' I said stubbornly. 'It's only a matter of a day.'

'Two days,' corrected Cheteshwar.

We wrangled about it for a bit and then I gave in, especially when he mentioned that he was suffering from constant fatigue and a spate of tiny niggles. I suspected that more than any physical discomfort, Cheteshwar wanted to get home and relax, because he knew that he would be heading for another long spell on the road. He was not alone. There were a few other cricketers who were also skipping the party to fly home.

Cheteshwar messaged Sachin paaji apologizing that we would not be able to attend the party. He wrapped up the missive with the following words: 'I have had an amazing time having conversations with you and missing your party is not going to change that.'

I still felt we were making a mistake. Parties were a good for networking but dragging Cheteshwar to one in my experience bore an uncanny resemblance to dragging a child to a dentist. It required a great deal of coaxing and cajoling, and sometimes even that failed.

My husband is an introvert. He finds it difficult to converse and large crowds make him uncomfortable. He enjoys his solitude and is happiest in familiar surroundings spending time with the people he knows. Over the years most of our arguments and differences have risen from my opinion that he needs to be more vocal and network better.

But he remains adamant.

'Rome was not built in a day,' he quips. It's his usual line of defence whenever we have this debate.

We caught the early morning flight back to Rajkot the next day, and got into an argument of sorts again.

'I think we should have attended the party,' I said. 'It's important to meet people in your profession and hang out with them.

'I want to go to Gondal,' he said quietly.

At heart, Cheteshwar is a country lad. He loves the countryside and smaller towns; he is not a big fan of metropolises as he is allergic to the long hours spent commuting.

'There's not much time between matches. This is the only window I have when I can meet Guruji and spend some time with Masi,' he explained.

I understood.

Masi, his closest confidante, friend, guide and lone mother-figure was suffering from breast cancer and Cheteshwar wanted to spend every possible moment he could squeeze out of his busy schedule with her. The rest was an eyewash.

'Why didn't you say so, earlier,' I chided.

I shook my head exasperatedly. When would my husband learn to share his inner thoughts with me?

I flashed a cheery smile, promising myself that I would work at it till one day, some day in the future, he would feel at ease sharing his innermost thoughts with me. It would be a challenge, but it was a battle I intended to win.

CHAPTER FOURTEEN

The Fitness Revolution Comes to India

The year 2013 was coming to a close. It was late November and there was a nip in the air in Johannesburg. The Indian test team was slated to play the opening match on 5 December and was practicing hard for the series. The ODI squad, which was also in the country, had travelled elsewhere for the one-day matches.

It was my first trip abroad with Cheteshwar and I was thrilled to be there, even though he had made it very clear even before we reached Johannesburg that whilst I could devote myself to endless hours of exploration, he was in South Africa to work, and his entire focus would be on the game.

'You can enjoy and explore. But I won't be able to go with you,' he warned.

His words would set the pattern for all our trips in the years to come. On most tours that I accompanied him, I would explore the city we were in, while Cheteshwar would divide his time between the stadium and our room. On his days off, my husband liked to recoup his strength and although he was usually willing to go out for a meal, sight-seeing was a big no-no.

I knew that since the team had arrived early, it was only expected to train in the first half of the day. I figured we would still spend time together when he was not occupied in the gym or the nets.

'Don't worry. I'm quite happy to explore the city on my own,' I reassured him blithely.

The security staff thought otherwise.

We were staying at Hotel Intercontinental and the security officer told us in no uncertain terms that we were not to go anywhere without informing him or unaccompanied by security personnel. This put paid to my ambitions to venture forth on solo jaunts, but group tours with wives of other cricketers were definitely on. I knew most of them were eager to discover the city with or without their husbands.

I ended up doing a lot of things with them, but Cheteshwar, as he had forewarned, did not accompany me. During the day, he was usually busy and I tried my best to stay out of his hair. The hotel was attached to a mall and when he was around, we would head there for our meals, patronizing a string of different restaurants—not out of a sense of adventure, but through sheer necessity. In our case, variety was definitely not the spice of life—vegetarianism was still a foreign word in South African, veganism was yet to be discovered and for herbivores like Cheteshwar and I, finding good food was a huge struggle.

There was an Indian restaurant at the mall, but the rotis and naans were so thick that we found it inedible. We started alternating between Mexican meals comprising beans, salad and rice or burritos and subway sandwiches. Italian cuisine was an option and sometimes we did eat pizza or pasta, but it was too cheesy and not particularly healthy. By this time, both Cheteshwar and I had started devoting ourselves to nutritious, wholesome and healthy fare during mealtimes.

The fitness revolution had found its way into Indian cricket earlier that year after England won the test series against India. The English players had been sharp on the field, the home team, less agile. The rout was a wake-up call and brought in a much-needed transformation in the team—fitness frenzy suddenly ruled the roost.

THE FITNESS REVOLUTION COMES TO INDIA

Cheteshwar too became a fitness fanatic at around this time and added gym and yoga into his already hectic training schedule. My husband had been practicing yoga for a long time, but earlier, he had done it for fun, intermittently. On this tour, he took it up seriously, without missing it even for a day.

There would be times during the tour when he would be too busy exercising. On these occasions, I would go into the mall to pick up food with other cricketers' wives. I think I spent more time with them on that trip than with my husband.

I voiced no complaints at my husband's absence most of the time. I knew what drove him: Cheteshwar had done well in the subcontinent but he still needed to fare well on foreign soil to prove his cricketing abilities to the rest of the world.

The first day of the test match. Dale Steyn, Morne Morkel and Vernon Philander were bowling at their very best. Cheteshwar survived the initial spells and was just beginning to look settled when his partner at the other end sold him a dummy and ran him out.

I was distraught. I had seen how hard he had trained for the series, and I was certain that he would be devasted when he came back to the hotel that evening.

I couldn't have been more wrong.

I was moping about in the room when Cheteshwar walked in after the close of day. He looked tired but calm.

'Oh, my goodness, I'm feeling so bad you were run out,' I said by way of greeting.

'There are things one can't control. You don't have to feel bad about it or feel sorry,' he said brushing away my anxieties nonchalantly. 'Such dismissals are part and parcel of the game. Of course, I didn't want to be run out. But I would be more upset if I had got out playing a foolish shot. These things happen in cricket. You should get used to it.'

My jaw dropped. How could he be so calm at a time like this? I reluctantly dropped the subject.

On day three, the match was equipoised. It could go either way. I was the only one who went to watch the game. I sat alone in the long room at the Wanderers. It was sparsely occupied, a fact that pleased me no end. At least I would be able to concentrate on the game without getting distracted by cheering crowds.

I sat glued to the long room throughout the day, warmly clad in a red jacket over a white shirt and a pair of trousers to keep out the chill. I kept praying hard for Cheteshwar, hoping against hope that he would make some runs in the second innings in lieu of the debacle that had taken place in the first.

I had come armed with photos of fielding positions on that tour and with the help of various commentaries on web platforms, I was slowly beginning to understand the game. This was a huge change from those early days of our engagement, when my knowledge of cricket would have barely filled a postage stamp!

The entire day passed; the tea break came and went, and Cheteshwar had still not reached his half century. Anxious, I sat at the edge of my seat waiting for him to reach that milestone. Naïve in the extreme, my understanding of cricket was still at a very preliminary stage. I did not understand at the time that a player could also contribute to the game by spending time at the crease. My idea of cricketing success still hinged on the notion that triumphs in the game were measured with centuries and half-centuries.

Post-tea, Cheteshwar picked up pace. I reckoned he had played cautiously till then because of the run-out in the previous innings. His half-century and century both arrived in quick succession in the same session.

It was a big relief! He had done it. He had proved that he could be as good on foreign soil as he was in India.

Cheteshwar and I were on cloud nine that evening.

'I saw you sitting in the long room clapping for me in that red jacket,' he said lazily over dinner.

I looked at him in surprise. He had not waved or given any indication that he knew I was there.

'Oh, I didn't know you could see me,' I said, slightly embarrassed.

While we were having dinner, a plot to go to sun city was brewing parallelly amongst the wives of other cricketers. They were planning a trip to the Pilanesberg Reserve and texted me an insistent message, asking me to accompany them.

I was in two minds. What if he scored a double hundred while I was away? But the others kept insisting.

'Come! Come! Come!' A flurry of messages beeped on my phone.

'You've already seen him score a century today,' stated one text.'

'This will be a good experience,' averred another.

'You should go,' said Cheteshwar who had been following the proceedings with interest. 'It will be a nice experience.'

'But you're batting,' I objected artlessly. 'What if you go on to score a double century? I don't want to miss that.'

If Cheteshwar thought this guileless observation was amusing, he took great pains to hide it.

'Don't worry about my double century. You should just go. You were already in the stadium today. What will you do there for the whole day all by yourself tomorrow. Just go and enjoy yourself.'

I succumb to his persuasion reluctantly and agreed to go for the outing. But I still kept worrying about missing the match. A voice in my head kept whispering insidiously: What if he scores a double century and you're not present? At that stage I still was under the impression that scoring double centuries was easy as pie.

The next day, we headed out to the Pilanesberg reserve. Cheteshwar and the others were right. The game drive was a riveting experience, not all of it pleasant. We came across a cheetah consuming a zebra, just moments after the kill. The sight was enough to turn my stomach.

Vegetarians, I concluded, could hardly be expected to witness such episodes with any kind of equilibrium. I would not be able get the ghastly sight out of my mind for the next three days. It creeped me out so badly. Towards the end of the safari, we came across a lion and lioness calling out to each other. It was pretty dark by then.

We first heard one roar and then another. Suddenly two silhouettes appeared from different directions before the they slipped into the twilight together and vanished out of sight. Our vehicle which had paused momentarily came to life and trundled down the small narrow lane of the game drive.

In the meantime, Cheteshwar was getting restless.

I had been out of range for the whole day and was still unreachable when the stumps were drawn. As soon as we reached the periphery of the reserve, my mobile phone went wild and started beeping manically. I punched it and a whole horde of missed calls and messages flashed on the screen.

The texts were along the following lines: 'All okay?' Then: 'All good?' Followed by: 'Can't reach you.'

I hurriedly called Cheteshwar to put him out of his misery.

'All's well. I'm fine,' I told him. 'We're just getting out of the park. We'll be stopping for dinner on the way, so I'll be late. You go ahead and have dinner and sleep.'

Johannesburg was still two-and-a-half hours away by road. We halted enroute for a hearty meal as we were all famished after our long day in the jungles. It was quite late when I tip-toed into the room. I need not have bothered because he woke up almost immediately. I apologized profusely.

'Sorry, sorry. Go back to sleep. You have an early day tomorrow.'

He grunted and shut his eyes.

THE FITNESS REVOLUTION COMES TO INDIA

The match finally ended in what I thought was a most fascinating draw.

South Africa had had a good chance of winning the match, but the Indians fought well and managed to push the game to a draw. I heaved a sigh of relief. So far, so good. Cheteshwar had done well in his maiden match abroad!

Before we left Jo'burg, I purchased PlayStation 3 for Cheteshwar. I was slowly learning how he actually liked to spend his time in between matches.

Initially, he tried to teach me the game—after he had scored two goals. I knew he possessed a strong competitive streak and flatly refused.

'No, thank you,' I said firmly, with a grin. 'I will never win with you.'

'I must win at all costs,' he confessed, grinning back.

I stayed firm and refused to yield to his persuasions.

Deprived of me as a victim, he soon found other quarry, mostly among his teammates in both test and domestic cricket.

The test team moved to Durban for the next match. It was slated to begin on boxing day. On Christmas eve, we discovered that everything was shut and spent a couple of hours frantically hunting for food. After a long, hard search, we eventually ended up buying subway sandwiches at a gas station.

The team had the day off on Christmas and the buildup for boxing-day test was huge as Jacques Kallis had announced his retirement from test cricket. India lost the match. It was a series loss and my disappointment was acute.

Cheteshwar shrugged it off with his usual sangfroid 'Winning and losing is part of the game. You shouldn't take it to heart.'

We flew out of Durban on New Year's Eve and reached India at around midnight, just in time to usher in the new year.

I wanted to go out and celebrate.

We were in Mumbai, a city I loved, and I was young enough to want to be part of the New Year's Eve revelry. Besides, at that time I was still a night bird.

'Shall we go out and celebrate? I asked.

'Where?' he inquired, reluctance writ large on his face.

'Just out somewhere,' I said wistfully.

'I just want to go to the hotel,' he replied laconically. 'I'm still tired from yesterday's match.'

'Fine,' I acquiesced, masking my disappointment, not realizing at that time that getting re-energized after a series took time.

But one thing was quite clear. While I was game to go out, my husband just wanted some peace and quiet as neither of us had slept on the flight.

At heart, I gradually realized, Cheteshwar is an old man; all he needs is his beauty sleep, his meals served on time—and that is all he needs. When it comes to food, there is no compromise; our repasts have to be elaborate. In the flight back home, all he had eaten was garlic bread. Now that we were back in India, he was dying to eat some good nourishing food after more than a month-long hiatus.

We celebrated the New Year with a wholesome meal of dal-khhichdi and took an early morning flight back home.

The South African tour was just a harbinger of the very long road ahead of us. The tour had been fraught with the highest of highs and lowest of lows. It began with a high—his century. It had ended with a low—India's series loss. I enjoyed the trip because he had done well. But not all trips in the future were going to be the same.

It was a marathon which we had just entered as a couple. Cheteshwar was aware of the hardships. I was not. I thought he would hit a century in every series. He was more realistic. But he never interfered with my illusions. He let me discover the real world in my own way, bit by bit. If I got carried away, he never restrained me. But gradually I learnt, what he already knew: that the sporting world like everything else had its peaks and troughs.

But at that stage, I was living through him; I saw my success in his success: even though I was taking care of the marketing and endorsement. Slowly, I too was doing what his father had done earlier, letting his career become the be-all and end-all of our lives. In a very passive way, it kind of got to him. The last thing Cheteshwar wanted was cricket to reign over our private lives.

When I entered the Pujara household, I was completely taken aback. Being a Gujarati, my palate only understood taste and never acknowledged nutrition as particularly important to my food intake.

It was an alien concept.

The food tasted bland when I married him. As a new bride, I was gently informed that Cheteshwar had jaggery and ghee with every meal. But a couple of months into our marriage, the fitness revolution hit us with a vengeance and now every morsel had to be carefully vetted for its nutritional value.

Always conscientious, Cheteshwar suddenly stopped touching all forms of sugar. He avoided sweets of any kind while he was training at home. Once I understood why nutrition was crucial to his career, I became as big a fanatic as he about consuming the right sort of food. But there was a catch—I did not know how to go about it.

In the meanwhile, Cheteshwar went through a BMI check-up and we learnt that with the kind of training my husband did he needed a minimum protein intake of 125–175 grams a day. I grew even more anxious. How was I going to ensure he received his required intake of proteins through his meals?

Just as I was grappling with this all-important question, I serendipitously came across Novak Djokovic's book, *Serve to Win*. It was an eye-opener! Djokovic lay emphasis on eastern medicine and the significance of food in any fitness regimen. I was inspired. Given the amount of work Cheteshwar was putting into his fitness and diet, it was clearly incumbent upon me to do my bit.

I instantly joined an online course on nutrition and a week later, I was in the market foraging for various varieties of millets that our forefathers had once consumed. To my intense surprise, it was extremely difficult to source them even in the old bazaars of Rajkot. A shopkeeper told me that only villagers still bought them. He also let slip that foxtail millet, the main staple of a village in a nearby taluka, had led to 'zero bone fractures'.

Over a period of time, my research intensified even as I started carrying out culinary experiments in the kitchen, trying out different preparations with various kinds of millets. One of my gastronomic triumphs was the soyabean and millet laddu which Cheteshwar could carry with him on tour. From what I had learnt, it would elevate his protein intake.

But the struggle to source recommended foods that were nutritious continued. Ten years back, sourcing buckwheat and tofu was a nightmare. They were just not available in Rajkot. I eventually realized that it was more sensible to eat what was accessible locally. As a result, we started consuming more jowar and bajra. Moong and chana became our preferred staples amongst pulses. The decision was a happy one, as our cooks found these items easier to prepare. All in all, it was a process, one that took about a couple of years to fructify.

During the height of the fitness revolution, all players went through a Dexa scan for a bone density checkup to screen their fitness levels and assess what kind of training regime they required. The

Board of Control for Cricket in India (BCCI) has now discontinued the practice, but at that time it was still de rigeur.

In the same period, to stay fit, Cheteshwar had started putting in more hours of training in the gym to strengthen his knees both of which had undergone ACL reconstruction surgeries. The two joints had been regularly cited as a major hinderance in his entry into limited-overs cricket.

Yoga and pranayama too had become a regular part of his routine to prevent his hamstring muscles and quadriceps from getting strained. He was training specifically to make sure there were no further tears, either of the ligaments or tendons.

We also sought help from a few friends in the medical fraternity who helped us understand the dynamics of what we were doing by bringing about a change in his diet.

'Trying to do too much all at once can do more damage than good,' cautioned Dr Ajay Patil, my father-in-law's cardiac surgeon. 'Any dietary changes you make should be gradual. The body has its own memory and you should not mess around with it.'

It was a phase when the entire family worked as a team and we all took our jobs seriously. His father kept analysing and observing his game, I helped him with his nutrition, managing all brand inquiries and he worked hard on his fitness, spending a great deal of time at the nets. There were almost no off days.

Every profession has a certain routine and high-pressure situations determine an individual's ability to handle them. For Cheteshwar, his routine was more important than any of his achievements. It is crucial to his existence.

To prepare for a match, he tried to make sure that the pitch in the nets was prepared in keeping with the forthcoming games he would be playing. To save time, he had a gymnasium installed at home. To combat his dust allergy, I would get his bedding vacuumed and ironed and the gym kept super clean so that his fitness was not compromised.

Food, sleep, training and recovery. These were small little changes that would help him in a high-intensity competitive environment; the tiny game-changers, once made, added to the success of his tour and if this meant shifting our schedule a little bit, we were okay with it because both Cheteshwar and I knew this was our priority.

As much net practice as possible was the go-to thing for Cheteshwar in the initial five years or so of our married life. He would head to the grounds to bat each morning. On his return, he would squeeze in a little rest, then follow it up with a gym session, before venturing out in the afternoon for another net session.

Cheteshwar was ignored for the Champions Trophy in 2013. The reasons cited were his agility and fielding. There is only so much of physical training an individual can do in the nets or at the gym in a day. To add to his woes, my father-in-law was very old-school in his approach. He believed that centuries are not scored by spending time in the gym. Net practice twice a day was an absolute must.

Cheteshwar, still a beginner, was perplexed between what he was taught and what he needed to do in order to succeed in international cricket. He was not recovering as he should have because he was putting too much load on his body. His father and he could not seem to strike a balance as the twice-a-day net sessions rule had been part of his training regime since he was very young. They had to let that go in order to make room for running sessions, gym and fielding.

Every time Cheteshwar did not do well, my father-in-law would say: 'Practice more.'

This remained a pattern till 2016.

One evening, in 2014, Cheteshwar and I went out for a walk in London and ended up at the Chelsea bridge. It was my first trip to England with him, where he played for the Indian team which would be locking horns with England in a five test match series and two practice matches.

On that particular evening, we set out for a walk with no particular destination in mind: it was his day off and the idea was just to work off our supper. When we reached Chelsea bridge, he had a flashback.

'I've walked through Chelsea bridge before, you know,' he said casually with that faraway look that sometimes creeps into his eye. 'Only that time I was alone.'

'Oh,' I said, wondering what he was talking about. 'When?'

'On the day of my ACL surgery. I walked here from the Crowne Plaza hotel first before I strolled on to the Westminster Hospital.'

For a moment, I stopped walking. 'How? Why were you alone?'

'Actually, the physio was supposed to be with me, but there was some visa complication. So, I went alone for the consultation. When the doctor told me I had to have a surgery, I agreed,' said Cheteshwar, seemingly unaware of the enormity of what he had just told me.

'What about the walk you mentioned?' I asked, still frozen where I stood.

He shrugged.

'No big deal. I woke up early, got ready. I had a lot of time to kill, so I decided to take a stroll and then went to the hospital and got admitted.'

I stared at him, completely nonplussed. He had casually taken a walk before getting admitted for surgery all by himself—at the age of twenty-three. I had never heard of such a thing! After we returned to St James's Court where we were staying, I sat down and pulled out all his email conversations and interviews from 2011. His courage left me stunned.

Cheteshwar has a very bad memory. He remembers things only in fragments, but back then, he had communicated a lot over emails and documented details that helped me gauge the extent of his pluck. I was overwhelmed. Yes, my husband has a difficult side, but it is these aspects of his character that leave me in awe of him.

⁓

After a terrible test series in England, where he got the first duck of his career in Manchester on Jimmy Anderson's home turf, for which no strategy to counter the pace and variable bounce offered by the English pacers seemed to work, beaten, we returned home.

The experience, however, left him seriously disturbed—enough to prompt him to consult a couple of cricketing legends. He was determined to correct the flaws in his batting against the English pacers. The two cricketing greats he talked to advised him to play county cricket. He heeded their suggestion and approached the Punjab Kings XI. The team was on the verge of playing the champions league and he was part of the playing eleven in some matches.

Cheteshwar asked the authorities in the Punjab King XI if they would relieve him so that he could play county cricket. They let him go, but the move, we suspect, cost him his IPL contract the following year: it was not renewed.

Papa was eager to accompany Cheteshwar to the county circuit as he wanted to observe the wickets in England. They both travelled to the United Kingdom. I opted to stay behind. It was going to be a short county stint of three four-day matches and my husband would be representing Derbyshire. I had just got back home from a long tour to the British Isles and was looking forward to some rest and relaxation.

'I'm done,' I informed them. 'I don't want to come. I'm tired of eating hotel food. I'm going to stay home and relax.'

I sorted out their visas and international driving permits, and saw them off at the airport. They landed at Derby and called me. It was late evening in England and around 2.30 a.m. in India.

'You must come,' Cheteshwar insisted urgently.

Cheteshwar explained that there would be away-games and he would not always be there to tend to his father. He felt I should go to keep an eye on Papa since he did not speak English.'

'Okay,' I said resignedly.

Then Papa came on the line and added his bit. 'It's a beautiful house. You will feel at ease.'

I was tired of hotel-hopping and had wanted to eat some basic home-cooked meals. I mentally said goodbye to these pleasant aspirations. I quietly booked my tickets the following day and flew off to London the day after, armed with some groceries. I knew the house provided by the club had a fully functional kitchen.

Cheteshwar and I had visited Derby earlier that year for a practice match and had fallen in love with the countryside. By the time I reached England, Cheteshwar was driving back to Derby from Worcester after his first match. His team had lost.

Papa had come to pick me up at Heathrow with a family friend.

When my father-in-law informed me that my husband was driving back to Derby and we would catch up with him there, I hid a smile. Cheteshwar being Cheteshwar is a most cautious driver. He is also the world's worst passenger, suffering as he does from an immense phobia when someone else is at the wheel.

We reached Derby at around the same time as Cheteshwar who had already ordered an Indian take-away for all of us. I insisted on making rotis but they politely declined. I had kneaded the dough but my husband made me put it back into the fridge.

'You've had a long day. There's no need to cook. I've ordered some naans,' he said gently.

Cheteshwar, of course, stuck to brown bread, while the rest of us consumed the naans. It was a happy meal.

The second match was an away-game in London against the mighty Surrey and we all traveled for it. Derby ended up winning the match and Cheteshwar was unbeaten at 92. The reason I mention this is because throughout that English summer, he played with conviction or so my father-in-law pronounced.

'He looked as if he was in the zone,' Papa said with a smile of satisfaction.

CHAPTER FIFTEEN

Snakes and Ladders

It was new year's eve. Everyone was making plans to celebrate the coming year. M.S. Dhoni had just announced his retirement from test cricket the previous day at the Melbourne Cricket Ground, Australia. We had travelled down to Sydney that very day and were staying at Hotel Intercontinental. The celebratory mood was catching.

'How will we bring in the new year? I asked Cheteshwar.

'Like every other day,' he said casually.

I did not argue. I knew he was worried, given what had happened at the MCG in the second innings. We both knew that there were some doubts about his selection in the coming match. The anxiety was a constant at the back of our heads, but it remained unacknowledged. Both of us were trying very hard to ignore the elephant in the room and went about our lives as if everything was normal.

Our room hotel overlooked harbour bridge and bang at the dot of midnight, fireworks lit up the night sky. It was a glorious sight. For a moment, I forgot our troubles.

The series had opened in Adelaide. I was not there. He scored seventy-two runs in one innings. I reached Brisbane in the middle of the second test match. Cheteshwar had organized a car to pick me up at the airport. He was beginning to learn how to make sweet gestures.

He had already left for the stadium when I checked into the hotel.

I entered the room and discovered that my husband had left an array of carelessly strewn gifts on the bed. I was greeted by the sight of a SIM card and a pin, a granola bar and a packet of nuts. He had also left a note. 'Bought a pair of shoes, they're in the closet. If you need cash, it's in the drawer. The local SIM has data so you can switch SIMs. There are some snacks in case you're hungry— they should see you through till food delivery gets sorted.' The note ended with 'Sleep it off. Rest. I'll see you in the evening.'

I grinned appreciatively before passing out. It was quite a welcome.

I was so exhausted after sixteen hours of travel that I slept like a log. I turned on the TV when I woke up, only to discover that Cheteshwar was already out for seventeen runs. I then switched SIMs and found my inbox flooded with messages from home: all informing me that the ball had hit Cheteshwar's helmet and he was given out when, in fact, he was not out.

The Australia tour which had started on a happy note had lasted just as long as my nap. Although I did not know it then it was going to be a long unhappy tour.

After two disappointing away series, the Indian team had reached Australia at the end of that year to rectify what had been a rather protracted dry run for the side. From Brisbane, the team headed to Melbourne.

I sensed something was afoot during the second innings of the third test match in Melbourne when Cheteshwar was sent four down which not his usual position. He usually batted at one down. In this match, K.L. Rahul batted at number three. I watched these proceedings nervously. Were they going to bench him? He had been getting starts but he had not been able to convert them into big scores.

1 January 2015 arrived. The Indian team was invited for high tea to Kirribilli House—the prime minister's residence—along with the Australian side. The morning was slow and everything was shut. Cheteshwar was a little low and nibbled indifferently at his breakfast.

'What's wrong? Why aren't you eating properly,' I asked.

'I have a bad headache,' he responded.

Later, at around noon, he said: 'I want a light lunch. I'm sure the high tea will be heavy.'

'You rest. I'll go and pick up some food for you,' I offered, not wanting him to go out in the heat, since he was unwell.

Cheteshwar agreed and I stepped out of the hotel. It was a typical summer day with the temperature hovering at around twenty-five degrees. The sun was scorching and I walked briskly keeping my eyes peeled for an appropriate takeaway. After trudging around the city centre for about forty-five minutes, I finally managed to find a subway sandwich outlet. I was just ordering a subway veggie delight when my mobile rang. It was Cheteshwar.

'Forget the food. If you're late, the bus will not wait and neither can I,' he warned.

'I've already bought a sub for you. I'll be back in a jiffy,' I assured him.

I quickly picked up the sandwich and ran back to the hotel as fast as I could in the deadly summer heat. When I entered the Intercontinental, I noticed that some members of the Indian team were already in the lobby. I sped past them and hurried to the room.

Cheteshwar was already dressed. I quickly handed him the sandwich.

'Eat!' I said, urgently.

'Not much time,' he responded, but ate half of it, because I insisted.

He had already kept everything in readiness for me—a black and white dress with a matching pair of sandals.

'You have two minutes to dress,' my spouse informed me lovingly. 'Or else I'll have to go alone.'

I quickly shrugged into the dress and strapped the sandals that he had picked out for me. I don't think I've ever got dressed so fast. We reached the bus in the nick of time and managed to board it with a few seconds to spare.

The Kirribilli House turned out to be a picturesque Gothic-style, twin-gabled heritage house overlooking the harbour bridge. I was enchanted by the steeply pitched roofs, fretwork, bargeboards and bay windows, and could not stop marvelling at its old-world charm. High tea was a lavish al fresco affair, consisting a vast variety of dishes, both vegetarian and non-vegetarian. There were scones, one-bite ice creams and lots of Indian snacks.

After it was over, I was glad I hadn't missed the bus! It had been a memorable experience, one that would stay with me for a long time. After all it isn't as if one has high tea at a prime minister's home every day!

The next day, the team went down for a net session. Even though I knew how things had panned out for Cheteshwar during the boxing day match at MCG, I was still not ready for the shock that lay in store for me. While the guys were at practice, most players' wives tended to hang around together. One of them called out to me and took me aside.

'The team has just been announced and both our husbands have been dropped,' she told me flatly. This had happened during the team meeting.

I looked at her disbelievingly, unable to absorb her words. There was nothing to say. I quickly excused myself and ran back to our room. In another forty-five minutes or so, I would be facing my husband and I needed to gather all my courage to support him. He was probably even more devastated than me.

I called up Cheteshwar's masi. And broke down.

'Pranam, can I talk to you,' I asked her in a wobbly voice.

'Yes, of course,' she said with that serenity that was so much a part of her.

'I've just got the news that Cheteshwar is not going to be part of the playing eleven for tomorrow's match,' I said, and all of a sudden, the tenuous control I had on my emotions snapped. 'I'm very worried about Cheteshwar, masi. How will he take it? I am so upset.'

I started weeping over the phone.

People who are spiritually elevated don't react like we do. They are detached and view the tragedies and ecstasies of this world with a different lens. To them, moments of intense joy and sorrow are just tiny blips in the cosmos—meaningless episodes that have little or no meaning in the larger scheme of the universe.

When she heard my tale of woe, she laughed. 'Don't worry about Cheteshwar, child. He's gone through so much and is still standing strong. This is all part of life. Success and failure are both part of living. Things change. Just take god's name and pray. Don't worry too much about Cheteshwar.'

Somehow, her words calmed me and when Cheteshwar returned to the room, I was ready to face him.

'I've been dropped from the team,' he announced. He seemed so indifferent.

'I know,' I said, equally stoic.

He went silent for a bit and then remarked, 'Our job is to put in the hard work and not think about the results.'

I kept quiet. He was taking refuge in the teachings of the Bhagavad Gita. If it helped him weather this storm, I was all for it. Over the next few hours, he reiterated this sentiment again and again. I looked on, troubled, not knowing how to reach out to him.

He then spoke briefly to his spiritual guru. It was something he did before every match. Their interchanges were usually brief with

Cheteshwar saying 'pranam' and his guru responding with 'Jai Siya Ram.'

In this instance, their interaction was slightly lengthier. After their usual exchange of greetings, Cheteshwar broke the news to his guruji. 'I will not be playing in the coming match.'

There was a momentary silence.

'Just keep working hard,' Guruji advised after that small pause. 'Everything will be fine.'

Cheteshwar's next concern was his father. He did not want his dad to find out that he had been dropped from anybody else.

He called up his dad.

'I'm won't be playing in the next match. I've been dropped,' said Cheteshwar, without beating about the bush.

'You don't worry about it. There's nothing we can do about this. We'll just have to work harder,' Papa said firmly.

They were both devastated but hiding it from the other, putting up a brave front. To onlookers it appears as if families of players have a great time on tours. But the reality is very different. Their state of mind depends on how the team is doing at the time and how their spouses or partners are contributing to the team. This is not specific to me—I have seen wives of other players going through the same highs and lows.

While everything looks very glamourous from the outside, on the inside, things are very different. When players hit troughs in their careers, their families are reduced to helpless bystanders—there is nothing we can do to help them through their emotional turmoil—and all that remains is our sense of dignity and the false smiles that we paste on our face to pretend that all is well when it is not.

I did not possess the emotional reserve to watch the game at the Sydney Cricket Ground. I was too heartbroken. I booked an early flight and went back home on the first or second day of the test match. Cheteshwar did not process the impact that the episode had on him. On the outside, he gave the impression that he was in control and it was only much later that we would discover how difficult that first drop had been for him.

He had lived with the public and private façade of strength for such a long time that it was difficult for him to acknowledge his vulnerabilities or accept that he was human. Cheteshwar tackled the situation just as he had every other misfortune in his life: he thrust it aside and refused to address it.

The first half of 2015 was one of the most difficult periods of his life—first he was dropped from the test team, then the IPL, and in July, he would lose his masi who was fighting a losing battle against breast cancer.

First came the IPL drop.

He learnt that he had not been selected for the IPL in March. This meant, he would have nothing to do in April and May. He tried to get into the counties but it was already too late—they had already picked their players. Things began to spiral after that—it was a frustrating time for him and his perturbation percolated down to his father and me. After almost two-and-a-half years of playing matches non-stop, he just could not unwind. He kept looking desperately for opportunities to play but there seemed to be none.

Late one evening, the phone rang. This was when nothing seemed to be working and we were valiantly trying to set up matches with domestic local players who were not playing the IPL so that Cheteshwar could keep up with his practice during the summer months.

The call was from Cheteshwar's agent. He was big with news. Yorkshire was on the lookout for a player because Younis Khan had pulled out from the team. There was an immediate opening to play three-to-four matches. Would Cheteshwar be interested?

I immediately consulted Cheteshwar and his father, and gave a go-ahead to the agent. A fortnight later, Cheteshwar was representing Yorkshire in the counties. The only other Indian player who had played for the team in the past was cricketing maestro Sachin Tendulkar.

The chance to play Yorkshire was heaven-sent and I concluded that god helped those who needed him and those who kept the faith. Cheteshwar had been telling me that god sent us troubles to test us. Perhaps he was right.

It took us some time to sort out the visa, so Cheteshwar missed the first match.

The weather conditions up north are very different. Firstly, northern England in April is very cold and wet. Temperatures are often as low as four degrees. Matches are very low-scoring and the wickets are tricky because of the movement of the ball.

Cheteshwar was aware of these factors, but the actual experience was very instructive. We were in Leeds for the entire month. One thing that tickled our funny bone no end was the fact that my husband would leave for the cricket ground at 8.45 a.m. all suited and booted each morning. It was an English tradition followed by the club and our very own Gujarati Englishman adhered to this rule. He would only change into his training gear when he reached the ground. Papa and I found the custom very weird.

After he left, my father-in-law and I would get ready and pack up our lunch boxes. The ground was about 1.6 miles away from our house and it would take us around forty-five to fifty minutes to cover the distance on foot. We timed ourselves so that we reached just before the start of play.

We usually paused to buy ourselves hot cups of coffee and my father-in-law made it a point to sweeten his brew with enormous amounts of sugar. This done, we would pick a seat that offered us the best vantage point of the wicket, usually by a wall or pole on the side, to block out the wind.

After that our focus would shift to the day's play, during which time we would religiously follow the game, ball by ball, session by session. My father-in-law kept a hawk's eye on how the other players were dealing with the pace and swing, constantly trying to figure out what his son's stance should be, how late was it okay to hit the ball, when he should play on the back foot, when he should go on the front foot and more technical assessments of this kind. It was at this point that I turned into an avid cricket-watcher.

During the lunch break, we would grab a quick meal from a nearby coffee shop—on some days, a sandwich and on others, a baguette or soup—whatever was available on the menu. Armed with our meal, we would go into the ground, at which time my father-in-law would inspect the grass on the wicket, the outfield, the sprinklers and all the visible equipment with a keen eye.

We would then eat our lunch, which was usually accompanied with one more round of coffee because of the cold. A lot of spectators would be sitting around enjoying their ice creams, a phenomenon that horrified my father-in-law.

'How can they eat ice cream in such cold weather?' he would exclaim each time he espied someone with an ice-cream cone or tub.

On days when it rained or during practice sessions, Papa would sit with me in the kitchen whilst I prepared food. He would help me organize the utensils, straighten out the dishwasher while trying to decode the areas that Cheteshwar needed to focus on to improve his technique.

My father-in-law loved to analyse and over-analyse the game, whilst his son just wanted to prepare and work in the nets. Cheteshwar was not only playing non-stop, he was also exercising constantly at the gym. He would come back in the evening dead tired and the last thing he wanted was cricket dominating each meal or conversation.

It was a tricky phase. The runs were still not coming and my father-in-law's analysis was exponentially increasing. Tensions mounted between father and son and the task to calm them down fell on me. It came to a point when I told Papa to discuss the game with me instead of Cheteshwar. It was a successful ploy and the friction within the household reduced noticeably.

It was at around this time that rescue arrived for Cheteshwar in the guise of a lady sports psychiatrist. The Yorkshire team had a mental-conditioning coach, and an hour's counselling each week was mandatory for all players, their personal preference on the subject notwithstanding. For once, my husband did not have the option of keeping his thoughts to himself. Besides, he was vulnerable at the time and unconsciously started unburdening himself during these sessions.

It began quite innocuously with an admission when he mentioned that he was under a lot of pressure.

'Have you tried deep-breathing and meditation?' asked the psychiatrist.

'I have,' admitted Cheteshwar. He also confessed that he tried to overcome his stress by sticking to his routine. As their sessions progressed, he grew more comfortable. He had not been looking for help, but now that it was there, he took the opportunity to find solutions.

'How do I improve my focus? How do I channelize my energy?' he inquired.

'Do you like any sport apart from cricket?'

'I like racket sports. I also enjoy video games,' he divulged guiltily.

'These are also good ways to reach a goal,' she told him. 'Because you're still chasing an end goal. When you're playing a sport, your thoughts will blank out because your entire mind will be on these games. They're the perfect stress-buster. You should play more racket games in your free time, or even video games.'

Her suggestion made sense, and he followed her advice with a vengeance!

It did not happen immediately, because on that trip, the PlayStation that had been purchased so lovingly in 2013 was still gathering dust back home in Rajkot mainly because till then, Cheteshwar had regarded it with a guilty pleasure. But now that he had the mental-conditioning coach's go-ahead, it became a vital part of his existence, a boon companion that would accompany him everywhere.

Badminton and video games dominated his free time in all his subsequent travels and it was soon evident that the psychiatrist's advice had been on the ball. Suddenly, Cheteshwar shed his reserve and his room became a 'gaming hub' where he and his teammates spent hours playing 'mission games'. The change in him was tangible and he was much more relaxed.

I was thrilled and quietly thought of the other suggestion that the psychiatrist had made. 'You should take a holiday every time you've gone through a long and exhausting series. When you've played a lot of cricket, you need to switch off completely. Getaways are a great way to unwind.'

I bided my time. He had come this far—surely, he'd be open to taking holidays as well? It was a delicious thought.

We travelled to Nottingham for an away game. The day was cold and windy and Cheteshwar called me up from the dressing room to ask me to get him more thermals from a sports store. He was carrying his skins, but he wanted to add more layers to his attire, as the cold was impeding his fielding. All the players were carrying heat bags in their pockets to prevent their fingers from stiffening; in their absence catches would have been an impossibility.

It was so cold that day that Papa and I got cold burns and my father-in-law eventually had to be taken back to the hotel in a cab. It was difficult enough for us to watch the game as spectators and I felt an aching sympathy for Cheteshwar. How was he managing to play in such cold conditions, when he hailed from the tropics where the temperatures went as high as forty-four degrees?

We braved the cold for a whole month and luckily after Nottingham, there was a home match. It was also Cheteshwar's last match of the season. He scored a wonderful century in the second innings and remained unbeaten on 133.

We left England on this joyous note and Yorkshire went on to win the championship that year.

CHAPTER SIXTEEN

Miracles Do Happen

Cheteshwar was part of the squad. But he had not played any matches for eight long, excruciating months after he was dropped in Melbourne. Once he was over the initial shock, he mustered all his inner resources and put his faith in god.

'My time will come,' he told me confidently whenever he spotted the anxiety in my eyes.

During the Sri Lanka series, even though he was not part of the first two games, he actually enjoyed his off-time by engaging in racket sports. He also spent an awful lot of time on PlayStation.

Every time I'd call him, I'd get a standard response. 'Is it urgent? I'll be playing games with some friends. I'll call you later at night.'

More often than not, he'd be too busy playing with his friends to keep a track of time. These gaming sessions would go on and on till late into the night with dinner being ordered in the room so that mundane things like meals did not hinder their play.

'Don't you want to sleep?' I would tease, when I actually managed to get hold of him.

'I'm trying to increase my focus,' he would retort, jokingly.

I held on to the thought, praying that he would be proved right. But I still worried. Perhaps because I could never match my husband's faith in the almighty. Then out of the blue, an opening turned up unexpectedly for Cheteshwar on the third and final match of the series. Both the Indian openers, Murli Vijay before the start of the series and Shikhar Dhawan at the end of second match, had been ruled out of the game due to injuries.

Cheteshwar had got his opportunity. But it came with a challenge. He had to open the innings in a game that was a series decider!

The match began on Raksha Bandhan day and for my husband, the time had now come to convert all those hours spent at the nets into runs. I kept my fingers crossed and Cheteshwar, I later learnt, kept chanting mantras at the crease whenever he was at the non-striker's end.

I was in Rajkot, he was in Colombo, and never had the physical distance between us felt so acute.

The wicket was tricky and after a shaky start, he settled down while wickets kept falling at the other end. India was 180 for seven when Cheteshwar decided to accelerate. He put up a 104 run partnership with Amit Mishra, the Indian leg-spinner who had come in at six down, and miraculously managed to bring the score to 312. Cheteshwar scored a century and remained unbeaten at 145. He went on to become the fourth batsman to carry his bat on a very bowler-friendly pitch.

When Cheteshwar reached his century, I was at my parents' house.

Tears of joy rolled down my cheeks and when they saw me weeping, my parents also became emotional. By tacit agreement, we had deferred the Rakhi-tying ritual till my husband scored his century.

Raksha Bandhan is a big event in my house because my dad has five sisters and my brother is the lone boy among several cousins. The entire clan usually gathers at my parental home to tie Rakhis. The ritual is always followed by a nice elaborate lunch.

But on this particular Rakhi, since Cheteshwar was playing, everyone was glued to the television. The living room was teeming with people and I was praying constantly, hoping against hope that he would do well. Lunch was postponed till he hit his century.

The end of the Sri Lanka tour culminated in another dream-come-true. After the match, we took our first tiny holiday to the Maldives for three nights with Cheteshwar's kitbag in tow!

En route to Sri Lanka, I met up with a friend at a restaurant as my flight was scheduled to take off a little later that night. The team had already won the match by 117 runs and the highlights were being played on television.

'*Kya mast khela na Pujara* (what a cool game Pujara played, no)!' said my friend playfully to the waiter who was serving us.

Our server was unimpressed. 'Next inning zero kiya! (he made a zero in the next innings),' he grumbled curmudgeonly.

We both burst out laughing.

But it was a salutary lesson. We tend to remember the errors that men make and often forget their triumphs. Yet the days of success are far less than the days of defeat and losses teaches us so much more.

Our visit to Maldives was a treasured trip and quite impromptu. I decided to join him on the last day of the series and travelled via Bombay. We caught the flight to archipelagic state in the Indian ocean the next morning armed with my husband's entire cricketing gear.

After our short getaway, Cheteshwar realized how important it was to take holidays, and this heralded a new phase in our lives. After every test series, we started snatching short vacations, usually for two-to-three nights to unwind, rest and reset.

There have been many occasions when Cheteshwar has been dropped and each time it felt as if there was no coming back, but against all odds, he has bounced back, making me realize that there is a unique connection between the crises he has faced and his unflinching resolve.

In the meantime, between Cheteshwar's first drop and his phoenix-like rise from the ashes of that disaster, a lot else happened. Professionally, he touched the very nadir of his career. He was dropped from the test team, the IPL and was not part of the playing eleven when the team went to Bangladesh in June that year.

When we returned to Rajkot from England, another misfortune loomed before us.

Masi took a turn for the worse the very next day and had to be hospitalized. She was admitted into the Sri Ram Sarvajanik Hospital, adjacent to the ashram, which had been established by Guruji. She lasted forty days and in hindsight, perhaps Cheteshwar's cricketing low was a blessing in disguise because it meant that he could spend a great deal of time with his aunt during her last days which would have otherwise not been possible.

Cheteshwar's attachment to his aunt cannot be viewed in isolation. It has to be seen through the prism of spirituality that ran in the distaff side of the family. His masi and mama were his closest confidantes and had stood by him through all the crests and troughs of his life. The link that twined them together was their shared spiritual guru who had inculcated the same value system in all of them.

Guruji was big on serving mankind and bhandaras were a regular feature in their lives. The core philosophy of his teachings revolved around leading peaceful lives while serving the almighty, feeding the needy and providing medical aid for a nominal fee. Honesty, spiritual discipline, service to society and simple living were the cornerstones of his philosophy and unlike a lot of modern-day gurus, he practiced what he preached.

Every time Cheteshwar encountered a dilemma or could not see the road ahead, he would call his aunt or uncle and ask them to pass on his queries to Guruji and seek guidance on his behalf. In the early days of our marriage, I sometimes felt that this overdependence on Guruji was robbing him of his decision-making ability. I felt like an outsider when I accompanied him to the ashram and often wondered why people sought Guruji's advice for solutions to their day-to-day problems instead of working them out on their own.

It took me sometime to understand that as Cheteshwar had been visiting Guruji since he was a child, seeking his advice was as natural as breathing. He felt he had the right to seek his Guru's guidance on matters for which he had no answers.

His uncle narrated one such incident.

In 2009, when Cheteshwar had his first ACL injury in South Africa, my father-in-law went to see Guruji at Gondal before flying out.

'His body is not meant for sports,' Guruji told Papa.

When Cheteshwar returned to India after his surgery, he sought his guru's darshan and pleaded with him. 'This is all I know. This all I have done. I want to make cricket my career. Please help me. Please bless me. I'm ready to put in all the hard work.'

At this point, masi intervened. 'He can't take it,' she pleaded. 'Please do something. Please help him.'

Guruji heeded her and blessed Cheteshwar. 'Okay, work hard and things will happen the way you want them to.'

This was one of the many instances when masi interceded on his behalf. There were times when Guruji was not available and since masi stayed in-house at the ashram, she became his intercessor, a sort of stand-in for his guru when he was away or otherwise engaged. Over time, Cheteshwar's connection to his aunt became deep and complex. After his mother died, the frequency of his calls to his masi increased; he started sharing every development—big and small—with her. She influenced him in ways that were not always visible and their conversations turned intense and seamless with no gender barriers hindering the topics they discussed.

When Cheteshwar started making money, it was masi's influence that played a role in his decision to donate to charity. It was one of Guruji's fundamental teachings. But masi's role in his life did not just stop there. She told him to keep his life simple and free of addiction and also encouraged him to give back to society. As a result, he started donating ten per cent of his net income to various charities and my father-in-law's academy.

Masi also guided him through rough times whenever events spiralled out of control. She would inspire him to do better when his game went through a lean patch. When someone wronged him, she advised him to rise above the episode. 'You must try and be big and stick to the path of truth. Be god's child. You do your bhakti and things will automatically fall in place.'

He would heed her and they always did.

Somehow, she managed to uplift him. She was central to his spiritual life and his faith in her equalled his devotion to Guruji. Masi was Cheteshwar's bridge to god.

By 2015, the cancer masi had been battling spread to her lungs. She could barely eat and we tried to be with her as often as we could. Throughout May and most of June, barring the days when India was playing Bangladesh, Cheteshwar and I travelled to Gondal to spend time with his aunt each evening. Cheteshwar's mama and mami were in attendance at the hospital during this period, tending to her needs, trying to ease her discomfort.

Masi's final days were uncomfortable and pain-filled, yet she was not ready to shuffle off her mortal coil for two reasons: she wanted to say a final farewell to Guruji who was on his usual summer trip to Pandukeshwar and she wanted to organize a bhandara before she departed to the other world. She had always accompanied him on these trips earlier. But this year, she was too ill to travel. She stayed alive through sheer will power and even managed to obtain both these heartfelt wishes.

Guruji came back to Gondal and masi asked him to fix a date for her bhandara. He gave us a date for a few days later and preparations began. Although she left the actual organization of the feast on healthier souls, the invitations were sent out at her behest. She invited everyone she could think of and the banquet turned into be an enormous event.

Masi's resilience amazed me. She had spent the last month struggling to breathe. She had been on oxygen, nebulizers and had slept sitting up because her respiration became affected when she lay down. And yet, during the bhandara, she summoned a sort of super-human strength from somewhere deep within and managed to participate in the feast. She even distributed food to the needy. How had she done it?

Dimly, even though I was not much of a believer, I realized that I was witnessing a miracle.

The next day, she passed away.

It was about half past eleven and I was on my way to Gondal. I had offered to go early so that mama and mami could get some rest after all the running around the previous day. Cheteshwar was still at Rajkot electing to attend his practice session before heading to Gondal in the evening with his father.

I was about ten minutes away from Gondal when I got a call from Cheteshwar's mama.

'Where are you? If you haven't started don't come,' he said tersely.

'I'm at the toll' I replied, surprised, wondering why he was asking me not to come.

The toll was just ten minutes away from the hospital. I had driven down to Gondal on my own.

'Oh okay, then come,' said Mamaji, without attempting any explanations.

By the time I reached the hospital, masi had passed away, and Cheteshwar and his father had already been informed.

Her room was on the third floor and as the lift usually took a long time to descend, I took the stair and noticed one of the ward boys who served her scurrying down. He did not spot me. I assumed there was an emergency and hurried up.

When I reached the third floor, I saw the hospital staff taking out the paddles on a tray. Cheteshwar's mama was standing by the window outside her room which was tucked away at the very end in a corner. He was looking very sad.

We entered her room. There was no need for any explanation.

'It happened just fifteen minutes ago,' said Mamaji.

Mami was not there. She had already left for the ashram to prepare masi's room so that her body could be laid there before her final send off.

Cheteshwar and his father reached Gondal a little over an hour later with a few other relatives. I was very worried about Cheteshwar's reaction to his aunt's demise. Masi had been his only solace during the recent series of events in his professional life. How would he react?

But by this time, several people had gathered and I could not snatch any private time with him or gauge how he was feeling. Besides, masi's room at the ashram was tiny and all the men had been cloistered elsewhere.

The last rites began at around five o'clock. Cheteshwar and his dad attended but I did not go. We finally headed back home to Rajkot at around half past ten. I had still not had a chance for a private chat with him.

After four days, he went back to his routine. I tried to make him talk, but initially, he was like a clam. He opened up after a week.

His reaction when it came surprised me.

'It was all part of God's plan, Puja,' he explained. 'She wanted to see Guruji before she went and she got that, she wanted to have a bhandara and that happened as well. But most importantly, her physical body was going through a lot of pain, and death put an end to her suffering. You must understand that while her physical body is not present, we're still connected at a spiritual level, and I will always feel her presence.

He then resumed his preparations for the Sri Lanka tour, not knowing whether he would actually play or not because he had not been picked for the playing eleven.

My husband was right. Masi's passing left no void; instead, a sense of calm descended upon us. This was also the time when he started heeding advice from doctors and began to learn how to unwind.

Cheteshwar started listening to his own body, became kinder to himself, and started playing video games, table tennis and badminton. He learnt how to relax and became more cheerful, joyful and expressive. When opportunity knocked in Sri Lanka, he was prepared and accepted the chance he was offered with both hands.

Faith has been the single most significant factor that has moulded Cheteshwar into the man he is today.

I have watched him from the sidelines, aware that our approach to religion is quite different. He is religious, I am spiritual. He often tells me, 'religion has helped me surrender to the divine and allowed god to lead me through life's untrodden paths. Faith should not be a matter of thought, but of belief.'

I had no difficulty understanding what Cheteshwar was trying to say, because my mother too is very religious. But unlike them, I cannot practice religion regularly or surrender to it as thoroughly. Fortunately, the Pujara family tree, though small, is very diverse in its belief-systems. All the members in the family worship different deities and practice their faith in the manner they see fit.

In a strange way, Cheteshwar's life has been an intermingling of faith and courage.

Perhaps, if Cheteshwar's beliefs had not been so strong, his life would have been much better or easier, and maybe even more successful. However, he believes that it is his faith which is leading him towards a consciousness for greater good and not just limiting him to the life he has led so far.

CHAPTER SEVENTEEN

Enceinte

Throughout the years that Cheteshwar played for the counties, we kept hoping he would be picked for the IPL. This was especially true in the year 2017 after he had had a particularly good season. The hunger to prove himself had become acute almost immediately after he had been branded as a test specialist. He tried to surmount this by opting to play for the Syed Mushtaq Ali Trophy and the Vijay Hazare matches which catered to T-20 and one-day cricket, respectively.

He soon became a visible fixture in these games and tried to shed the test-specialist tag that dogged him relentlessly through the years by playing aggressive shots to make a case for himself.

It did not work.

But in the meantime, Cheteshwar and I had devised a strategy between us. I would get in touch with agents for the upcoming county season in the month of December each year and Cheteshwar would sign the contract only after the IPL auction.

We lived in hope, even though year after year, season after season, the story remained the same and Cheteshwar continued to be ignored by the IPL franchisees.

In 2017, after being overlooked for the IPL yet again, Cheteshwar signed up with Nottinghamshire. We had heard a lot about the famed charm of the Midlands and were aware that Trent Bridge Cricket Ground in Bridgford—the headquarters of the Nottinghamshire

Country Cricket club—was one of the finest cricketing stadiums in England, notable for its elegant architecture and close proximity to river Trent.

It was a prominent test venue which suited Cheteshwar's needs because at that stage, he was trying to play in grounds that were popular in the international test circuit. He felt that in the long run, the experience would help him improve his game. His stint was divided into two parts; he would play four matches in May–June and another four at the end of the season.

Cheteshwar was in a good headspace and my father-in-law and I joined him for the tour. We were allotted a house which was about two kilometres away from the cricket ground. The back end of our temporary residence abutted a canal fringed by lush green grass and a narrow, tarred lane peppered with pale-yellow benches for weary wayfarers. Throughout our stay, we would take the canal road and trudge to the Trent Bridge grounds on foot. A left turn would lead us to the bridge that spanned the river, where kayakers and canoers were a common sight.

The stadium had two entrances and one of them was a five-minutes' walk to a café which we patronized quite frequently. The second match was a delight, because Cheteshwar hit a brilliant century; it was the first on his home ground. The weather too was so much better and it was much easier for us to acclimatize to it this time round. Memories of the chill we had encountered during his previous season in Yorkshire still had the power to make me break out in goosebumps.

We had settled down when the Indian team arrived in England for the Champions Trophy accompanied by a bevy of journalists. Cheteshwar did a couple of interviews with them and held forth on life as a local and how the county matches were preparing him for future series.

After the first four county matches, Cheteshwar and I decided to travel to Scotland for a week before heading home. A three-match series in Sri Lanka loomed before him and this was the only window-period available to us for a much-needed break. Even though this was our fourth trip to the country, we had never really explored England.

Determined to make the most of our snatched vacation, we approached a car-rental service. We quickly loaded up the said vehicle with our belongings and drove off for our maiden trip to the Highlands.

Our first stop was Edinburgh.

It was a delightful city and we spent a couple of hugely enjoyable days exploring the town. During one of our many walks, I caught sight of John Lewis, a one-stop shop, in a three-storied building.

'Perfect!' I exclaimed aloud. 'This is the ideal place to wrap up our shopping. I can pick up some clothes for myself and we can also buy gifts for everyone back home.'

Cheteshwar, less enthusiastic, followed me into the store with a resigned expression. Shortly afterwards, when I headed to the home section to purchase a suitcase, he finally decided, he had had enough.

'Call me when you're done,' he muttered, ennui writ large on his face. 'I'm going to grab a coffee.'

That's not all he did. He also ended up buying a coffee machine!

After settling the bills for my new acquisitions, I headed to the coffee shop on the third floor in search of my husband.

'I've also decided to pick up something,' said Cheteshwar by way of greeting.

'What?' I asked, surprised.

'Come let me show you,' he said, excitedly.

He grabbed my hand and took me to a shelf in the coffee shop.

'Let's buy this coffee machine,' he said with an ardent gleam in his eyes.

I looked at its size and gulped.

'How will we carry it?' I demanded flatly.

'I've already got it figured out,' Cheteshwar reassured me confidently.

I gave up. This was a battle I was clearly not going to win.

'Okay, fine. Buy it,' I said, with a sigh.

The next day we took off to Loch Lomond.

It was a beautiful drive. The month of June was coming to a close and the countryside was lush green, ribboned with little streams of crystal-clear water. The highlands seemed to be full of shimmering lakes and to my delight, I discovered that our hotel at Loch Lomond was just adjacent to one.

We discovered wonderful walking trails over the next few days and spent most of our time hiking; when we weren't trekking around, we cycled to our selected destinations. We tried to take the cruise across the Loch Ness, but it was fully booked and we filed it in our to-do list for the future.

In the meanwhile, Cheteshwar's coffee machine was a bit of a flop.

I made this grand discovery when he proclaimed that he wanted a sandwich.

Room service took ages so I offered to go out and get some.

'Should I get some coffee as well?' I asked as I prepared to leave.

'No need. I'm going to get the coffee machine,' he announced.

'What if we're not able to pack it back?' I objected.

'We will,' said Cheteshwar with his usual assurance. 'It's not rocket science.'

The coffee machine was percolating by the time I returned with the sandwiches. Cheteshwar's beloved appliance turned out to be quite shoddy. The coffee was tepid.

I did not say a word, but the expression my face was a dead giveaway.

'At least it's hot,' insisted Cheteshwar defensively, refusing to acknowledge that it had been a bad buy.

When we returned to India in July, we discovered I was pregnant with our first child. Thrilled to bits about our forthcoming offspring, the discovery was mingled with a touch of dejection because it meant I would not be able to accompany Cheteshwar for his upcoming series in Sri Lanka later that month.

I was in my first trimester and magnanimously decided to forgo the trip because I thought I would hinder his game with bouts of morning sickness.

Besides, my mother had already given me a piece of her mind on the subject.

'Stay here!' she enjoined. 'What if something happens when you're there.'

Acknowledging the justness of her decree, I stayed back, only to discover that our apprehensions had been unwarranted. I did not suffer from any spells of nausea and seemed to be in the acme of good health. My sacrifice has been needless! My grievance mounted when I discovered from the sports media that Cheteshwar would be playing his fiftieth match. I felt the injustice of it even more acutely when he went on to score a century in that match and I was not there in the stands to cheer for him.

September arrived and Cheteshwar prepared to return to England for the second stint of the season. Since I was now in my second trimester, I was allowed to go with him. My sense of triumph lasted only till we reached England. The weather conditions had changed!

The Midlands in autumn were a far cry from summer! It was very wet, cold and gloomy. I discovered that it rained a lot here as well.

My general sense of gloom and doom was exacerbated by another unpleasant occurrence—morning sickness.

After escaping spells of morning sickness during my first trimester, I was finally stricken by bad bouts of nausea in my sixth month, just when I was certain I had been spared the affliction. I found it difficult to retain any food in my belly. Constantly beset with an acute burning sensation, the only items I could safely ingest were Greek yogurt, granola (nuts and oats and raw cacao) and blueberry. Sour comestibles went off my menu, perforce I stuck to very basic fare. Facing the first half of the day became a dire affair and the only way I could weather it was by staying home.

In the mornings, before heading to the cricket grounds, Cheteshwar would try his best to mother me.

'Do you want breakfast in bed?' he would ask anxiously. 'Just tell me what you need. I'll get it for you.'

I spent most of the day lounging around in a beautiful large conservatory that came with the house. It had large bay windows painted white, overlooking the lawn. Beige-coloured venetian blinds matched a roughly woven carpet of similar hue on the black tiled floor. It became my favourite haunt and I spent an inordinate amount of time listening to music with both feet up. I used to read a lot in those days and the Bhagawad Gita became a source of peace and solace during this phase.

It was not all bad.

My pregnancy heralded the beginning of a new chapter in our lives. Cheteshwar and I were on top of the world. Given the amount of stress that came with cricket, my husband and I had resolved quite early in our marriage that we would only bring a child into this world when we were in the right headspace. September that year turned out to be one of our happiest times together. We spent hours indoors and even though he had back-to-back matches, I stayed away from them.

There was an away game in Brighton against Sussex that month and it was our first visit to the town. Hotels were heavily booked in the city because of some big-ticket conference. Under the circumstances, we were billeted at a resort some fifteen miles away from the cricket ground. Our balcony afforded us a wonderful view of the wide verdant expanse that surrounded the building.

There was a golf course nearby and at lunch time, the restaurant at the lobby became quite lively with famished visitors looking to appease their hunger pangs. But the fare on the menu was largely non-vegetarian and my own options were limited to sandwiches and coffee. When I wanted a change, I ventured out to pick up some snacks and fruits that were available just a kilometre away from our temporary digs. But in the evening, once Cheteshwar was back, we would drive to a small town that was about three miles away to pick our meals from an Indian takeaway.

On the last day of the match, we had to check out, so I took a taxi to the City Centre at Brighton and wandered around till the match was over.

There were two more matches: one in North Hampton and the other, a home game. At this point, I was completely dependent on home delivery and desperate to return to Rajkot. I was tired of my morning sickness and completely done with fending for myself.

We flew home, quite oblivious that county cricket would play a defining role in his career in the future.

Once we were back at Rajkot, we learnt that the two-match series against Sri Lanka in India had been cancelled in the last minute. I was thrilled because this meant that Cheteshwar would spend Diwali at home. We made the most of this unexpected break and organized a memorable baby shower, celebrating it with family and friends.

At the end of the year, on 26 December, when he was leaving for Bombay to attend Virat and Anushka's wedding reception before the Indian team left for South Africa, I had tears in my eyes for the first time in our five-year-old marriage. My gynaecologist had forbidden me from travelling. I was now in my last trimester and had just entered the eighth month of my pregnancy. Parting with Cheteshwar was hard.

Anxious, he tried to soothe me. 'Don't worry, there are a lot of people around to look after you.'

But my teary-eyed reaction disturbed him and he did the unprecedented. He took his father aside and said, 'Look after her, she's very emotional.'

Still dissatisfied, he called up my mother.

'She's a little emotional. Be close to her,' he requested. 'I think she'll be happier with you at this stage. She's so chatty and light-hearted with her siblings. I'm going to try and convince her to stay with you.'

True to his word, he tried to persuade me to shift to may parents' place. I was non-committal.

'I'll think about it,' I said, trying to maintain a stiff upper lip.

I did not drop Cheteshwar to the airport as it was an early-morning flight and my husband thought that prolonging our farewell would just add to my emotional strain. He attended the reception and the team flew to Cape Town in the wee hours of the morning on 28 December.

The South African series spelt the start of the away season. India lost the first two games and Cheteshwar was run-out twice in both innings during the second test. By the time the third match started, I was a nervous wreck. The resurrection of the Indian team was under intense discussion and his performance in the last two matches was under scrutiny. I knew just how vital it was for him to make a big score. I kept my fingers crossed.

By this time, I had moved in with my parents and, as usual, I was glued to the television. The first wicket fell very early. Cheteshwar walked in to bat at one down and made a slow start. I was used to this and knew that with so much at stake, he would be chary of taking any chances. In any case, this was how he usually approached the game at the beginning of his innings. Even after ten dot balls, I thought it was okay—until another wicket fell at the other end.

He immediately retreated into his shell and slowed down even further. It was a tricky phase. The bowlers were on top of their game and the ball was doing a lot. At this point, he showed the first signs of taking it on the body. The dot balls reached twenty, and then thirty with zero runs on the scoreboard. I started panicking.

I tried to read his body language. He looked peaceful, as if he had settled in and was ready to stand his ground and weather the storm. It was cold comfort; the thirty dot balls had climbed to forty and then escalated to fifty. My alarm levels shot through the roof. The rest of the family had been eyeing my reactions with grave misgivings after the dot balls had touched thirty-five. My mother, who has a disconcerting inbuilt antenna, mysteriously displayed her awareness of my mental state and called out to me from the first floor.

'Switch off the TV and come up, this not good for you,' she hollered.

I refused to budge.

'I'll get even more stressed out if I don't watch the game,' I insisted stubbornly.

There was no let-up in the excitement and my tension kept rising. Another wicket fell. Virat walked in. We were now two down. A couple of dropped catches off Virat's bat at the other end added to the stress levels. There was worse to come. Cheteshwar faced over 53 balls without a run, but, thankfully, he struck lucky with a missed LBW chance. If South Africa had called for a review, it would have spelt the end of his innings.

He finally scored his first run on the fifty-fourth ball and was greeted with loud cheers from the dressing room and spectators alike—almost as if they were applauding a milestone. Vernon Philander had bowled so well that he had made Cheteshwar toil hard for that first run.

India was looking to build a partnership and Cheteshwar's score did not really reflect a fraction of what he encountered. It was a long innings and a defiant one. He batted for nearly five hours, faced 179 deliveries, and when he got out after hitting a half century, India was at 144 for five. Some fifteen overs later, the entire team was all out at 187. This demonstrates the quality of his knock. It was his birthday gift to himself and bittersweet torture for me—an unintended punishment for not being with him on the day he turned thirty.

India won the match.

Cheteshwar returned from the series with some bruises that seemed like a lot at the time. He came armed with a whole horde of diapers and baby clothes. My friend Prithi, Ravichandran Ashwin's wife, had helped him out with the baby shopping.

We were now all set for the arrival of our little one.

He spent less than a week at home and then went off to captain Saurashtra for the Vijay Hazare Trophy. He was back at Rajkot around 15 February after the team had qualified in the leagues. He wanted to go to Gondal to seek Guruji's blessings for the next phase of the tournament.

On the way, I pulled his leg. 'If you go for the qualifiers, you'll miss being there for the birth of our child.'

Since we'd just been to Dr Amee Mehta, my gynaecologist, he was unimpressed.

'Nonsense! Your due date is still twenty days away and the doctor has said the baby will be on time. I'll be back then.' He spotted my grin as he shifted gears and continued. 'In any case, I can always fly back to be with you since I'm in India.'

At 4.30 a.m., on 22 February 2018, on the very day of his quarter final match, my amniotic fluid broke. I was sleeping next to my mother. I changed and waited till 5 o'clock. I only woke her up when she started twisting and turning, as she transitioned from slumber to wakefulness.

I told her what had happened.

'I think your water bag has burst,' said my mother, looking at the clock. 'It's too early. Let's wait for a bit before calling Dr Mehta.'

We waited till a quarter to seven and then called the doctor.

'You'd better come over to the hospital. I need to examine you,' she said at once.

My mother then went to my brother and shook him awake.

'Get ready,' she said. 'The baby is on the way.'

'You'll have to deliver today,' pronounced Dr Mehta after she had examined me. 'We'll have to do a C-section since the baby is in a tilted position. But if you want to try for a normal birth, we can wait till one o'clock. If your labour pains arrive by then, fine; we can't wait longer otherwise it can get dicey.'

I broke the news to Cheteshwar. He had just boarded the bus to head for the match. 'I've just been examined by Dr Mehta. She says the baby will have to be delivered today. She's told me that there is no point in waiting for twenty hours, as at that point it can become touch and go.'

'What should I do?' he asked, completely flummoxed by the news. 'Should I come back?'

He was obviously in no state to take decisions. I sighed, upset that my premonition was about to come true. I thought logically.

He was captaining Saurashtra and since our child was going to be delivered by caesarean section, he would not make it in time. There were no direct flights from Delhi to Rajkot that day. He would have to fly out to Ahmedabad first which was a good 225 kilometres away. It would take him at least four and half hours by road to reach here. This was not counting the travel time between Delhi and Ahmedabad. It just wasn't feasible.

'Don't come back,' I told him. 'There are so many people here. If I'm going to have a c-section, what does it matter if you are here or not? Go, win the quarter final.'

He went ahead and played the game. Cricket was still priority number one in the Pujara household and today was no different. But it was a fine weapon to have for future arguments, even though, honestly speaking, it had been a collective decision and not his alone.

'I told you that the baby would come early,' I would later tease him.

In the meanwhile, in Rajkot, we waited till 1 p.m. and then opted for the c-section. There had been no labour pains, and waiting further was futile. I was wheeled into the operation theatre without further ado and shortly afterwards, Aditi was born.

In Delhi, the same afternoon, Cheteshwar's team won the quarterfinals. My brother sent photos of our little one to my husband. He called up as soon as the match was over.

'How's Puja?' he asked anxiously. It was his first question to my brother.

'Congratulations!' said my brother. 'Puja and the baby are both fine.'

'Is it a boy or a girl,' my husband then queried.

'It's a girl,' replied my brother.

'Waah!' said Cheteshwar, sounding very pleased.

My brother then handed the phone to me.

'I'm coming to see my little one,' he said, tenderly. 'I'll be there with you tonight.'

It was easier said than done. There were no direct flights to Rajkot that day, as I had surmised earlier. He booked one to Ahmedabad and only managed to reach Rajkot at 1.30 a.m. We cried with joy when we saw each other and he shed a few more tears when he had his first glimpse of Aditi. He had been up since 6 a.m., had won a match and travelled 700 miles to see his little one.

But she made him earn his paternal privileges, making him wait patiently before she deigned to open her eyes for him. We tried everything. We switched on the light, tickled her, but she refused to relent for a good thirty minutes, almost as if she was penalizing him for not being there at the time of her birth. Like a true daughter, she was testing her father's patience, unaware that he had plenty of it!

'Go home, get some rest,' I whispered. He had had a long and exhausting day and he looked dead tired.

'No,' he refused stubbornly. 'I want to see her eyes.'

'What's the use? She's not cooperating.'

'She will,' he said obstinately. 'I'll wait.'

Aditi opened her eyes a short while later and exchanged her first glance with her father. Satisfied that he seen her fully at last, he finally agreed to go home.

Never big on emotional displays and bound by a strong sense of duty, Cheteshwar values the privilege of playing for his nation more than anything else. He left for Delhi the next evening to play the semifinals. It would have been so easy for him to have missed that match. He could have stayed back and spent time with us, but instead he chose to strike a balance between his two worlds.

On the fourth day after her birth, Aditi was wracked by a series of tremors and jerks while she was asleep. Everyone around me panicked and I was terrified. I suddenly remembered that one of Cheteshwar's aunts had suffered from seizures as a child. Was our daughter going through the same thing?

Filled with foreboding, logic fled out of the window and my fear-levels went through the roof. I broke down. The only thought that flashed through my hazy mind was that I must somehow get in touch with Cheteshwar and tell him what had happened. He was still in Delhi for the Vijay Hazare Final.

Sobbing uncontrollably, I called him up. He was in the middle of a gym session. When he heard me weeping wildly, he quickly stepped out of the gymnasium.

'Take a deep breath,' he ordered.

I complied.

'Now, tell me what's wrong?' he asked, once I had calmed down a little.

I described what was happening to Aditi in graphic detail. My voice was still a little wobbly.

'Nothing is wrong with her,' he said confidently. 'She's a blessed child and loved by everyone. Calm down and just take a video of these jerks and send it to the paediatrician. He'll tell you what I'm telling you, that you're getting needlessly frightened.'

I got off the phone and followed my husband's instructions. The doctor confirmed Cheteshwar's assessment. The baby was alright!

'Nothing to worry about,' proclaimed the paediatrician. 'The baby is just twitching. It's quite normal and it happens when infants are trying to adjust to the world outside the womb. Just relax. Your little one is fine.'

I heaved a sigh of relief.

And then all of a sudden, I wondered—how could Cheteshwar, who was miles away and had seen the baby for just six hours, be so confident that she was alright? He had been so calm and rational while I had had a meltdown. He had been a pillar of strength: unfazed, unshaken, and so serene. Not for the first time, I envied him, his faith. It gave him the courage and conviction to stare down every disaster; to meet every triumph with indifference, every sorrow with stoicism and every joy with thankfulness. Perhaps, it was time to tread my husband's spiritual path and seek some enlightenment.

PART FOUR

CHAPTER EIGHTEEN

Separate Rooms

In the year 2018, Cheteshwar could have easily been dubbed a British citizen. He spent almost half the year in England playing county cricket for Yorkshire and a five-match test series as part of the Indian squad against the English team.

It was his first chance to play against England in England after amassing so much experience at the counties.

Our world, in the meantime, had expanded seamlessly to embrace Aditi into our fold and by the time she was three months, we discovered that we were parents to a most accommodating infant—she was sleeping through nights! The process began when she turned seventy-five days old and I decided to travel with her to England to join Cheteshwar during the county season. Even though my sister, Dhara, had agreed to accompany me for the trip, I still displayed all the signs of an anxious new mother, wondering how I would deal with such a tiny baby during the long flight to London.

I had spent the past three months cocooned in my parents' house, pampered by my mum, Geeta didi and an ayah, who were always at hand to help me with the baby. I was quite unused to managing Aditi on my own. Looking after her in England would be a different ball game altogether. For the first time, I would be solely responsible for Aditi and even though Dhara would be around to chip in, truth be told, we were both a couple of novices and the prospect was petrifying.

I was haunted by terrifying visions of an endlessly squalling infant throughout the flight, a traumatizing prospect. Aditi surprised us both and turned out to be a model passenger. She slept throughout the flight with nary a squeak, much to our intense relief!

After landing at Heathrow, we drove down to Leeds. It was cold and cricket took a backseat for me. I spent most of my time taking care of my daughter and hardly went to the stadium. All I knew was that Cheteshwar was playing a mix of four-day and one-day (RL50) matches.

A couple of weeks later, my father-in-law arrived with my brother. The atmosphere at home became light-hearted. For once, Papa's attention was on Aditi instead of cricket, a marked shift from yesteryears. In mid-June the rest of us flew out of England. Cheteshwar stayed behind and came back home on the last day of the month.

Papa was not the only one who had changed. My husband too had gone through his own evolutionary process.

He shocked us with an unexpected announcement—he had decided to go on his first mancation at the ripe old age of thirty!

I was impressed. He was gradually shedding the shackles of his childhood and learning how to loosen up. It was such a positive development. Something deep inside me rejoiced.

He took off to the Gir National Park with his pals from the Saurashtra team. The monsoons were at full pelt, the downpour heavy and the Safari closed. It was a fun trip with no agenda. They just lounged around in the resort, spending most of their time either karaokeing, swimming or playing volleyball.

He came back looking relaxed and happy.

I was fiercely glad.

The test series was due to begin on 31 July and Cheteshwar flew back to England with the Indian team on the twenty-third of the month.

I already had my own plans in place. Now that I was something of a veteran at handling Aditi, I was ready to brave England again, though not quite on my own. Prithi Narayanan, Ravichandran Ashwin's wife, and I had decided to join forces and travel to England together. She had two girls, Akhira and Aadhya, who were two and three years old at the time, and their nanny was travelling with them.

We plotted over the phone.

Prithi and I are good friends and share a lot of common interests. Both of us follow our husbands' games fanatically and she too manages his career. We often talk to each other on the telephone when we are not hanging out together during the cricketing season, discussing everything under the sun, while our husbands are busy on the field. We know each other's families and there is a genuine trust and affection between us. Our children too are extremely fond of each other.

She rang me up when I was back in India from England and mentioned in passing that she was planning to go to the UK for the test series.

'When?' I asked.

'Sometime close to the second match,' she told me.

'I can also go at the same time,' I said excitedly. 'Let's go together.'

She was game.

As soon as I got off the telephone, I asked my travel agent to figure out our itinerary for the agreed dates. In the meantime, I started looking for an AIR BNB near St James Court, Taj, where the team would be staying. A three-bedroom apartment looked particularly promising. I sent her the pictures and she gave me the go-ahead.

Neither of us would be staying with our spouses. Cheteshwar in fact had been quite vocal on the subject.

'We need separate rooms throughout the series,' he told me unequivocally. 'My attention has to be on the game. I cannot compromise my sleep, come what may.'

I had not argued. Even though Aditi was sleeping through the night at this stage, there were no guarantees that she would not wake up at some odd hour to demand a rare nocturnal feed during the tour. We just could not risk it. My husband simply could not afford the distraction.

This situation was not unique to Cheteshwar and me. It was common practice among cricketers who often asked their families to stay in separate accommodations so that they could concentrate on their game.

In the meantime, the first match of the test series began in Edgbaston, Birmingham on 1 August on an infelicitous note for Cheteshwar. He was randomly dropped from the playing eleven. England won the match by thirty-one runs. The second match, at Lords, was not much better. He was involved in a bad run-out in the first innings with just a single run to his name and scored a mere seventeen runs in the second when he was bowled by Broad after facing eighty-seven balls. India was routed with an innings defeat.

It was at around this delicate stage of the series that Prithi and I landed in London with our children and her daughters' nanny in tow. Our husbands were busy at practice so we took a cab and received a huge shock. We thought we had booked a ground-floor apartment. It turned out to be the lower basement!

'Oh my God!' exclaimed Prithi, taken aback, as she gazed down at the stairs leading to our apartment in horror. She had a double pram; I had a stroller. How on earth would we manage to lug them up and down every time we went out?

My own feelings were completely in sync with hers. The steps, though only five or six, were nevertheless large and steep. It was not just about the strollers. How were we going to manage to drag our luggage down? Both of us had travelled with humungous suitcases, stuffed with our children's requirements and the guys were not even around to do the heavy-lifting!

Our lodgings were definitely not ideal.

Somehow, we managed to lug our baggage down to the front door. Both Prithi and I devote time in the gym and neither of us are particularly fragile. But that interminable period spent up and down those steps was a chastening experience. We were panting profusely by the time we managed to accomplish the entire operation.

Our husbands finally caught up with us after practice. It had been a long, exhausting day and we were all dead tired.

That first day set the pattern for the rest of the tour.

Our husbands would come and meet us bearing food after practice sessions. On days when they were bushed, Prithi and I would go to the hotel to have dinner with our respective spouses in their rooms and taxi back together to the apartment in the basement.

The third test was at Nottingham where Prithi and I had found a beautiful penthouse near the Trent Bridge cricket grounds. I would babywear Aditi and walk to the stadium. But the weather was unpredictable and the authorities did not allow children in the box. I soon realized that with Aditi so young, it was no longer possible to watch the game out in the open, something I would have done unthinkingly in the past. I opted to follow it on television at the penthouse instead.

The game began on 18 August. Cheteshwar did not make too many runs in the first innings, but scored a respectable seventy-two in the second. India won the match by 203 runs. I was thrilled. In the last couple of days, I had managed to get into the box with Aditi and I had the pleasure of watching India win the test.

After the match we had a victory celebration of sorts. Aditi had turned six months and Cheteshwar felt he was back in form. The team had a four-day break till the next match. Prithi and I made the most of it, and shifted to the Taj at St James Court with our kids so that we could spend time with our husbands.

For the first time during the tour, Cheteshwar and I were at peace.

Till Southampton, the venue for the fourth match of the series.

Cheteshwar and I do not normally quarrel and when we do, it rarely spirals—except on matters of cricket. In Southampton, we squabbled over an accidental error.

We bussed it down with the team to Southampton, a port town in the South of England. The coach drove straight to the Rose Bowl where the players got off for a practice session. A mini-van had been arranged to take the rest of us to the Harbour Hotel where the team was staying.

By the time we reached the hotel, it was about half-past three in the afternoon. It was a stunning place, built right on the waterfront, on a private marina with an incredible view of the Solent, a strait that overlooks the Isle of Wight.

But I was in no condition to appreciate its beauty. I had just discovered that the additional room that I had counted on was just not available.

How had this happened?

Tired of moving back and forth from our AIR BNBs to the hotels where our husbands were parked, Prithi and I thought we would book additional rooms in the same hotel as our husbands instead of kipping at yet another AIR BNB.

Amenable, Cheteshwar had requested the logistics manager to do the needful while we were still in London.

To my intense dismay, the hotel was fully booked.

'Sorry, we're sold out,' said the receptionist, when I went to inquire after freshening up in Cheteshwar's room.

I was in panic. Cheteshwar would be furious.

I tried for an AIR BNB. There was nothing available that day. Weary, upset, I wondered how we would manage.

Noticing my unease, the receptionist offered a solution. 'We'll give you a bigger room,' she offered.

Faced with a lack of options, I politely accepted.

The room was largish, with a rather big passage, where the staff placed a cot for Aditi. I knew at once that it was a bad idea. I could just imagine Cheteshwar's reaction. Of late, Aditi had been waking up in a panic because of the frequent shifts. I quietly asked them to remove the cot and install a bed instead.

When Cheteshwar returned and discovered us in his room, he was distinctly unamused.

'Today we'll adjust, but this will not work tomorrow,' said Cheteshwar coldly. 'You can't stay here. I told you so right at the start'

I looked at him ruefully. I knew I was partially responsible. I was the one who had told Cheteshwar he need not worry about my travel plans, because I would be staying in AIR BNBs and now because I was finding the whole process fatiguing, I had changed my mind. I knew this situation would have never arisen had the logistics manager been given sufficient advance notice for the additional room.

Guilt-ridden, I initially tried to placate him.

'I'm sorry, I did try to find a place,' I explained. 'There's no hotel nearby and the city centre is four kilometres away, so what can I do?'

'You can plan better,' he returned icily.

'I tried,' I snapped, beginning to get irritated. Why couldn't he be more empathetic?

He looked at me exasperatedly. 'Plan ahead.'

It was obvious that he thought I was displaying an acute lack of understanding to his point of view.

'There's nothing I can do about it tonight,' I said pointedly, by now feeling a strong sense of ill-usage.

'I've already said, tonight we'll manage but tomorrow you have to find something, because the match starts the day after and I need my sleep.'

'I could figure out something today but I have the little one to think of,' I griped.

'I'm not telling you to figure something out today, you can do it tomorrow,' he retorted.

'Don't worry about tomorrow. Tomorrow, I'll be out of the door,' I said angrily. Tomorrow, I'll make sure I find a place. You don't need to worry about me.'

After venting our mutual grievances for a little bit longer, we declared a ceasefire and went for dinner at a café outside the hotel.

This is typical of us. We have our spats, but they usually blow over quite quickly. We try not to carry our differences forward.

The next morning, still raw from the events of the previous evening, I went on a manic internet search in the breakfast area. I was tired, overwhelmed and overcome by a longing for home.

'Let this week get over,' I thought to myself. 'And I'll go back home. There's no point in staying for the last match in London.'

Luckily, by afternoon, I found a two-storied house some five hundred metres away from the hotel with four bedrooms and a harbour view.

Prithi wanted the upper floor as her family was coming over for a visit.

'We'll take the house if you can babyproof the doors,' she said to the landlord. He agreed and I heaved a sigh of relief. At least Cheteshwar would calm down now that he would get his beauty sleep!

The storm had blown over.

~

The match began on 30 August. England won the toss and elected to bat. Cheteshwar was in a much better mood since he had managed to get two nights of uninterrupted sleep. I too was upbeat when I took Aditi to the stadium to watch the game. When we returned home after the end of the day's play, I discovered that my daughter had developed a mild fever. She was fine the next day, but I decided to stay home, only to discover that I was stuck in a house with no Sky Sports. Cheteshwar was to bat that day so I followed the match on a digital platform on my phone.

Cheteshwar came to bat at around the drinks interval. He made a decent start and played an impeccable innings, staying unbeaten at 132, after cementing sufficiently lengthy partnerships with lower order to put India in the game. It was his first century in England in an international match.

The moment was special and I was overcome by the thrill of it. The only other time I remember weeping was when he had scored a century in Sri Lanka in 2015.

I don't know why I cried.

I was in the same city but not at the stadium. I was happy, but maybe I was exhausted and worried because Aditi had been unwell. That evening, he came home bearing some scrumptious Indian food. He wanted to see Aditi because she had been sick and he wanted to celebrate his century with me.

He was grinning from ear to ear when he arrived, not only because he had hit a ton, but because he had had the well-deserved rest which had facilitated it!

'Carry on with your beauty sleep if it keeps the runs coming,' I joked exuberantly.

We had a happy peaceable meal and Prithi was impressed that he had made the effort to come to the house, instead of calling us to the hotel despite his undeniable exhaustion after such a long, hard day at the grounds.

Aditi and I left for India after the match and my husband joined us not too long afterwards.

CHAPTER NINETEEN

The Test

A lot of people define Cheteshwar's cricketing success by his triumphs during the 2018 Border-Gavaskar Trophy in Australia. Lesser-known are the personal battles he was engaged in at the time, making his achievements even more remarkable.

The onset of his struggles began without prior warning when he was wracked by a neck spasm during a practice session, a month before the impending tour. Anxious, he called up Patrick Farhat, the team physiotherapist, an Australian, who had more than three decades of experience in his field and was a dab hand at dealing with sports injuries.

'I have a bad neck spasm,' blurted out Cheteshwar. 'I thought I'd discuss it with you.'

They had a long chat during which time he went on to describe his niggles in great detail.

'Since you have a big tour coming up, I think it's best if I assess you in person,' said Patrick finally after patiently hearing him out. 'I'll be in Mumbai, two days from now. Why don't you meet me there?'

It was Diwali time and they fixed up to meet the day after the festival. We duly rushed to Mumbai at the appointed time and Cheteshwar met Patrick at the gym at Taj Land's End, where we had booked a room. From there, the duo proceeded to a hospital for a scan. Matters did not appear to be very serious but Patrick advised him not to play domestic matches as a precautionary measure. He, however, permitted Cheteshwar to practice at our academy in Rajkot 'provided he did not overdo it'.

Even thought this meant that he had to forgo his usual match practice (Cheteshwar usually played at least two before each upcoming series), he nevertheless heeded Patrick's counsel and concentrated on simulating the conditions in the academy to resemble those he would encounter in Australia.

Bowlers at the academy were requested to bowl bouncers from a distance of sixteen to eighteen yards instead of the usual twenty-two, and these were hurled at him with the help of coated balls on wet concrete pitches to generate pace and bounce so that Cheteshwar could put bat to skidding balls. By the time the team took off, my husband was well-prepared for the coming tour.

But the neck spasm remained.

My English experience earlier that year had been a chastening one, leaving me disinclined to accompany Cheteshwar on the tour. Aditi was now nine months old and had just begun to take her first steps. When she was not attempting to walk, she would crawl all over the place. Besides, she was also teething and consequently, cranky. I deemed it politic to give the trip a miss.

Cheteshwar reached Australia late in the evening. I woke up the next morning to a series of pictures that he sent to my phone. It was his usual practice to inundate me with photographs when I was not there with him, so that I could still be part of his overall universe.

On this particular occasion, he had sent me a picture of himself watching a show, followed by an image of an iPad with a keyboard printed on it, which turned out to be the case of the new iPad he had bought.

I grinned.

My husband is not particularly flamboyant, but his abstemious predisposition usually goes for a six when he comes across the latest available gadgets. They are his only weakness. Video games, tablets, phones—any gizmo that hits the market usually catches his eye and he must have it. I find it amusing in the extreme that he carries two phones, an iPad, a PlayStation, fancy headphones and AirPods on his travels.

Slightly slow that morning as I was not yet fully awake, it took me a little while to cotton on to the back story behind that beaming smile. My husband had sailed forth to an Apple Store the first thing in the morning to fortify himself with the most up-to-date iPad that had caught his fancy, together with a very expensive case. This latest addition to his already colossal collection I surmized was to serve as his close companion on a tour in which most of his teammates were accompanied by their families; which meant very little video-game time. His latest toy would fill the gap and help him kill the empty hours by watching shows, at least that was how I read the situation.

It was a good omen. His tour was starting on a high—with the purchase of the said tablet—something he really enjoyed. The only other thing he bought on that tour was a neck pillow. This too was the latest-of-its-kind and its procurement was inspired by Patrick, who had been keeping a sharp eye on his patient's strained collum.

'The neck pillow will really help your spasm,' Patrick told Cheteshwar with a kindly glance. 'Let's go and get it.'

Patrick was right and the said pillow helped. He recovered from the spasm but the cervical strain did not go completely and the soreness in the afflicted area persisted. I kept worrying about it.

'Are you okay? Are you better,' I would ask constantly.

'I'm taking treatment for it. It's being managed,' he would reply.

'How are you feeling?' I asked after a warm-up match, worried that the pain would be back after such a long innings.

'I'm sleeping much better with the neck pillow,' he told me patiently. 'Just chill. You don't need to worry. I'm fine.'

Then came the first test at Adelaide on 6 December. It was memorable. India won the toss and elected to bat on a pitch that appeared tailor-made for batting. It seemed like a good portent, until the top order fell in quick session.

Despite the top-order collapse, Cheteshwar scored a match-winning century that included crucial partnerships with the lower middle order and a remarkable sixty-two–run partnership for the seventh wicket with Ravichandran Ashwin. It was Cheteshwar's sixteenth test hundred on a day when the temperatures touched forty degrees Celsius.

I had my heart in my mouth throughout the match, especially when he pulled his hamstring while diving to complete a second run, towards the end of the match. He was on eighty-two runs at the time. At first, Cheteshwar thought it was just a cramp, but he later discovered that it was a hamstring niggle. However, since India won the match, it seemed worth it.

The boys at the academy too woke up early to watch their 'Chintu bhai' bat and were pumped up when they saw Mitchell Starc bowling a bouncer that Cheteshwar countered with ease.

I was extremely amused when one of them said, 'Arrey, Starc's bouncers won't bother Chintu Bhai, he's been preparing for them.'

But I was also touched. The boys at the academy had worked very hard with Cheteshwar during his preparations and were now celebrating his success as if it was their own and it was, because they had put in a lot of effort to help him get there.

Cheteshwar was spending a lot of time with Patrick in rehab to deal with his niggles before the second test match and I was hoping against hope that his pulled hamstring and strained neck would survive the rigours of the upcoming game.

Even as I worried over Cheteshwar's fitness, fate delivered a major blow, back home—my father suffered from another episode of tachycardia!

On the eve of the second test match, in the wee hours of the morning, my father-in-law called me on my mobile from his room on the first floor.

'Puja, I'm feeling very uneasy, can you come down,' he requested, in a thready voice.

I was on the second floor. Aditi was sleeping in her cradle, close by.

'Of course, Papa,' I agreed, on the alert immediately. 'I'll be right down.'

I glanced at the time. It was 2.30 in the morning. I fought down the fear that threatened to overwhelm me. I was on my own—would I be able to manage, I wondered nervously, sending a quick prayer heavenwards, asking the gods to give me the strength to cope with this latest crisis—whatever it was.

I snatched my slippers and rushed down to the first floor, switched on the lights and grabbed his blood pressure machine. It was not a particularly fancy contraption, but it was efficacious enough to keep tabs on his blood pressure on a fortnightly basis.

'What's wrong, Papa?' I asked urgently.

His BP appeared normal, but his pulse rate had shot through the roof and was hovering at around 204.

I panicked.

'I don't know,' he replied, shakily. 'I'm feeling giddy.'

I checked his pulse again. It was still the same.

I did not bother to re-check his BP.

'I'm taking you to Synergy,' I said. 'Lie down quietly till I've arranged everything.'

He nodded.

I ran up to my room and called Kuldeep.

He lived three blocks away, was something of night bird, and likely to be up at this hour. Besides, Cheteshwar had instructed me to reach out to him if this sort of emergency ever cropped up.

I briefly told him what had happened and he promised he would be there within the next few minutes.

I then called up my sister, as I quickly shed my nightclothes and wore the first half-way decent garments I spotted.

'Papa's feeling giddy, Dhara. His pulse rate is very high so I'm rushing him to the hospital with Kuldeep. He'll be here any minute. Aditi is sleeping in her cradle. I'm going to get Naina bua to keep an eye on her till you arrive. Just come to the house with Jeet and take her home. He can join us at Synergy later.'

This done, I quickly gathered my father-in-law's files and walked rapidly to Cheteshwar's bua's room and knocked. She was in bed, fast asleep, but she woke up at once.

'Naina bua, I have to go to the hospital with Papa. Dhara will be here in ten minutes. Can you please watch over Aditi till then? She's asleep. But I don't want her to be alone, just in case she wakes up.'

Cheteshwar's aunt rose at once. 'You go. I'll keep an eye on the child.'

I thanked her and ran down. I had already called up Dr Ajay Patil, Papa's cardiac surgeon, and primed him about the situation. He had promised to inform the doctors to be in a state of readiness for us at the hospital.

My sister and brother arrived just as Kuldeep and I were heading to the hospital with my father-in-law. Dhara collected Aditi and Jeet dropped them home before rushing back to join us at Synergy. As soon as we reached, the doctors injected Papa with a blood thinner. Within fifteen minutes, he started feeling better. He was then put through the ECG and echo tests. Some forty-five odd minutes had elapsed and he seemed quite comfortable.

'He's had another episode of tachycardia,' said the attending doctor. 'You can take him home now. There's nothing to worry now. He's quite stable.'

It was his second episode in three months, so I was familiar with the drill. At that time too they had released him after injecting him with blood thinners. We were back home at half-past three. Aditi was still at my parents'.

The second test was beginning that very morning, so I freshened up, took a short nap and woke up in time to wish Cheteshwar luck for the match. I carefully omitted all mention of the events of the previous night, not wanting to take away his focus from the impending game.

'How's the hamstring,' I asked casually.

'Fine,' he answered, insouciantly.

'Best of luck for the match,' I wished him, with a spurious attempt at jollity.

'Thanks,' he replied, distractedly, his mind already on the game ahead.

Later that afternoon, I took Papa to Dr Patil.

'This is happening too often,' he proclaimed after scanning Papa's reports. 'And it can be dangerous.'

He spotted the anxiety on my face.

'There's no need to be so anxious. It can be cured with a heart ablation procedure,' he asserted and then noting my mounting tension he held up his hand and added. 'There is nothing to worry about, it's a very short procedure.'

'Will you do the procedure?' I asked.

'No,' he said, firmly. 'The best doctor in the field is Dr Yash Lokhandwala, in Mumbai. You should go to him.'

India lost the second test at Perth by 146 runs, despite Virat Kohli's century in the first innings. It was Australia's first victory since its match in Durban earlier that year. Cheteshwar struggled during the match as his afflicted hamstring was now really troubling him. But I was battling a bigger worry. How was I going to tell Cheteshwar that his father needed a heart ablation procedure?

Nothing seemed to be going right. My father-in-law needed medical attention, my husband was sporting a limp thanks to his aggravated hamstring after the game at Perth and I still had not told him about Papa's impending ablation.

I finally broke it to him when he reached Melbourne. The team had a tiny break between matches and I knew that I could not keep him in ignorance any longer. He took it on the chin and agreed with me: there was no point in delaying the procedure till his return. We settled between us that Papa and I would travel to Mumbai and get the procedure done as quickly as possible.

Relieved that Cheteshwar was in the know at last, I finally got in touch with Dr Lokhandwala. Christmas was round the corner and the earliest date we could get for the procedure was 3 January as the doctor was off on a vacation for the festive season.

In the meantime, Cheteshwar made the most of his three-day break and did not step out of his room much. He alternated between resting his afflicted limb and getting his strained hamstring treated. On the lone occasion when he did, he overheard someone engaged in an intense conversation on the telephone, stating that he did not want my husband to play in the coming match because he was unfit. It was an unpleasant incident. But Cheteshwar gave no sign that he had accidently become privy to the said exchange. Neither did he tell anyone about Papa's medical condition.

I only learnt of the incident accidentally on Cheteshwar's birthday after the tour was over.

It was around half-past-two in the afternoon, the lights were off and the room was quite dark. Aditi was napping and Cheteshwar and I were reclining on our bed as I scrolled through our social media pages reading out birthday greetings. One message posted on Instagram was particularly effusive and touching.

I read it out aloud to Cheteshwar, remarking, 'Such a sweet gesture—what a lovely message!'

There was complete silence. He did not say a word. Puzzled, I looked up from my phone and caught a most peculiar expression on Cheteshwar's face—one that was simultaneously secretive and pitying. I had no trouble translating his mien—it was his vintage you're-so-naïve-and-trusting look—I had seen it before and was therefore quite familiar with it.

My antenna went up at once, and I immediately sensed that something was not right.

'What's wrong,' I asked.

'Nothing,' he said, at his taciturn best.

But I was not buying it. I knew quite well that when Cheteshwar went completely quiet, it usually meant he was concealing something. It was a frequent occurrence. I usually learnt of on-field gossip and politics from other players' wives, never from him. Throughout my marriage, Cheteshwar's description of his various trips had been limited to three unvarying sentences: 'We had practice, a team meeting and then I returned to the room.' Day in and day out, year after year, I had been treated to the same standard lines. He was ready to talk about everything but his professional life. There were times when I would wonder if he even knew what was happening in the world around him.

But in this instance, I was not about to let him clam up on me.

'Tell me,' I pestered.

He tried to fend me off, but I was nothing if not persistent and I finally wore him down.

'This guy you're praising,' commented Cheteshwar laconically, 'wanted me to be dropped from the team because of fitness issues.'

I gaped at him.

'Why didn't you tell me earlier? Why did you go through it alone?'

'Such things happen,' he shrugged, 'and not everything deserves a reaction. I played and played well and that's what matters. You don't need to dwell too much on the incident. But it's important that you learn not to trust everything that takes place on social media.'

'I'm a work in progress, remember?' I joked, throwing back one of his favourite lines at him in an attempt to lighten the atmosphere and veil my outrage. 'You need to mentor me.'

The Boxing Day test was quite thrilling. Cheteshwar scored a century in the first innings almost as if he was sending out a message to his critic that he had plenty of cricket left in him. India set a massive target of 443 runs for seven and made Australia toil hard for their 151 all-out when it was their turn to bat.

The Indian second innings appeared to be an exercise in widening the run target and both Cheteshwar and Virat were dismissed for ducks. India piled on another 106 runs for eight and declared, setting the Australians a mammoth target of 399 runs for a win. They were already eight down for 258 runs at the end of day four and it took India just over four overs to wrap up the match on the final day.

Cheteshwar had hit another century, India had won the match and was leading 2-1 in the series and even better, it had managed to retain the trophy even though it lost the next match.

I was elated—for the moment.

I was anything but happy when I accompanied Papa to Mumbai, fighting hard to keep my emotions in check. I was leaving my ten-month-old baby behind with my parents and wondering how she would fare without me. Adding to my stress levels was my father-in-law's imminent procedure that was slated to take place later that evening and if this were not enough, it was also the opening day of the final test match at Sydney and I was hoping that Cheteshwar would retain his form going into it.

Before flying out early that morning, my father-in-law and I had dropped Aditi at my parents' place. She had thrown up just as we were leaving and I had hurriedly cleaned up the mess, hoping she was not falling sick. I did not tell Papa, because he I knew he would panic.

I thrust my daughter on to my mother and hurriedly gave her a string of instructions in hushed undertones. 'She has puked. Feed her. If she's not well, just call Dr Sameer, her paediatrician. You have a list of medicines and her medicine kit. You can give her whatever she needs as an SOS. I'll be back soon.'

When we got to the airport, Cheteshwar had just come in to bat. We had no check-in luggage, so we quickly went through security and waited near the gate for the next forty-five minutes. There was no connectivity on my mobile and I could neither check on Aditi nor get any update on the match. My unease surged.

I called up my parents as soon as we touched down in Mumbai. Aditi was fine. I relaxed—at least one of my anxieties had been laid to rest. I then combed for the latest updates from the Sydney Cricket Ground. More good news. Cheteshwar looked quite settled at the crease. My spirits rose and the day suddenly looked brighter than it had earlier that morning.

By the time we reached the Holy Family hospital in Bandra, Cheteshwar was approaching a century. I cheered inwardly and took my eyes off my phone for the first time since we had landed in Mumbai to absorb our surroundings. Holy Family was a big hospital, spacious, sparkling and super-clean. We went to the reception with our meagre baggage.

'My father-in-law has a heart ablation procedure scheduled this evening with Dr Lokhandwala,' I informed the receptionist.

She checked her register and nodded. I paid up the tentative bill and completed all the formalities. It was just noon. We went to the elevator as Papa's room was on the third floor. The liftman was busy watching the match, as he punched the button. I couldn't blame him, because I was equally engrossed in the same match on my mobile.

Dr Lokhandwala's assistant came in once we were settled and we briefly chatted about Papa's procedure, which would be taking place one floor below.

At around 11.30 a.m., India time, Cheteshwar struck a century and suddenly all hell broke loose.

As soon Cheteshwar got his ton, one of the commentors announced that Papa was due for a surgery the same day and all of a sudden, we were flooded with phone calls from family, friends and—the media! Till then, we had not told anybody about Papa's procedure outside the immediate family. But somehow, word had got out and now, instead of watching the match, I spent time fielding calls, accepting congratulations and commiserations at the same time.

Relatives and friends called up to ask after Papa's health, fans and members of the press corps wanted to know the details of Papa's procedure. I patiently answered them all, even though I could have done without the distraction. All I desperately wanted to do at this point was to concentrate on the game.

However, there was an upside to all this: Cheteshwar's century and the series of phone calls kept Papa occupied and served as a great diversion, keeping his focus squarely off the game and the looming procedure.

Dr Lokhandwala walked in during the middle of all this commotion, putting a temporary halt to all the phone calls. He examined Papa and seemed satisfied.

'You don't need to worry,' said Dr Lokhandwala. 'You won't even need to go under full anaesthesia. The procedure will take about forty–forty-five minutes. But we'll keep you there for an hour or so for observation.'

His reassuring words went a long way in allaying our fears.

The staff wheeled Papa to the OT at around four o'clock, to prep him. It was late evening in Australia. Cheteshwar was batting overnight at 130 and the Indian score stood at 303.

He called me up to ask after his father.

'They've taken him into the OT,' I informed. 'So, there's nothing much to tell. The doctor has met us and examined Papa. There's nothing to worry about,' I added, repeating the doctor's statement. 'He won't even be going under full anaesthesia. Just go to sleep and relax. I'll update you in the morning.'

Cheteshwar's cousin, Avani, kept me company while Papa was going through the procedure. She lived in Mumbai and figured I could use a spot of handholding while I waited. Once it was done, Dr Lokhandwala came to inform me that the ablation had been a success.

'You can go back home tomorrow. Your father-in-law will be completely fine in two-three days.'

I felt as if a load had lifted off my shoulders and thanked him profusely.

Avani and I chatted idly till Papa was wheeled back into the room. It was around 8 p.m. Avani rose at once to leave.

'Stay back for dinner,' I invited.

She shook her head. 'I need to go,' she said ruefully. 'My little ones will be wondering where I am.'

The next morning, I was up at 3.30 a.m. to inform Cheteshwar that the procedure had been a success. I tried to speak to him in hushed tones, but this ploy was a failure.

'Go get a double hundred,' I whispered.

As soon as I hung up, I noticed Papa was awake, looking bright-eyed and bushy-tailed.

By tacit consent, we whiled away the next few hours, following the scores on a website, cheering loudly every time he scored, quite forgetting that we were in a hospital. Cheteshwar did not get a double ton. He got out caught and bowled by Nathan Lyon for 193. I had read somewhere that he seemed a little tired and restless post-lunch.

I was a wee bit disappointed, but perked up when my father-in-law remarked: 'This is even bigger than a double century. He has done well for his country and the team.'

Coming from a man who was difficult to please, this was a huge compliment!

Papa and I flew home that evening as happy as clams.

India played well, forcing a follow-on upon Australia. The hosts were six down on day four, and we would have definitely bowled them all out if the rains had not come to spoil the party. The game was abandoned and the match ended in a draw.

But it was a magical moment because this was the first time ever that India had lifted the Border-Gavaskar Trophy on Australian soil. The team had also garnered its first-ever test series win in Australia in cricketing history. It was a tremendous achievement!

The whole country rejoiced and I exulted with it. Cheteshwar was named the player of the match and series. When he was described by commentators as the Australian team's worst nightmare whose batting had left the Aussies with no answers, my cup of joy overflowed. What more could I ask for?

A vacation? A teeny-weeny break—as a treat for all the sleepless nights I had endured?

These dreams lasted till Cheteshwar's next phone call.

He had already booked his tickets to travel to Kanpur for Saurashtra's quarter-final game.

'Yay!' said my normally unruffled spouse in a state of great excitement. 'Saurashtra has qualified for the quarter-finals. *Yaar, isme toh jaana hi padega* (Pal, I will have to go for this)! The team will be stronger if I'm there. I hope we qualify for the semis.'

At that moment, I quietly packed away my dreams.

I knew the holiday wasn't happening and I didn't have the heart to protest.

CHAPTER TWENTY

The Year of the Pandemic

A year had passed since Cheteshwar's epic series in Australia. It was early February, 2020, and my husband had already left with the test team for New Zealand. There was a bustle of excitement in our house at Rajkot as I ran helter-skelter to take care of the last-minute details that needed my attention.

Aditi and I had stayed behind to attend a family event and were due to follow Cheteshwar by mid-February. I had missed the Australian series, deeming Aditi too young for the rigours of a tour at the time, a decision I subsequently came to rue. I was determined not to repeat the error by skipping yet another series. I did not know then that we were standing at the cusp of the most debilitating pandemic of the twenty-first century—Covid-19.

In fact, till that point of time, 'pandemic', a word that would dominate lexicons in several languages over the next two years, was an alien term, with which none of us were familiar. We had no idea how close we stood to one of the most widespread worldwide outbreaks of any disease, one that would go on to claim millions of lives.

Covid was already a health emergency in China and corona cases had now started erupting in Singapore. It did not take me long to realize that it was unsafe to travel and I reluctantly cancelled our tickets.

'I've cancelled the tickets,' I informed Cheteshwar over the phone. 'It's not safe to travel anymore.'

Cheteshwar endorsed my decision and we resigned ourselves to a month-long separation.

By the time Cheteshwar flew back to India via Singapore in early March, Covid had been declared a global health emergency and restrictions on air travel were beginning to tighten. The intervening month had marked a slow but radical shift in the way the world functioned. China was already under lockdown and a few Indians who had flown in from Wuhan were in quarantine.

I watched the rapid progress of events with severe misgivings.

Cheteshwar returned home in a state of excitement. Saurashtra had qualified for the finals and he was raring to have a go at the game. The team had also reached the finals in 2019, but had lost to their rivals.

This time round the finals were taking place against Bengal on our home ground in Rajkot and Cheteshwar's hunger to win was even greater. He had just a couple of days left to practice, beat the jet lag and be prepared for the big game.

On the day of the match, Cheteshwar came down with fever and a runny nose. He elected not to bat in his normal position. Worried, I checked his temperature as soon as he came home that evening after the day's play. It was still high.

'We'd better get you tested for Covid,' I said, in a steady voice, bringing up the dreaded 'C' word between us for the first time. 'There's no point in taking any chances.'

I had already dropped Aditi at my parent's house as a precautionary measure.

We were having this conversation in the early days of the pandemic when nothing much was known about the disease even within the medical fraternity. The general outlook at the time was that Covid was equal to death even among doctors. It cost me a great deal to raise the possibility that he might have contracted the illness.

Cheteshwar was inclined to brush away my fears. 'I'm sure it's just the change of weather and fatigue.'

'There's no evidence to support your claim,' I argued, stubbornly. 'Besides, you've travelled from Singapore. How can we be sure, until we get you tested?'

'It's just a gut feeling I have,' Cheteshwar stated, perversely.

I stared at him, speechless.

My father-in-law then jumped into the fray. 'Puja is right,' Papa averred sternly. 'You should not take your fever so lightly. It's better to get a test done, so that we can rule it out.'

We wrangled on and on until Cheteshwar finally gave in to our implorations.

What nailed it was my final argument.

'You could put the entire match in jeopardy,' I chided, pressing the one button I knew would never fail. I appealed to his sense of social responsibility. 'Just imagine what will happen in the off-chance that you're Covid-positive—you'll put everyone at risk—the other players, the staff, the groundsmen. Do you want to take that chance?'

Cheteshwar shook his head. 'No', he conceded quietly. 'I would not like to take that chance.'

I had finally got through to him!

Relieved, we took him to our family physician, Dr Chirag Matrawadia. He carried out some blood tests and Cheteshwar's parameters all seemed to be within range.

'Everything seems normal,' Dr Matrawadia finally pronounced. 'It seems to be a viral. I'll give you some medicines for it.'

Thank god, I thought, heaving an inward sigh of relief, finally convinced that Cheteshwar's gut instinct had been right.

But Papa looked unhappy and unconvinced.

'How can we be sure until he's been tested,' he told Dr Matrawadia plaintively. 'I still think he should be tested.

The doctor did not react at the time, but it was obvious to everyone concerned that Papa's entreaty had left him patently uneasy. Half an hour later, he called me up.

'I think you should get Cheteshwar tested. It's best to be safe in these matters,' he advised.

'But how?' I asked, blankly. 'Who do we go to? How do we go about it?'

That's when we made the disconcerting discovery that Rajkot had no Covid-testing facility!

'You'll have to go through the sarkari circuit. Only the government can help you,' said Dr Matrawadia.

I recounted the doctor's advice to Cheteshwar. He thought about it and decided to tap into the government machinery. He called up the personal assistant of a senior member of the state government who put him on to his boss within minutes.

Cheteshwar quickly told the gentleman in question of the straits we were in and appealed for help.

'Fine,' said the man on the other end. 'Give me a few minutes. I'll get back to you.'

A few minutes later, the phone rang. 'Get a swab done at any hospital here in Rajkot and go to the Jamnagar civil hospital. It's the only place near Rajkot which is carrying out Covid tests. The hospital has already been informed about your case and somebody will be waiting for you.'

Cheteshwar was still thanking our benefactor profusely for his prompt assistance, when I swung into action and called up my brother. He was playing box cricket at the time.

'Leave home quietly and come to Gokul hospital at once,' I instructed. 'I'll tell you all the details when we meet.'

Cheteshwar and I headed to Gokul. Our biggest concern at that time was keeping the whole thing from the media. Covid-testing was nascent at this time and if the press got wind of tonight's events, it would have a field day.

Jeet caught up with us at the hospital.

'We're getting Cheteshwar tested for Covid. We have to take the swab from here and go to the civil hospital in Jamnagar,' I told my brother rapidly. 'And all this has to be done before the start of play. Otherwise, he'll have to withdraw from the match.'

While we waited for Cheteshwar to take the swab, we overheard some doctors joking about Covid. '*Cheen ma ghana lokana mota thaya che*' [so many people have died in China], they jested in Gujarati.

My brother and I were outraged.

'How can they be so insensitive!' I thought indignantly.

I kept my mouth shut, not wanting to create a scene. Once the swab was taken, a weary-looking individual at Gokul handed us Cheteshwar's swab in a thermocol box.

'The thermocol box will help to maintain the swab at the right temperature,' he explained.

It was 11.30 p.m.

I clutched on to the said box as if it contained priceless diamonds and thanked the man for his help. I hurriedly left the medic to catch up with my husband and brother who were already on their way out. Cheteshwar, as had been decided earlier, drove back home in our car to get some much-needed rest, while Jeet and I took off for Jamnagar.

We reached the Jamnagar Civil Hospital at around 1.30 a.m. It had been a long day and it promised to be an even longer night. I quickly rang the contact number I had been furnished with for further directions and was told to head to the third building on the right. We drove through a longish driveway noticing that the hospital was situated in an enormous campus with large rustic-looking buildings. Jeet parked the car and we walked towards our destination. It was dark, quiet and lonely. There were hardly any cars around.

We entered a long high-ceilinged hallway that had definitely seen better days, and after asking around for more directions, we entered a tiny room with a door made of wood and some old wooden furniture that looked the worse for wear. There were a few resident doctors munching chips and biscuits with cups of tea. But they immediately abandoned their nocturnal feast to attend to us.

I apprized them of the purpose of our visit.

They nodded and fished out a form and a pen.

'Name of the patient?' one of them asked, with his pen poised over the form.

'No name', I replied firmly.

They stared at me in surprise. It was obvious that they were wondering, 'what's wrong with this woman!'

'You talk to your superior, I've already had a word with him,' I said defensively, feeling a little foolish, but still determined to protect Cheteshwar's identity. By now, I was feeling very tense and every bone in my body was aching with fatigue.

'But we have to put some name,' objected the resident doctor, his pen still hovering over the form.

'You can write my name,' I conceded, surrendering to the justice of his comment, after a short pause. 'It's Puja.'

He waited for me to elaborate for a moment, but when he realized there was no further information forthcoming, he conceded and rapidly filled up the rest of the form.

I handed him the thermocol box and asked one last question. 'How long will it take for the results to come?'

'Four hours,' said the young doctor. 'Don't worry. You'll get a call.'

'Thanks,' I said courteously, extremely glad that the formalities were complete. But we still had a four-hour wait and it would be a long and worrisome one for me.

'I'm hungry!' I announced, once Jeet and I were back in the car.

'This is Jamnagar. Only gathiya and chai will be available at this time,' Jeet warned, knowing I was not particularly fond of the former, a popular Gujarati deep-fried snack made of gram flour, which Cheteshwar liked.

'I don't care, let's just eat something. If we don't like the gathiya, we'll just have some biscuits and chai. But I need to eat something. I've not had dinner or anything. Moreover, I want to keep my mind off the test.'

Eyeing me sympathetically, Jeet pressed his foot on the accelerator. He drove slowly as we kept our eyes peeled for some eating joint that was still open. Some two kilometres away from the hospital at a crossroads on the outskirts of Jamnagar, we finally spotted two-three dhabas on the right side of the road that were open; they were all selling gathiya and chai just as Jeet had earlier predicted. I was too starved to care. Jeet picked up the said fare and placed it on the boot of the car. I wolfed down the usually unwelcome snack with a piping hot glass of tea, as if it were haut cuisine.

We resumed our journey once our stomachs had been appeased, and were just about to reach Rajkot when I got a text from Cheteshwar. 'Where have you reached? All okay?'

He was obviously still awake. I eyed his text in exasperation.

I had already tried to assuage his fears earlier, on the way to Jamnagar. At that time, I had said, 'From the way you're describing your symptoms, it's probably nothing. You have a match tomorrow, so please go to sleep.'

I called him up.

'Why are you awake?' I asked sternly.

'I just woke up,' he replied defensively.

But to me it was quite clear that he had not slept. I had intended to sleep over at my parents' place that night, because Aditi was there, but since Cheteshwar sounded so worried, I changed my mind.

'I'll be there in ten minutes,' I promised. 'We're quite close to the house.'

'Change of plans,' I told my brother. 'Drop me home. It's better if I go and check how Cheteshwar is doing.

I reached home at around 3.30 a.m. and Cheteshwar was still wide awake.

'You'd better sleep in Aditi's room,' he advised.

'Not required. I'll just pull a mattress and sleep on the floor,' I said with a yawn.

Once I had arranged my makeshift bed, Cheteshwar and I spent the next twenty minutes talking. I must have slept for another twenty when I got a call from the civil hospital. Both Cheteshwar and I woke up instantly.

Cheteshwar looked at me questioningly as I hung up.

'Well, what's the result,' he asked, although the answer was written on my face.

'It's Covid-negative!' I beamed, as I quickly texted the good news to Jeet before going back to sleep.

Cheteshwar slept for about three hours and then rose to get ready for the day's play. He was sleep-deprived, had a runny nose and was still feeling weak. I had barely slept either, but I was anxious to inform my father-in-law that Cheteshwar had tested Covid-negative.

My husband left for the stadium and I sallied forth to my parents' house to fetch Aditi. Later, that day, I packed some home-cooked food and lemonade for Cheteshwar to help him battle his dizziness. Only five people had been aware of the previous day's events.

Cheteshwar fought hard for his half century that day, facing 266 balls to score sixty-six runs on a slowish track. He had walked to the crease when the team was four down on day one and had retired hurt after a dizzy spell. He returned to bat on day two after five wickets had fallen. By this time, I felt the worst was over and I was prepared to enjoy the match as Saurashtra was in a decent position.

The following day, on 11 March 2019, there was a public notice from the city corporation declaring that the match would not be open to the general public. Cheteshwar was feeling slightly better, and Bengal was batting. Just as I was beginning to relax, I got a call from Cheteshwar before the start of play, asking me to come to Dr Nirbhay Shah's clinic.

'What's wrong?' I asked, a frisson of fear darting through me.

'Back spasm,' said Cheteshwar shortly. 'Just come.'

I rushed to the clinic only to discover that Cheteshwar was in acute agony. Dr Shah sent him for an MRI to get to the bottom of the problem, especially since my husband had been complaining of mild niggles of late. I waited anxiously for the scan to get over. But it took a lot longer than usual because he was in excruciating pain.

Over the next three days, it would take three people to help Cheteshwar out of bed. It would take almost ten minutes to get him to recline from a standing position. During this period, sitting up was an impossibility. He watched the entire match from the dressing room, standing, as he was in no condition to field.

The scan results were depressing. Cheteshwar had strained his L-4 and L-5 discs which were causing compression to his back. He would need at least two months to recover! The only respite was that it did not look like he would have to bat for Saurashtra again. The wicket had slowed down considerably as the game progressed and the match seemed to be crawling towards a draw.

It was a frustrating time for Cheteshwar, reduced to watching the game from the sidelines, segregated from the team strategy even as he ached to be part of it. Bengal inched close to the first innings total—if no wickets fell, the team that had a lead would win the match—I cringed at the thought.

By this time, Cheteshwar was sending frenetic messages to the field: 'Try this, try that'. On the morning of 13 March, Saurashtra captain, Jaydev Unadkat, who had bowled exceptionally well that season, managed to get the three crucial wickets which would eventually lead the team to its maiden Ranji Trophy title; the margin was just forty runs. Saurashtra came in to bat and it still had to go through one-and-a-half sessions before it could be declared the Ranji champion.

Families of players, we were granted permission to go to the stadium. I took Aditi with me to watch the tail end of the match. We cheered the team until we were hoarse. Aditi, too little to understand what the moment meant to her father when Saurashtra lifted the trophy, napped in my arms. The last five days had been like a roller-coaster ride with sharp highs and steep lows. Cricketers play matches and win them; their families live through the emotional graphs with them!

Covid turned everyone's life upside-down and the transformation it wrought was long-lasting. Some of the changes were immediate and short-lived, others were gradual and more permanent. India initially declared a twenty-one–day nationwide lockdown on 24 March but later extended it to about fifty-five days. There were not many cases in Rajkot and the outbreaks that occurred were limited largely to one particular area. By the time the lockdown lifted, our lives were no longer the same.

Tasks, once impossible to carry out from home, were done with unbelievable ease. The health of our loved ones became the single-most important issue in our lives and all our plans revolved around it as we sought to adapt to the new reality along with much of the world. We realized how little we needed to stay happy and healthy. The days when we had hustled for endorsements and the like now seemed senseless and unnecessary. Shorn off its glitz–glamour, the very simplicity of our existence became a thing of joy.

Covid meant so many different things to different people. For Cheteshwar, at least initially, it was a blessing in disguise. Wracked by a bad back, for the first time in his life, he could rest and recuperate peacefully without worrying about the matches he would be missing.

'It's almost as if nature has decided to let me know that I deserve this rest,' he observed wryly.

In the beginning, we all thought that the pandemic was going to be a two-to-three-month affair. It was only later that doctors would announce that Covid was here to stay. We took things as they came and Cheteshwar took to the lockdown like a duck to water because the days that followed were closely aligned to his ideal life, which roughly translated to lots of privacy, no socializing and plenty of cleaning.

For the first time, there was no staff and all the household chores fell on us. A borderline germophobe, Cheteshwar enjoyed doing his own cleaning. He felt the house was so much cleaner when he was in charge of the cleansing process. His fixation to keep a spotless home seemed to inspire our daughter and Aditi decided she wanted to give a hand to her dad to keep the place sparkling. I had taken over the cooking and watched their labours from the sidelines with affectionate amusement and a deep sense of gratitude that we were getting so much time together, for a change.

'We will make it through this marriage when there is boredom and not much happening in our lives,' I jested wryly, after we had lived together like every other normal couple, a few weeks into the lockdown.

'Yeah, I think we'll make it when I retire,' he retorted jocularly.

I smiled. I am the one who tends to overthink situations, Cheteshwar always knows what he wants and lives in an enviable state of certainty. He never entertains the notion that we will not be together or that we will not be living in a state of bliss at any phase of our lives.

One evening, just as we were about to shut the doors of our house, a bat flew in. Creeped out, Cheteshwar ran up with Aditi to our room. I had darted up with them, amazed to see my big, brawny husband frightened out of his wits.

'I think you should go down and switch on the light so that the bat can find its way out,' he coaxed. 'You take care of the bat and I'll stay with Aditi and make sure she doesn't get scared.'

I hid a smile and gave him an old-fashioned look. Aditi's dad was far more scared than Aditi was at the moment! But I refrained from commenting aloud, as I descended down the stairs to switch off the lights, marvelling that my grown-up husband was not a big fan of the darkness and would do everything he could to avoid getting something from the kitchen at night, unless the circumstances were extremely dire!

It was at around this time that Cheteshwar and Aditi bonded together. She had just turned two, and loved to play. The father–daughter duo spent a lot of time inventing childish games and sometimes he would regale her with tales about lord Hanuman, which she would listen to with rapt attention. She had started talking and expressing herself quite clearly at this stage.

Slowly, after a month had passed by, Cheteshwar and his father decided it was time to head to the nets to practice on the bowling machine at the academy. The lockdown was still in place but by then, we had acquired a car pass. Aditi and I would tag along to get some fresh air. I would do my bit and fetch the ball while my daughter would run merrily round the grounds.

Slowly, things started to reopen but there was still no update on when cricket matches would resume. By late August, when his teammates left for the IPL, he started getting somewhat restless. It was the longest he had ever gone without playing cricket.

One evening, just before bedtime, I broached a sensitive topic and suggested that he should consider doing commentary or coaching after retirement.

'I'm a hundred percent sure I'm not going to do it,' he enunciated, rebuffing the idea outright.

The inevitable argument ensued.

'You should at least consider giving it a try instead of rejecting it. If you don't like it after you've tried it, you can always give it up. It would be a pity if you fail to build on a career to which you've devoted so much time and energy.'

'I want to do business, after I retire,' he declared obstinately.

'You don't have any experience in business,' I pointed out.

We argued for an hour, but Cheteshwar did not cede ground (he generally never does) and I finally dropped the subject, realizing that I had picked the wrong moment. My husband usually reacts negatively when he is not well-rested or if he is in physical pain or if he is taking longer to recover than he anticipated.

'Okay, we'll talk about it later,' I said resignedly.

There was another change that Covid effected in Cheteshwar. He started taking an interest in finance and investments. Earlier, he had an interest, but no time, but now that he had plenty of it, he started following market movements. Heartened by his interest, I encouraged him.

~

After a seven-month hiatus with no cricket whatsoever, we finally travelled to Dubai to quarantine for the Border-Gavaskar Trophy 2020-21. We quarantined there for a week at the Al Habtoor Palace, an opulent Hilton-owned property situated next to the Dubai water canal. A bio-bubble, originally known by the less attractive nomenclature 'germ-bubble', had been created to facilitate the movement of players within its premises, but it was still very much a gilded cage.

Cheteshwar was indifferent to the luxurious surroundings as his adrenaline levels, though sky-high, were devoted exclusively to the prospect of playing cricket again. Although, initially, the players had to stick to their rooms where they been provided with training equipment, after five days of incarceration, they were finally allowed to go to the nets.

The Dubai heat did not deter Cheteshwar; he was that delighted to be practicing with his teammates. But the times were still uncertain and it was not yet clear whether players' families would be allowed to accompany them. At this point, Australia was still Covid-free and had firmly shut its borders.

After the team concluded its requisite week-long quarantine in Dubai, it was permitted to fly to Australia en famille. But I discovered that quarantine rules were even stricter Down Under. Players were allowed go out for practice after two negative Covid tests, but their families were expected to stay confined to their rooms. Meals were placed outside their doors and the occupants inside had to wait for thirty seconds after the customary knock before opening them. Guards were stationed outside, and all outward movements discouraged. Individuals found lurking outside their chambers were summarily escorted back to them.

The pandemic not only ravaged human health around the globe, it also messed up the game of cricket. A lot of batsmen struggled post-Covid. It was a time when matches became low-scoring and hardly any centuries were hit. Cheteshwar spoke at length about the phenomenon, explaining how each time players tried to get back their rhythm, quarantines would wreak havoc on their practice sessions forcing them to start slowly to avoid risking injuries. By the time they got used to the conditions, the series would already be halfway through, placing immense pressure on cricketers who had failed to perform.

CHAPTER TWENTY-ONE

The Ultimate Test Series

It was early December 2020. Covid times. The Border–Gavaskar series was still a couple of weeks away. Words like masking, social distancing and superspreader had already entered the English lexicon. We were parked at a hotel in Sydney, Down Under, languishing in quarantine and ennui like all cricket players and their families, when Aditi and I ran into the Australian coach, Justin Langer, at the hotel elevator.

He recognized us almost immediately and once he had placed us as members of Cheteshwar Pujara's family, he grinned. 'We won't let him trouble us this time.'

It seemed like a promise and a warning.

A week later there was another portent. I was leaving for India the next day. We were seated at the breakfast table when Cheteshwar accidentally dropped his fork. As he bent down to pick it, his back went into spasm. He tried to move from the chair; no dice; the pain was just too excruciating.

By the time we made it to the room, he was in agony.

'I think it's the same problem I had earlier this year during the Ranji finals,' he groaned.

I held my peace knowing that I would be offering no value addition with any comment I made. Besides, speculating on the nature of his injury was plain stupid. In the meanwhile, Cheteshwar called Nitin Patel, the physio.

'Skip the second practice game,' he advised. 'You need to rest that back.'

I was perturbed. My sister was just about to get married. I was leaving for India the next day. How would Cheteshwar cope on his own with a bad back?

Cheteshwar and I exchanged helpless glances. We were stuck between a rock and a hard place. I had to get back to India to help with Dhara's wedding arrangements and he had to stick around for the series.

Before I left, even though I knew he wouldn't like it, I gave him a bit of advice. Langer's words were niggling in my head. In the previous tour, Cheteshwar had been Man of the Series and India had bagged its first ever series win in Australia—there was no way the Aussies were going to give him a free run this time around.

'Australia may not allow you to score so freely in the coming matches or let you make the kind of runs you did in 2018. Just hang in there, survive and tire them out,' I counselled.

As if it's so easy! He didn't say it. But it was obvious that that's what he thought.

As I was leaving that day, I just got a nod from him and not a nasty stare. He hates it when I pick up stuff from the media and quote it to him. He loathes it even more when I convey his father's cricketing advice. He believes I should just enjoy the game and leave the analysis to him. Given that I have never even played cricket for fun and do not really understand its technicalities, I can't really blame him. Communicating everything that I hear does not help. It plays in his head and he needs zero thoughts when he heads into a series.

Cheteshwar normally avoids social media like the plague when he's on tour. Good days, bad days, worst days—the I-will-shun-social media rule applies even to his own handle. Monitoring it is left to a team that has access and only important items filter to him in a closed-group messaging site to which only a select few are admitted. It is here that he reads whatever is deemed fit for his eyes, it is only here that any exchange of communication takes place. This strategy has been devised to garrison all the superfluous noise on the outside, so that he can focus on his game.

Then came the series—one of the most exciting in test history—starting with the historic collapse of the Indian team that had everyone writing it off, followed by a startling comeback, a nail-biting draw to an unexpected series win at Fortress Gabba! A poll run by the International Cricket Council 'crowned' the 2021 Border–Gavaskar Trophy as the 'Ultimate Test Series'.

Also adding to the general ferment off the field was the steady exodus of several top Indian players, thanks to a string of injuries. It had begun even before the opening ball of the series had been bowled when India lost its veteran pacer Ishant Sharma and opening batsman Rohit Sharma to injury. Virat Kohli had already signalled that he would not be available for the last three tests as his wife and he were expecting the birth of their first child. By the end of the series, the Indians would be playing without key players like Ravichandran Ashwin, Ravindra Jadeja, Hanuma Vihari, Mohammed Shami, Jasprit Bumrah and Umesh Yadav. This facilitated the entry of the young brigade.

The series began at Adelaide with a day-and-night match. Captained by Virat, India won the toss and elected to bat, putting up a fairly respectable score of 244 runs in the first innings. In reply, Australia was bowled out for 151, giving India a fifty-three–run lead. The game was evenly poised and nobody anticipated what would happen next: the India team fell like a house of cards with just thirty-six runs on the scoreboard. It was the lowest completed innings for India in test history and the lowest test total posted by any team in the twenty-first century; no Indian player reached double-digits in the match.

The first players to exit the playing eleven were Virat Kohli and Mohammed Shami. Shami was ruled out of the coming matches because he had fractured his forearm, courtesy a short ball from Pat Cummins.

After the defeat at Adelaide, Cheteshwar certainly needed to keep the noise out for the upcoming match at Melbourne.

It began on Boxing Day, Ajinkya Rahane was captaining the side. Derided, written-off, very much the underdogs, the Indians went into the match pushing the memories of the motherless rout at Adelaide where it belonged—in the past. Two feisty youngsters—Shubham Gill and Mohammed Siraj—made their debuts. Australia won the toss and chose to bat.

The Aussies were skittled out for 195 and the Indian team ended up with a lead of 131. In the second innings, the Indians bowled out the Aussies for 200 and had a target of seventy runs to win, which they achieved easily with eight wickets in hand.

It was a stunning comeback.

India had levelled the series to one win apiece to each team—but it came with a cost. Umesh Yadav was out of the series, courtesy a calf injury. India was now without three of its frontline bowlers.

After their triumph at Melbourne, the psyche of the Indian team underwent a sea change. It triggered a hunger for victory and there was a collective desire to push for a series win.

Parallelly, back home, hectic preparations were underway for my sister's wedding. We had just found out that Cheteshwar would be allowed to come home for four days after the series. It was to be a short break before the home series against England started. Having an international cricketer in the family comes with its own baggage. Dates for important family functions have to be decided keeping India's cricketing itinerary in mind!

In the meanwhile, the India–Australia time difference was playing havoc with my schedule. My days would start at 4 a.m. so that I could catch the live test telecast from Australia. I would then go for a thirty-minute run in the morning, followed by more cricket and then a marathon stint of wedding preparations at the end of the day's play. It was an exhausting time.

By the end of December, Covid had spread in Australia. At the start of 2021, the teams travelled to Sydney, only to learn that they would be living in a bio-bubble.

Just after the match at Melbourne, Cheteshwar injured his index finger during a net session. He later told me that the skin near the nail had come off and his finger had bled a lot. Assuming it would be 'manageable' before the Sydney test, given that there was gap of a few days between matches, he consciously decided not to get any scans.

'If it's broken, I don't want to know,' he told me over the phone. His reasoning? The Sydney test was very important and there were already a couple of forced changes in team because of injuries among players.

The third match at Sydney was vital. The series could still go either way. It was a tense, thrilling squeaker that went down right to the wire. The Australians amassed 338 runs all out in the first innings. India in response fell short with just 244 runs. The hosts piled up the agony by posting a mammoth 407 runs for India to win and almost four sessions to survive.

India was at ninety-eight for two when it went into day five. All four results were still possible at that point—Australia could win, India could win, there could be a tie or a draw. Rahane's early dismissal by Nathan Lyon put paid to the chances of an Indian victory and Australia looked very much on top the game. However, a rapid-fire ninety-seven from Rishabh Pant and a more circumspect seventy-seven from Cheteshwar made while he took a volley of body blows turned the situation around. Could India win? The game see-sawed yet again when both their wickets fell before the final session. An Australian triumph seemed inevitable.

Jadeja, then nursing a broken thumb and padded-up, looked on from the balcony as Hanuma Vihari with a pulled hamstring and Ashwin, nursing a bad back occupied the crease. Nobody expected them to last. The Australians were just a wicket away from exposing the Indian tail, when the unthinkable happened. The two managed to stick around for forty-two overs, consuming 289 deliveries and forcing a heart-in-mouth draw! It was a draw that was celebrated by India like a victory. It had been culled in unimaginably difficult circumstances. India still had a chance.

Yet, the fate of the series was still uncertain. The fourth and final match would take place in Gabba, better known in cricketing circles as the Gabbattoir or Fortress Gabba where Australia had not lost a match in thirty-two years! It was an all-hands-on-the-deck kind of situation.

There was more bad news in the Indian camp. Their dogged fight in Sydney had come with a high price. India had lost six more players. Ravindra Jadeja, Jasprit Bumrah, KL Rahul, Ravichandran Ashwin and Hanuma Vihari were ruled out for the final test.

India would now have only two of its original eleven players who had played at the opening match and would be fielding a bowling line up that had the combined experience of four tests and thirteen wickets before this match. Net bowlers who had never expected to be in the playing eleven were now part of the team.

The match in Gabba did not begin on a happy note for India. Australia won the toss (a crucial element) and elected to bat. Australia batted the entire day and made 369 runs. The Indian innings seemed to totter when it was reduced to 186 for six till a strong lower order partnership brought India to 334. The difference was not much but Australia still had a lead and the psychological advantage. It set India a target of 328 runs to win on the final day.

18 January arrived, bringing with it a spell of rain. I spent hours frantically scanning meteorological sites and discussing the weather reports with anyone who was willing to lend me an ear. On the

eighteenth evening, rain stopped play after India had batted two overs. It seemed likely that it would rain on nineteenth as well but to my surprise, the sun was out.

On the morning of the last day of the four-match series there was still no clarity which way the match would go or who would take the trophy home. India had to bat the whole day to win or draw the match. That morning, TV broadcasts showed that the cracks on the pitch had widened and the ball would probably drift a lot, a bad omen of how the ball was likely to behave.

The first wicket fell early. Cheteshwar joined Shubman Gill. They built a solid partnership. Shubman had been playing positively right from the start. Cheteshwar was, meanwhile, trying to anchor the innings.

At some point, the opposition felt, Cheteshwar was looking to defend and was not take any chances to score runs. To provoke him into making a mistake, they started bowling bouncers and short balls. When he was batting at six off sixty balls, an Aussie commentator stated: Pujara looks to be in the zone. The Aussie bowlers should try and rough Pujara up. They should try and rip the helmet off by bowling short stuff!

The things that happened on the field that day were horrifying and the emotions that we as a family underwent cannot be described in words. I was, however, not surprised at this line of thought amongst the Aussies. Cheteshwar, the press had reported at the time, had been the difference between victory and defeat in 2018 and they would do anything to change things this time around.

I knew from the first blow that he took on his body that he was there to stand and fight, no matter what was thrown at him. Such was his body language, his aura that day. He would later state: 'You can punch me as long as you can. Then I'll punch back.'

I thought of the 1932–1933 Ashes (Bodyline) series all those years ago that had created such a storm that it had not only threatened the tour itself but also political relations between Australia and the United Kingdom. I took heart from the fact that Bodyline had been outlawed the following year and repeatedly told myself: 'I hope it will all be worth it at the end of the day.'

In a state of high tension, I invoked god's name, incessantly asking the almighty to give Cheteshwar the courage to bear the pain. I also prayed and prayed that he would not sustain any major injury, while trying to win the game. He took thirteen visible body blows that day.

Even our two-year-old could sense her father's pain and our tension. We watched on, cringing at every blow and yet proud at how far he was willing to go to win the match and the series for India.

At 3.20 p.m. Brisbane local time, Cheteshwar was hit so badly on the finger he had injured earlier that he threw his bat. At 4.20 p.m. local time, his logistics manager finally replied to the multiple messages I had sent seeking an update on his injury. 'He was hit on the same finger at the same place as Melbourne a few days back,' I was informed.

Later I would discover the extent of the injuries he sustained that day. The first injury occurred just below his shoulder. The second was on the ribs, and he took another blow below the shoulder again, and 'that's when the pain became really bad,' Cheteshwar later told me.

The blows on the helmet were scary but they were not actually that bad. The most painful hit he bore was on his already injured finger when the ball collided with the exact site of his previous injury. Cheteshwar was in so much pain that he could no longer hold the bat with five digits. He took recourse to closing four fingers round it, keeping his index finger away from the handle.

But why had he endured so many body blows?

Because he did not want to get caught at leg gully. The Australians had placed a player at leg slip and Cheteshwar was reluctant to take his hands away from his body in case the ball hit his gloves and ballooned over to him.

Shortly after lunch, Hazlewood delivered a ball that did not rise much. It hit Cheteshwar above his left elbow. He walked away from the crease, grimacing. His strategy was the same. He was very confident that as long as the ball was hitting his body, he was fine. But this particular hit had been more painful than the others, so he called for Nitin Patel, the physio. He needed a break to cope with the pain.

When his index finger took the second blow, Nitin came again.

'I think I've broken my finger,' he told the physio during the drinks break.

'You'll be able to bear the pain. You've done it in the past,' said Nitin encouragingly. 'Do you want a painkiller for it? Or a strap?'

'No painkiller,' said Cheteshwar. 'It makes me woozy.'

Cheteshwar, by now, had had enough time to figure out how he wished to tackle the injury. He decided to bear the pain. 'I knew it was an important time in the game, so there was no way I could back out. Even if it was a fracture, I didn't want to get bothered about it or think about it. I just wanted to carry on batting,' he would tell me later.

He had played with a fracture against Australia in the past as well during the home series in 2012-13, in Delhi. In Brisbane, he was not yet sure if it was a fracture or not, and at that stage he just did not want to know.

The second new ball was taken, and Pat Cummins was bowling to Cheteshwar when Bruce Oxenford gave him out LBW. It could have gone either way, but he had raised his finger and Cheteshwar had to depart after a valiant fifty-seven.

I remember shivering and sweating simultaneously. India needed another ninety odd runs with six wickets to win the match or bat twenty overs to push for a draw. Rishabh Pant played an unbelievable innings and India won the match creating history.

After the match, when I figured out that Cheteshwar would be back at the hotel, I spoke to him. He was just about to leave for the team celebrations. Aditi, jumping up and down in excitement, innocently assured her father that she would kiss his wounds and chase the pain away. Usually his words, his job when she hurt herself.

Later that evening in India, when it was well past midnight in Australia, I messaged him in the off chance that he was still awake.

He quickly reverted back: 'Yes'.

'Why are you still up?' I queried.

'I haven't had time to pray, what with the get-together and packing to travel back to India tomorrow, that's why I'm late. I'll message you back after I've finished my prayers.

I couldn't believe it! Despite all the body blows, the adulation and accolades that had come his way in the wake of India's victory, he was still stuck on his routine. What kind of man was this? I thought of Kipling's lines to his son in 'If':

> If you can dream—and not make dreams your master;
> If you can think—and not make thoughts your aim;
> If you can meet with Triumph and Disaster
> And treat those two impostors just the same

Kipling might have written them for Cheteshwar, I thought dazedly. When the world celebrated, he was calm; when it was moved to excitement, he was still. He stubbornly stayed in the present, pushing every victory to the past, unmoved, unstirred by the moment as he grouted each day with new goals, fresh horizons.

My phone rang. 'You can sleep in peace now,' he told me. I could almost see his grin. 'Because you don't have an early morning match to wake up to.'

Cheteshwar did not sleep much that night. His body was in too much discomfort. His throbbing finger and painful shoulder made every toss and turn a trial. Even in slumber. Besides, as he later confessed, 'the adrenaline rush was so strong it did not allow his body to switch off'.

He came home with a body full of bruises, bang in the middle of the family wedding, the first he attended in all these years after his own. When he reached Rajkot, Aditi kissed his injuries and scolded him for standing his ground and playing when he was hurt. '*Dadda tu kem ubho ryo, tare hotel vayu javai*' (why did you stand there and get beaten, you should have left for the hotel).

Cheteshwar did not celebrate; he did not check his social media account even after he returned. He took no notice of the media plaudits. But he seemed at peace despite his bruised and battered state. When we had his index finger examined, we discovered that he had played both the Sydney and Brisbane tests with a tear.

Of course, there is a psychological advantage in living in a state of ignorance. He often says that he dislikes adventure sports of all kinds because there is an element of risk involved—but if this is not a risk, then what is? Perhaps, in Cheteshwar's head, the normal rules don't apply when it comes to cricket. Even though his run tally in the 2020–21 series was nowhere close to his previous tour, Cheteshwar says, for him it was just as satisfying because this time it had been more about the triumph of the spirit; a victory of the mind over body.

CHAPTER TWENTY-TWO

Coping with Covid

After attending Dhara's wedding, Cheteshwar flew to Chennai to gear up for the approaching Test series against England. It was his easiest quarantine yet, and he spent all five days of it, dishing out back-to-back interviews to the media about India's recent triumphs in the Border–Gavaskar Trophy, 2020–21. When he was not engaging with the press corps, he trained hard.

The world had become a lot smarter in dealing with the pandemic in the past one year. People had become accustomed to the new normal and had gone about adjusting their lives to keep up with the rapid changes that were taking place in all walks of life around the globe. The cricketing world too had adapted itself to the exigencies of the times.

Stationary cycles, weights and other devices tailored for quarantines had now become de rigeur stock in players' rooms to ensure that their training programme did not suffer during frequent stretches of enforced isolation.

The four-match test series against England had been divided into two parts by cricketing authorities: the first couple were to be played in Chennai and the remaining two in Ahmedabad. Cheteshwar appeared at ease in the first match in Chennai and was batting fluently when the ball hit the short-leg fielder's shoulder and was caught by the fielder at mid-wicket.

It was an unpropitious moment that heralded the beginning of a long dry run-spell for Cheteshwar.

—⁓—

Aditi's third birthday was around the corner and we wanted to spend it en famille. I checked in with Aditi at the Hyatt Regency in Ahmedabad six days before the team reached so that we could merge into the bio-bubble. As far as ideas went, it was peerless, but our ensuing experience was distinctly unpleasant: both of us got stomach infection on our very first day and we spent the initial period of our self-imposed quarantine throwing up.

When we recovered, I had my hands full. Aditi was an active child and looked to me for entertainment unlimited. Fortunately, I had possessed the forethought to pack plenty of games and art and craft kits. I somehow managed to keep pace with her.

By the time Cheteshwar landed, Aditi and I were ready to scratch walls. His approaching presence spelt an eagerly awaited and highly welcome change in our thus-far monotonous stay at the hotel. We had been lodging in a different wing of the hotel earlier and I was in the process of switching rooms when the team arrived.

Our Covid reports had been delayed, so Aditi and I met Cheteshwar in his room only after he after had checked in. Since the series was still on, we adhered to the 'adjoining rooms only' rule to protect his precious sleep.

We knocked and my daughter flew exuberantly into her father's arms when he opened the door, overjoyed that the days of making do with my sole companionship were finally over.

'Dadda, I've got you some dhana dal,' she said excitedly, referring to a traditional savoury post-digestive mouth-freshener made up of the soft core of coriander seeds, which is very popular among Gujaratis.

Just as she was expressing her delight in being in her father's arms with vigorous vertical movements, both our phones started buzzing non-stop. Cheteshwar had been picked for the IPL by the Chennai Super Kings after six years in the wilderness and the announcement triggered an avalanche of congratulatory calls.

Happy days are few and after nine years together, we have learnt to be kind ourselves. I prepared for Aditi's third birthday—the reason for our presence in Ahmedabad—and Cheteshwar trained for the match. Unfortunately, both tests were low-scoring and Cheteshwar's wicket fell to left-arm spinners in each of them.

It gave my husband pause for thought. His run average against left-arm spin till this series had hovered at around seventy. This was the first time he had been dismissed in two consecutive matches by left-arm leg spinners. By the time we returned to Rajkot, he had given himself a new task. He was now determined to take corrective measures to prevent it from becoming a pattern.

Although he was part of the IPL, Cheteshwar but did not play any matches. He worked a lot on his fitness and observed the white-ball game closely. Covid cases began to surge and in response to the sudden spike, the IPL was called off after a member of the support staff and a few others tested Covid-positive.

⁓

Cheteshwar came back home and went through another obligatory period of quarantine; for the first time in our almost decade-long marriage, we lived under the same roof without meeting each other and our interactions took place over the phone!

I shifted into Aditi's room during this period and although all our private conversations were telephonic because Cheteshwar was such a big stickler for privacy, my daughter and I did hold short but noisy tête-à-têtes with him at predetermined times across different floors. Cheteshwar would appear on the balcony jutting out of our room, while my daughter and I would stand on the terrace garden on the first storey for these fleeting trysts.

―⁀⁔

The Delta wave swept across India in the months of April and May that year, with terrifying speed; it was even more lethal than its predecessor, Alpha, wiping entire families, wreaking terror wherever it went. There was not a single person in the country who could claim that they had not lost someone they knew. It was a terrible time.

An immediate fallout of the Delta wave was its impact on sports. Net practice and domestic games that had served players to prepare for matches in the past had all but evaporated in the prevailing scenario and took a toll on a number of cricketers. Forms dipped, scores plummeted and match fitness and training went for a toss.

A few days after the IPL, we had to leave for England for the World Test Championship (WTC) Final. To avoid an additional quarantine in that country, we gave the staff a five-day break and isolated rigorously before driving down to Mumbai. We had access to the home-gym and garden, but as hard-core match preparations went, it was scarcely enough.

The drive to Mumbai took us a good twelve hours. Fortunately, Aditi was a good traveller and seemed to enjoy the journey. We went armed with food and did not stop on the way. In Mumbai, we checked into the Hyatt and went through another five-day quarantine. By this time, we were heartily bored of our seemingly endless seclusion.

―⁀⁔

The team reached England after quarantining in Mumbai for fourteen days. Following a Covid-negative test result, a soft quarantine was imposed on players and their families. We were staying at the Hilton Aegeas Bowl in Southampton which was situated within the stadium itself. We were back in a bio-bubble but at least we were not incarcerated in our rooms. Even better, the team had access to the nets and gym at allotted times. But no practice games were played.

We were confined in the bio-bubble for twenty-five days. During this period, Cheteshwar fought hard to get back his rhythm. It had been a long quarantine and he was worried about his lack of practice. The WTC final was to take place in another two weeks, and the players kept practicing in the nets, aware that the New Zealand team, which they would be facing, would be going in with an advantage: it was scheduled to play two test matches against England before it played India.

―∽

India lost the WTC final badly and I saw Cheteshwar spiralling for the first time in the nine years I had been married to him. He was devastated and unreachable. Although, he never expressed his anguish in so many words, his mental agony was obvious. In the past, he would have dismissed certain unpleasant episodes that took place on the field decisively and would have never allowed them to trouble him. But now he began to brood over them. He turned increasingly insecure and started agonizing over the things that people were whispering about him behind his back.

For the first time in his life, Cheteshwar, who had always lived in the present, found it hard to remain there. He was just not himself. It was almost as if he was getting pulverized by his painful emotions. True to form, instead of letting it out, he chose to retreat inwards. I sensed a restlessness in him, coupled with desperation and despair.

The thought that he had not been able to keep to the standards he had set for himself was killing him and there was nothing I could do to pull him out of his abyss.

I stood by helplessly and watched Cheteshwar struggle with himself. I wanted to breach his fortifications, but I instinctively held back, understanding intuitively that he needed space to work things out in his head. I stayed and quietly tip-toed round his grief.

But when the bio-bubble was deemed over, I made my move. It was tactful, subtle and indirect.

'I think we should take that six-day break we had planned earlier. We already have the bookings. It would be a pity to waste them,' I said casually and held my breath, waiting for his reply.

'Okay,' he responded, dully. 'If that's what you want.'

I exhaled in relief. It was a step—a small one—perhaps a change of scene would do the trick.

The journey to Oxford would have been unnaturally quiet, but for Aditi chattering nineteen-to-a-dozen, as she treated us to a running commentary of the various sights that caught her fancy. Cheteshwar was still truculent and withdrawn. I maintained an outward serenity, pretending not to notice his elongated silences.

The three days we spent at Oxford brought no change in Cheteshwar's mood. He moped around, looking completely lost and spent most of his time inside, emerging outdoors just once to accompany Aditi and I on a pre-booked farm visit.

We spent the next three days at Centre Parcs, a resort with wooden cabins in the Woburn Forest at Bedfordshire. It was just an hour away from London and offered plenty of activities such as pottery, painting, boating and hiking.

Nature appeared to have a calming effect on him and he eased up a little. He resumed his running sessions and played a couple of games of badminton. I noted the change and relaxed slightly. I was still baffled by his moods, and kept wondering why he was so triggered by the recent events when he had never let similar instances affect him in the past. But I bided my time and refrained from intruding. I had decided to wait until he was ready to speak.

I finally managed to pierce his armour.

'What's troubling you so much? I asked.

'I really wanted to do well—especially after 2021—I had such high hopes,' he paused, gazing into the distance. 'Maybe if I'd played some matches in advance, I might have done better. Who knows? I feel bad that I couldn't contribute. It was my first chance at a world cup, and it meant so much to me. It was supposed to be my redemption, my one chance to make up for not being able to play ODIs and IPLs.' His voice drifted away into the evening air and I finally understood why he was so upset.

'I can understand that, but why are people getting to you—they never did in the past?' I probed, trying to comprehend why he was acting out of character.

He grimaced slightly.

'I'm not sure. Maybe it's because its I'm finding it difficult to digest this loss and all these nasty whispers are just adding to the pain,' Cheteshwar said wearily.

'It's not your fault Cheteshwar,' I stated, firmly. 'It takes eleven people to lose a match. You can't blame yourself for it.'

'Everyone else is,' he said wryly, referring to the media which had gone down heavily on him and another Indian player.

'Let them! We're on a break, let's try and shut out the outside noise,' I told him gently. 'Let's be in the moment and just enjoy ourselves in small ways.'

We tried, but it was easier said than done. Cheteshwar was attracting a lot of negative publicity and every time we tried to switch off, some well-wisher or the other would call up and accidentally prick the fragile hard-won serenity we were striving for reopening his unhealed wounds all over again.

After a few days, we came to a tacit understanding: we would control the things we could and ignore those we could not. On this sombre note, we returned to London. Striving to be positive, Cheteshwar spent the next six days commuting for a total of two-and-a-half hours daily to a cricket academy near Oxford, which belonged to an acquaintance.

On day seven, we headed to Durham for the training camp that had been scheduled ahead of the test series.

One afternoon, a few days later, I rang up my father-in-law, who was in Rajkot. I made it a point to call up him up daily to chat with him. It was also my way of keeping a benign eye on the state of his health.

When he failed to respond, despite repeated rings, I sensed that something was not right. I checked the cameras in the house on my phone and suffered a shock. There was no one around. I turned to Cheteshwar who was sprawled on the bed. 'When did you last speak to your dad?

'It's been two days. Why?' he queried.

'There's something wrong. There's no one in the house. I spoke to him just yesterday, everything was fine then,' I said, mystified. 'Wait, let me catch the parking camera.'

There was no staff movement visible, which was unusual because there was always a flurry of activity in the house at around six in the evening.

'Why don't you video call?' Cheteshwar advised.

'Good idea,' I said, motioning Cheteshwar to take Aditi out of the room.

He nodded and gently escorted our daughter out, as I video-called Papa. Fortunately, for my tension-levels, he took the call.

'How are you, Papa?' I asked casually.

'Everything is good,' he responded.

He did not look good.

'Why didn't you take my call? I demanded. 'Where are you?'

'I'm at home,' Papa replied, without missing a beat.

'No, you're not at home,' I contradicted. 'I've checked the cameras.'

Cheteshwar walked in, mouthing that he had left Aditi at a friend's room.

'Talk to Nirbhay Shah,' he suggested, trying to fend me off.

'What's happened? I inquired, persistently.

'Talk to Nirbhay Shah,' he repeated.

'Where are you, Papa,' I asked, beginning to panic.

'Here, talk to your father,' Papa said thrusting his phone on my father.

My father appeared on the screen.

'What's wrong, Dad?'

'You know, he was not feeling well, so a neighbour called me,' said my father. 'We're at the Harmony Hospital.'

'What are you doing there?' I asked.

'He's had a brain stroke,' my dad said carefully and as if sensing my panic, he quickly added. 'A minor one.'

'How long has he been there?' I probed.

'For the last four hours,' my father replied.

'Four hours! Get off the phone, Dad. I'm calling you on audio.'

By this time, Cheteshwar was already talking to Dr Nirbhay Shah.

I dialled my dad and asked him to tell me what had happened in detail. It turned out that a neighbour had spotted Papa walking in a wobbly fashion when he returned home, at around two o'clock in the afternoon. Worried, he called up my folks. They rushed him to Harmony where he had been diagnosed with a mild brain stroke by the attending doctor, a neurophysician called Dr Mehul Patel.

Cheteshwar spoke to Dr Patel, who confirmed that Papa had had a minor brain stroke and he had been admitted because it needed monitoring.

'I'd better take Aditi and go back,' I said worriedly. 'At least that way you can focus on your game and not worry about Papa.'

We waited for a few days before travelling back home. Cheteshwar's headspace was still very delicate and only Aditi's liveliness seemed to draw him out. I also sensed that he was tired—weary of relentlessly pursuing his goals, of constantly needing to prove himself at each phase of his career to convince selectors that he was worthy of being picked, of justifying his position in the team and defending his approach to the game, even though it had brought home so many wins on several occasions.

At one stage, I thought he would hang up his boots and quit. But he surprised me and dug in his heels, determined to work harder and play the sport he adored in a manner which may have been uncharacteristic. He had resolved to quit, but only at a time of his own choosing and he had decided that he would not go without a fight.

The series was also the beginning of the 'nervous nineties' in terms of the number of matches he had played. The road ahead looked thorny and his fight to survive meant phoenix-like, he would have to virtually rise from the ashes.

Cheteshwar approached the series with two different strategies. In the first innings, he would play the way he was known for and in the second, he would accelerate.

When I reached home, I discovered that Papa too had undergone a radical shift towards cricket. His doctors had banned him from activities that made him anxious. As cricket topped the list, especially when Cheteshwar was at the crease. He did the unthinkable.

He stopped watching cricket.

For the first time since Cheteshwar had picked up a bat as a tiny tot, their conversations stopped revolving round his game. Whenever Papa spoke to him over the phone, he would instead ask him about his well-being. It was liberating for Cheteshwar. Instead of facing his father's disappointment and incessant analysis after a bad day of cricket, he could just relax and let go.

He had finally reached a stage in his life when he was on his own, with no suggestions from his father about his game; no chastisements because he had not done well in the first two matches, no discussions that he had survived a difficult phase or even the possibility that he would be dropped from the team-this last was something Cheteshwar was unaware of as he had stopped following the news.

Despite his ignorance, he was still feeling the heat. On the eve of the third test match, a cricketing legend who played alongside him messaged Cheteshwar telling him not to think and just play his natural game. He scored ninety-one in the match and was batting overnight, although he got out the next morning.

In the fourth match, too, he played decently enough and India won the game. The series tally stood at two apiece when it was abruptly shortened after some members of the support staff in the Indian side went down with Covid. The final match of the series was deferred for the following year.

The Indian team left England for Dubai for the IPL. As part of CSK, Cheteshwar trained regularly, although he was not part of the playing eleven. He focussed on his fitness and kept up with his routine. But with plenty of time on his hands, Cheteshwar spent large parts of his day reflecting. It was at this stage that it dawned on him that eventually everything came to an end; while it was important to give the game his best, it was foolish to use his performance in the sport as a barometer for happiness. He had another flash of insight: there was life beyond cricket and he needed to cherish how far he had come from those early days at Kothi compound.

From this point on, Cheteshwar would take everything in his stride: failures and triumphs as he had always known instinctively were both flip sides of the same coin, and they were both equally instructive. The acme of success, he now understood, could never really be appreciated without hitting rock-bottom and vice versa.

CHAPTER TWENTY-THREE

The Fight for Form

Cheteshwar's life has always resembled a cardiogram—full of ups and downs. In 2021, he was hit by the 'nervous nineties' syndrome which all but skidded his career-graph to a snail's pace, heralding the onset of a three-year long, agonizing uphill climb and a century-drought that would last for 1,443 days.

It began when he played his ninety-first match against New Zealand that year. From this point on, the runs dried up and every time he looked to consolidate and cross the magic figure of ninety, he failed to convert it to a century, something that had not happened to him since his iconic innings in Bangalore in 2017—in that period, he had converted all his nineties to hundreds.

The game against the Kiwis in India was his first since the final match in England had been deferred the previous year and five matches and a series later (this last against South Africa), Cheteshwar was dropped. He had managed to cross a half-century only once in the interim and his run average had plummeted from twenty-five runs per innings against New Zealand to twenty against the South Africans. In five matches, he had totalled just 219 runs and the pressure on him was at an all-time high. When Cheteshwar returned from South Africa in mid-January 2022, it seemed he had reached the end of his career in international cricket.

In any case, he had already decided to go back to domestic cricket, his usual nostrum, when he lost form. Saurashtra was playing a couple of matches in Ahmedabad and Cheteshwar headed there. I insisted on tagging along with Aditi because our anniversary was round the corner and I saw no merit in our spending the day in separate corners. Bio-bubbles were still around, but I was willing to brave them even if it meant we would end up cutting a cake and eating dinner within the hotel.

I left Ahmedabad with Aditi on 14 February and the Ranji Trophy match between Saurashtra and Mumbai began on the seventeenth. Mumbai won the toss and opted to bat, putting up a total close to 500 runs. When Saurashtra came in to bat for its first innings, Cheteshwar got out for a duck. Coincidentally, India had announced its squad for Sri Lanka and Cheteshwar's name was missing. He had been dropped from the Indian test team and this time round, it looked like he had been dropped for good.

This was his first drop from the Indian team since 2012. He had been dropped from the playing eleven on several occasions, but never from the squad. How would he take it? I wondered anxiously.

But I needn't have worried. Time does not stay static and Cheteshwar had already faced his demons the previous year. He took the news stoically, expressing no disappointment or despondency. 'I want to score runs. I want to find my rhythm and I want to do well. The rest can go hang,' he told me over the phone.

In the second innings, he scored ninety-one runs, but a century still eluded him. The match ended in a draw.

The period that followed was one of the toughest in his life, but he soldiered on. It was not as if he was doing anything different. He was following the same routine, working just hard as always and, yet his efforts did not reflect the outcome. He responded to the situation by meditating thrice a day instead of twice.

'At least he is not dejected,' I thought thankfully, grateful that he was taking it on the chin.

He had a month off before his county stint started at Sussex. We decided to reward ourselves with a small break and travel to the Netravali Forest in Goa for three nights to unwind and relax. We had planned a trip to Ranthambore earlier, when he had returned from South Africa, but I came down with Covid and we had to cancel the trip.

One afternoon, in early March, I got a call from Dr Prashant Shah, the homeopath who had treated Cheteshwar for his clogged sinuses all those years ago. Since then, my husband had ceased to be his patient, although I had been consulting him on and off for my migraines.

'Why have you not called?' Dr Shah demanded.

He sounded worried and angry.

I was stumped. It had not occurred to me to call him because I had been busy with Aditi.

'Sir, I've been busy with my daughter,' I responded feebly.

'I found out from the newspapers that Cheteshwar has not been selected for the test team for Sri Lanka and I have been waiting for you to come to me. I know what's wrong with him,' he said in a milder tone.

'Sir, Cheteshwar is in Ahmedabad. After that we're going to Goa for a short break,' I said apologetically, hoping this fresh piece of information would not annoy him further.

It did not. In fact, he appeared to approve of it.

'Good. Go for a break and come and see me with Cheteshwar after you return,' he said, giving our plans his seal of approval.

'Sure,' I promised, meekly. 'We'll certainly come and see you once we're back.'

Goa turned out to be very relaxing. We had left Aditi behind in Rajkot so, for once, our vacation did not revolve around her. We both loved nature and revelled in our verdant surroundings. We hiked in the forest, went for swims, cycled to an orchard, visited an orchid plantation and had high tea by a lake. It was great fun and by the time our holiday came to a close, we were feeling rejuvenated.

Just before we left Goa, Cheteshwar's mama called us with some bad news.

'Guruji has lost consciousness,' said Mamaji, somberly.

'When? Where?' Cheteshwar asked.

'This morning. In the Ashram in Gora,' replied his uncle.

'I'll join you there,' Cheteshwar promised. 'We're taking the flight to Ahmedabad in any case. I'll drive down to Gora from there.'

We spent the next few minutes arranging the logistics. Cheteshwar called for two cars from Rajkot, instead of one, deeming it wise for me to return straight home to Aditi.

'I'll be back tomorrow,' Cheteshwar said, as we parted ways at Ahmedabad. I nodded as I got into the car. His journey to Gora—a small village on the banks of the Narmada river—would be swifter than mine to Rajkot as the former was just two-and-a-half hours away.

Cheteshwar came home the next day, looking grim. Guruji's health had deteriorated rapidly and he was still unconscious. We looked at each other silently, fearing to voice the unspoken dread lurking in the shadows of our minds: would Guruji recover?

The news from Gora remained the same and, in the meanwhile, my promise to Dr Shah bothered me. Unsure of Cheteshwar's reaction to a proposed trip to Dr Shah's clinic, I broached the topic cautiously.

'Yeah, let's go and see him,' he said casually, to my immense surprise.

Relieved by his unexpected reaction, I duly made an appointment.

Dr Shah's clinic was situated in the heart of the city at Limda Chowk. It was a basic-looking edifice, with a glass-door entrance, a waiting area and a reception on the right side, abutted by a tiny window that opened into Dr Shah's cabin. He used this aperture to pass on prescriptions so that medicines could be prepared on the spot. There was another cabin on the left side, which was occupied by another homeopath.

'Why haven't you come all this while?' Dr Shah asked bluntly as we entered his cabin.

We offered him a sheepish look and pleaded a busy schedule by way of alibi.

He waved, motioning us to take our seats and then turned to Cheteshwar. 'Do you know what's wrong with you? Do you know what's the actual problem you're going through?'

Cheteshwar listed out his understanding of the difficulties that beset him. 'There are the frequent quarantines, then once they are over, I find it difficult to transition into a match to find my rhythm. Sometimes I feel sore, because of lack of exercise. I feel I don't get enough fresh air because of the bio-bubbles.'

I intervened at this point, interrupting him. 'Sir, shall I say what I think?'

It was apparent that by now Cheteshwar thought we were ganging up against him, but he was familiar with Dr Shah's ways of old and knew that he had called us out of love and concern. He was old-school and authoritative, but at the same time, he was very fond of my husband and had never charged us for consultations.

'Yes, yes, go ahead,' he encouraged.

'I think it's because of his fear of injury,'

Dr Shah rose, delighted that I remembered his earlier diagnosis.

'Good, good, I'm glad you remember,' he approved delightedly. His glance then returned to Cheteshwar. 'You know, everything you're facing or feeling right now is just a by-product of your emotions. The decline in your performance is a result of the psychological burdens you are carrying not because there is a problem with your game. You suffer from anxiety of judgement and fear of failure and injury. Because you're an introvert, you find it difficult to express yourself fully and this lack of expression transfers itself to your body and makes you indecisive—and this is causing the dip in your form.'

Cheteshwar had not been under Dr Shah's care since 2014; he had not needed it. But post-Covid, the situation had changed, and it was reflecting in his game. He was once again afflicted by disturbed sleep cycles, longer recoveries from injuries and stuffy sinuses. Bio-bubble fatigue, his slump in form and his manic attempts at the nets to regain it without success had got to him.

Dr Shah's pronouncements compelled Cheteshwar to take a good hard look at himself and forced him to acknowledge the truth in them and this very acknowledgement brought about a considerable change in him. For the first time, he started playing cricket for the sheer enjoyment of the game. He drew definitive boundaries at this stage and allowed no one to intrude into his inner space to heap unwanted advice regarding the way he approached the sport.

Sadly, Dr Shah, whose prescience helped Cheteshwar come to grips with himself, passed away in 2023. It was a huge loss for both of us. He had been our mentor and friend for so long; it was hard to accept that he would no longer be around to chide and guide us in the future.

Four days after he had lost consciousness, Guruji was brought to Gondal and Cheteshwar spent the next sixteen days alternating between the nets and the ashram. On 28 March, Guruji breathed his last. Papa broke the news as I walked down the stairs that morning.

'Guruji is gone,' Papa said in his forthright manner.

My first thought was—how will Cheteshwar take it? But he was calm when he heard the news.

He nodded and asked, 'Where will the last rites be held?'

'In Gora,' informed Papa. 'They will be taking the body there tonight.'

My husband nodded absently, appearing lost in thought. 'Let's go to Gondal first' was all he said.

We went to Gora the following morning to pay our respects. The last rites were performed at the ghats of the Narmada river, which flows just behind the ashram. I stood beside Cheteshwar watching the flames curling over his pyre. It was like witnessing the passing of a pillar. He had been the single-most influential person in my husband's life, the rock he had turned to whenever he was overcome by despair or dilemma.

I stuck to Cheteshwar throughout the funeral, saying very little; it was a huge personal loss and one of those occasions when words were meaningless and superfluous. Grief is usually a solitary state.

Cheteshwar did not mourn his loss but kept reiterating that we, as his followers, should carry forward his legacy and continue his work for the underprivileged. On our way to the ashram, he had already started outlining how he would handle the donations we made.

'I want to focus on education and medical aid for the underprivileged after I retire,' he said, gazing ahead, at some place I could not reach. I heard him out quietly as he kept discussing his plans for the future.

Within a week after Guruji's death, the county season was upon us. Given the state of his career, it was a crucial event. He would go on to display his innate resilience and mental strength that summer. He was not yet ready give up his desire to play for India again. Besides, he was far from content to call it a day when his match kitty stood at ninety-five—he was determined to drag it kicking and screaming to a hundred games!

He had been written off by almost everyone at this stage and very few people realized the dedication and passion with which he continued to play the sport or that he was humble enough to hang up his boots when he felt he could no longer contribute to the team's success.

Cheteshwar had decided to play county as early as December 2021. At that time, he had no idea of the outcome of the South Africa series or how his future with the Indian team would hang on a frayed thread. But once he was dropped, unwilling to undergo a repeat of the emotional distress he had gone through the previous year, he accepted what the gods had dished out and resolved to do his best for whichever team he represented.

Due to the significant backlog in the visa office, Cheteshwar arrived in Brighton on the day of the first match of the season, which was a home game.

As he was not playing in the opening match, he had enough time to get acclimatized and prepare for the upcoming away-game against Derby which would be his first in the season; he got out cheaply in the first innings but went on to score a double ton in the second. Later that night, he travelled back to Hove to an overexcited family. We were relieved that the burden of disappointments that he had been carrying for so long had finally been shed.

The summer of 2022 had begun on a high. This was probably because at the time, Cheteshwar felt that he had nothing to lose or prove. He focused on his enjoyment of the game, leaving behind the constant search to find his rhythm, the main reason behind his failure to deliver at the international stage.

Hove was a fresh start in a lot of ways. It was a reset button after a pause. After that first match against Derby, he felt as if he had found the missing part of the jigsaw puzzle he had been grappling with for so long—his rhythm was back with a bang.

Aditi and I had arrived in England just then, and each day when he was not training or playing a match, our collective goal was simple—to bring joy to our four-year-old who had taught us how to live in the present and cherish it. Children possess the enormous felicity of being incredible teachers if one just stops to listen to them because they have not lost the art of finding joy in simplicity.

After four hard days of cricket, all the energy that Cheteshwar could summon up was building a Marble Run at Aditi's insistence lying down on the couch and collecting a BRP (Biometrics Residence Permit) card from the post office. For the first time in our marriage, we did not discuss the future, content to enjoy the present and adhere to the routine he had chalked out for himself: it was simple—get ready, eat breakfast, go to practice or to the gym, if the latter was part of the schedule for the day, order lunch, take a walk in the park, do yoga, pray, have dinner, watch a show to unwind and then sleep.

Cheteshwar has a very rigorous time-table and his intensity towards each match he plays, whether for the country or a club, remains the same.

Cheteshwar had a few away-games but Aditi and I stayed back in Brighton, a seaside town, full of beaches and parks. The school holidays had not commenced in the UK, so the parks were relatively empty. Every time Aditi said 'I'm hungry' or 'I want to go to the ground', I would carry some additional layers of clothing for her and take her to a park or a beach to enjoy our day-time meals out in the open.

Once Cheteshwar returned, he started preparing for his first home game. When the match began, I took my daughter to the park, armed with popcorn and fruits. I was just enjoying a pizza when I learnt that Cheteshwar had scored a century and was still going strong. When the congratulatory calls started pouring in, Aditi got excited 'You know Dadda has scored a century. Do you want to go and cheer for him.'

'Yeah,' I told my daughter. 'But can I finish my pizza first?'

She nodded magnanimously.

Once I'd finished my meal, I wheeled Aditi's pram towards the stadium so that we could watch him get his double ton. But by the time we had reached half-way, Aditi fell asleep and it became very cold and windy. Deeming it pointless to press ahead, I turned the pram around and headed back to the flat. The next day, Cheteshwar scored his double ton.

He was on the field for almost ten sessions during that match and he was tiring. On off days, it was difficult to get Cheteshwar to move from his spot on the couch. Every time we went out to pick groceries, he would wait in the car and rest whilst our enthusiastic child and I would shop to stock up the kitchen. He had narrowed down four to five eateries and would rotate his delivery orders from these outlets, convinced that they were helping him recover from his exhaustion. Our go-to dessert had become mango cream and strawberry cream.

'I need to fuel up on carbohydrates after all the physical exertion,' he explained defensively when he spotted the amusement on my face.

I did not comment even when he started ordering sandwiches and salad for lunch to avoid home-cooked meals.

Like most players, Cheteshwar latches on to the notion that a particular thing is bringing him comfort. This usually happens when he is in the zone and things are working for him; and having arrived there after a lot of trial and error, no power on earth can move him to change it even by an inch. It is not really rooted in superstition. It is just a strange belief that a certain kind of food or a changed approach to his sleep is a catalyst that helps him to perform better.

There were times I would make tactful attempts to wean him away from his boring meals. 'Do you want to try this new place Aditi and I went to?' I would ask, without much hope of being heeded.

'No, I'm happy where we go,' he would reply, obstinately.

'Fine,' I would mutter and back off.

When two matches remained in the first leg of the county season, I started planning our first proper vacation in years opting for a road trip to France and Netherlands, reckoning it would provide us with the flexibility we wanted.

Cheteshwar's idea of a vacation was to rest well, eat well and explore if there was time left over from these activities—the exact opposite of mine.

'What's the point of going to a place if you don't see it?' I asked reasonably.

Cheteshwar stood his ground. 'I'm really tired after two months of cricket. I want to take things really slow and easy. I don't want to do anything hectic. I know you'd like to explore, so you can carry on. I'll stay back and take care of Aditi.'

Jeet joined us for the trip and it went along the expected lines.

We had booked a service apartment in the suburbs of Paris that was situated quite close to my cousin's house. She had children who were around the same age as Aditi and I thought it would be fun for her to go to Euro Disney with them.

Cheteshwar and Jeet were too comfortable to move.

'The two of you go ahead, we'll join you later,' Cheteshwar told my cousin and me.

They fixed up to join us for lunch.

At around noon, I texted him: 'It's very crowded.'

At around one o'clock, Cheteshwar sent me a message. 'If you think it's too crowded, then let it be. In any case, it will take us one-and-a-half hours to come and you guys will be very tired by then. So, do you still want us to come?'

Irritated, I wrote: Don't come.

And he actually didn't!

When I reached home, I was fuming. 'How could you do this to me?'

He looked puzzled. 'But you were the one who said 'don't come.'

'There's something called sarcasm, okay,' I snapped.

'How am I supposed to know?' he protested. 'If you're in front of me, I can figure out you're being sarcastic from the expression on your face. How do you expect me to know when you're not there?'

I contented myself with a dirty look and swept past him into our room, while my husband and brother exchanged that bewildered look that men often get when they can't keep pace with the workings of a woman's mind.

The next day, Cheteshwar tried to make amends. 'I'll go where you want to. I'll be ready whatever time you want,' he offered, trying to cajole me out of my sullens.

'Fine, let's go to Notre Dame,' I said, willing to abandon my sense of grievance.

And that's when my daughter decided to ditch us. 'I want to play here. You continue.'

I tried to coax her. 'We're going to the Eiffel tower and Notre Dame.'

'No,' she stated intransigently. 'I'll stay here and play.'

I looked at her in disbelief! Nobody in the family seemed to want to exert themselves!

I gave up, remembering what Cheteshwar had said when we had reached Paris. 'I don't mind if I have to come back again to see this place. I don't mind even if I don't see anything!'

Prescient words! Even when we went to Amsterdam, it is safe to say that we will have to travel once again to actually explore it.

We were in a zoo in Amsterdam enjoying the antics of Thong Tai, the elephant, who was showcasing his skills with a basketball, when the message notifications in our phones started beeping continuously. The squad for the one-off match against England which had been pending from last year was out and Cheteshwar was back in the Indian team!

We had hoped for it but it had not been the fulcrum of our existence as it would have been back in 2021.

We went on a cruise in the canal that evening, when Aditi decided to throw a fit. 'I want water!' she hollered.

It was one of those rare occasions when I had forgotten to carry a bottle. I tried to convince Cheteshwar to cadge a bottle of water from one of the boats that swept by. Cheteshwar pronounced the idea as 'most improper' and Aditi's howls became louder and louder. An argument ensued, and I told my husband that he should try for a little spontaneity. I don't know what worked but, in the end, he did manage to procure a bottle of water from someone in a boat close by.

The next day, Cheteshwar caught a mild cold and it rained all day forcing us to stay indoors. It was the final day of our vacation. The next day, we went back to England and from there, we took a flight to back to India.

Cheteshwar had only a fortnight before he was slated to fly back to England. I wanted to go with him, but my daughter was about to begin her own innings in academia and I had to stay back for the epic event; Aditi's school commenced the same day Cheteshwar left for Delhi. I promised to join him later.

'I'm not part of the playing eleven,' he informed me, once he reached England.

'Let's forget it then. I'll come when you go to the counties. No point making Aditi miss school if you're not playing,' I said pragmatically.

Later, I would wish I had not been so dismissive.

Somehow, in an uncanny resemblance to his 2015 comeback during the Sri Lanka series, the gods seemed to be ranged on Cheteshwar's side.

Both the regular openers were unfit on this occasion as they had once been during the Sri Lankan Series, and this gave my husband the chance to play his ninety-fifth test match for India as an opener. India lost the match, but Cheteshwar scored a half-century in the second innings.

After the test match, Cheteshwar joined the Sussex team and was all set to start from where he had left off. He had built an amazing camaraderie with the young and talented boys at Sussex and he decided to skip the IPL and enjoy county cricket for the next few summers. Some places just feel like home and Hove was turning into one.

After a few days of practice at Hove, the team played a home game in which Cheteshwar scored sixty-six runs, setting a target of 370 for England. On 19 July, the Sussex team travelled to London and faced one of the worst heatwaves that had ever hit the city.

Cheteshwar scored a double ton at Lords and what a mighty innings it was—full of resilience and character. He scored 231 runs and faced 403 balls at a time when the temperatures had broken all summer records. But Cheteshwar was used to the heat and it had been easier for him to adjust to the rising mercury. It was a really good innings and his first century at Lords. He had finally found a place in the honours board for county centuries at a time when he was captaining Sussex in place of Tom Haines.

But the severe weather conditions did take a toll on him, leaving him so severely dehydrated and fatigued that all he could do after he reaching Hove was eat and sleep.

Aditi and I came to the UK just in time to witness the commencement of the RL50 (One Day) tournament. He exhibited a new avatar and was in the zone, as they say. The designated captain, Tom Haines, had been ruled out due to injury and Cheteshwar ended up leading the team.

Cheteshwar has been a leader at various stages in his career, and he really looked forward to working with the youngsters from Sussex, who were almost half his age. He feels that the right professional guidance during adolescence is the key to building and sustaining better careers.

In a game at Birmingham, he piled up twenty-two runs in an over to change the course of the match and went on to score a century, but he regretted the fact that he could not take the team to the finishing line and they lost the match.

We drove back from Birmingham after playing a hundred overs of enthralling cricket. He was tired out but the team was on song. For another match in Durham, he decided to travel by train instead of the team bus so that he could spend more time with us as we were leaving for India.

Unfortunately, the trains had been cancelled because of the heat wave and he had to take an uber from London to Durham for a hefty sum of 500 GBP for a four-hour ride! I was aghast, concluding that the logistical luxuries at home were peerless and nothing abroad could match them. Cheteshwar merely shrugged at my observation. For him, the game is supreme.

The Sussex team was awash with a whole new energy, and it showed in the way they had approached their white ball tournament.

Every week they delivered record breaking performances and surprised everyone by reaching the semi-finals. They lost the match but won a number of hearts across England.

It was time for my husband to come home. The summer of 2022 was over, but it had given Cheteshwar so much more than he had hoped for.

Cheteshwar came back at the end of August. Because he had been away from home for the entire summer, a week later, we went to Varanasi and then on to Chitrakoot to organize a bhandara to honour Guruji. When we returned, he did a couple of endorsements and began to prepare for the Bangladesh tests that were to begin in December.

He left for Bangladesh in the first week of December and the first match began on the fourteenth in Chattogram. He scored ninety runs in the first innings—once again, that longed-for century had evaded him. It was his ninety-seventh match and he had scored his last ton in January 2019 in Sydney against Australia. Although he scored a couple of nineties during this period, he had failed to score in triple digits for fifty-two consecutive innings in the last three years.

In the second innings, Cheteshwar finally broke the jinx and scored his fastest ever century, remaining unbeaten at 102. He hit thirteen boundaries to reach his nineteenth test hundred, which came off just 130 deliveries.

The next test took place in Dhaka. It was a low-scoring match which India won although Cheteshwar did not make a lot of runs. However, by the end of the series, he had become the eighth Indian to cross 7,000 runs.

I smiled from the sidelines.

Envoi

Winter was not yet dead and spring was yet to arrive. The month of February was at our doorstep and Cheteshwar had a new milestone coming up—his 100th test match—some thirteen years after he made his debut, in 2010, in Bengaluru.

I kept thinking about his mother. How happy she would have been—how proud—if she had been around to witness how far her son had come since those days when he had started playing cricket under the gigantic neem tree in Kothi compound! He had gained so much through the sport, but he had also lost a great deal to reach here, I thought, and struggles we had faced in-between.

When Cheteshwar started playing cricket, the Pujaras had pursued their dreams against formidable odds, chasing their aspirations with limited resources. His mother had sacrificed so much to make sure he reached where he did.

I felt a sliver of sorrow.

How I wished she could watch her son reach yet another major milestone. She had done so much for him—she had prodded him to dream, to dare, to reach out for the goal that was the sum total of their collective desire—a chance to play cricket for India. It was such a pity that she had not lived to see Cheteshwar achieve it all.

Her absence haunted me.

It was so unfair that she would not be there for the big day—when Papa, my mum, dad and siblings would all turn out in full force. Was there no way to honour her memory? I thought and thought. I was quite certain that we should do something to let her know, wherever she was, that she was still a much-loved, much-remembered member of our family. But what?

Suddenly, it struck me that if she had been alive, perhaps she would have invited her own family, the Kananis, to attend the occasion. Maybe we could invite Mamaji as a sign of love and respect to her. Mamaji had become Cheteshwar's closest confidante after his mother and Masi had passed on—surely, my husband would approve of my idea?

By this time, my parents, Uncle Nirbhay and Aunt Saloni had already declared that they would be coming to Delhi for the match. There was no reason for the Kananis to not attend, unless they had other pressing engagements.

I caught hold of Cheteshwar and told him that I had been thinking of his mother and where my thoughts had led me. 'Why don't we invite everyone—whoever can make it?'

'Do you think they'll come?' Cheteshwar asked doubtfully. 'The match will be taking place on working days.'

'Let's ask, and leave the decision to them,' I returned, reasonably.

'Okay—go ahead and ask,' he said, before adding predictably, 'But I won't be able to help you manage anything. I have to focus on my cricket.'

'Fine, don't worry,' I replied, unsurprised by his reaction. 'I'll take care of the logistics.'

The invitations were duly made. I began with Cheteshwar's Mama and his family, including his son and daughter-in-law in the invite. They accepted. I then asked my husband's chacha—once again taking care to include his entire family. He too assented.

After that I spoke to his bua. 'Will you come?' I queried.

'Of course, I will,' she averred.
I smiled.
There had been no refusals.

———

Cheteshwar's 100th test match began on 17 February 2023. It was the second match of the Border-Gavaskar trophy and took place at the Arun Jaitley Stadium in Delhi on a slightly nippy morning. The early morning mist had lifted by the time the game began, but the cricket field was dewy.

Cheteshwar's dad, who had stopped watching cricket on medical advice was among the twenty odd members of our group attending the match. He had elected to make an exception for the upcoming occasion. Papa looked overwhelmed and extremely proud, when Cheteshwar received the 100th match cap—the thirteenth Indian to achieve it. But lately, the dynamics between the two had changed—they were no longer mentor and mentee—they were finally just father and son. Not very expressive, but extremely close.

The match began. Australia won the toss and elected to bat.

Papa seemed calm. It was one worry off my shoulders. But I was jumpy as usual. Cheteshwar had worked very hard for the series, but for me, every time a new series began, it was like going back to square one—there was a lot of hope and excitement and with it, a tremendous amount of nervous energy. I was never sure how things would unfold. It was like stepping into a new adventure—not knowing whether there was disappointment and scrutiny ahead or joy and contentment.

The wicket in Delhi was a typical turner which aided the spinners. Australia was dismissed all out for 263 by evening and India had to bat for nine overs. The openers survived but the first wicket fell the next morning and Cheteshwar came in to bat.

I had my heart in my mouth.

Nathan Lyon was having a terrific spell and I desperately kept hoping that my husband would survive his onslaught. On the very third ball he faced, Nathan, who had been bowling round the stumps, appealed but the umpire ruled Cheteshwar not-out. It was not reviewed. Four balls later, Nathan appealed again, the umpire turned him down and the Aussies called for a review.

Cheteshwar was ruled LBW by the third umpire. Cheteshwar was out on a duck on the seventh ball in his 100th test match!

He looked down and started walking back, his face impassive. My husband is not given to animated reactions at the crease. Back at the stands, none of us said a word. Papa's expression was easy to read. It was an unusual such-things-happen kind of a look. He later told me, 'It was a very good ball. There was not much Chintu could have done with it.'

When I met Cheteshwar with Aditi that evening, I had sense enough to discuss everything but cricket with him. The game was still on and I deemed it prudent to keep my mouth sealed. The Indians were all out for 262 in the first innings.

The Aussies came back to bat and India bowled them out for 113 runs. In reply, on day 3, India posted 118 for 4. Cheteshwar came in at around lunch, and by teatime, it was all over.

Cheteshwar hit the winning runs against Australia and remained unbeaten at 31. I was elated. My husband was more circumspect. For him, the personal milestone was irrelevant—what counted was India's victory!

We flew back to Rajkot even before the Indian team left for Indore for the third test match of the series. India lost that match but Cheteshwar hit a crucial half century—in the second innings, becoming the fourth Indian to score 2000 runs in the Border-Gavaskar trophy, joining the august ranks of Sachin Tendulkar, V.V.S. Laxman and Rahul Dravid who had attained this landmark previously.

India won the Border-Gavaskar trophy 2-1. Both teams had qualified for World Test Championship Final and would be facing each other at the Oval in June, later that year.

Cheteshwar had bit of a break before he flew to England to represent Sussex for the county season. He had a great county season, while captaining the side. Ironically, Steve Smith who would go on to become Australia's second highest run-scorer with 121 runs in the WTC finals, also played a couple of matches for Sussex during the season.

Three weeks later, they would both face each other in the World Test Championship Final at the Oval in London. But that still lay in the future. In the meanwhile, my parents and siblings came to Sussex and Aditi and I had a great time with them.

Towards the end of May, Papa and my parents flew back to Rajkot and the Indian team arrived in England ahead of World Test Championship Final to prepare for the match. Cheteshwar started driving down to Arundel Cricket Ground, which was 45 mins away from Hove, each day to practice, till the team moved to London on 3 June.

Aditi, my siblings and I joined Cheteshwar a couple of days later.

The World Test Championship Final began on 7 June 2023 and sadly, the Indian side received a thorough drubbing. India won the toss and elected to field conceding 469 runs as well as the match. We were 269 runs all out in the first innings. The Aussies declared their second innings at 270 forcing India to chase a mammoth total of 444—an impossible task. The Indian side was summarily dismissed for 234 runs.

Cheteshwar did not have a great time with the bat. He made 14 runs in the first innings and 27 in the second. Ajinkya Rahane was top scorer at 89 and 46. It did not matter that the rest of the team also had a poor showing with the bat— once again, Cheteshwar became a convenient scapegoat and was dropped from the team!

The chief selector called him up after the match and said, 'I just wanted to let you know that we want to take a younger side for the upcoming West Indies series, so you will not be part of it. But you will be in contention later if you perform well in domestic cricket.'

Cheteshwar was calm when he recounted the conversation. I was not.

I was outraged! And overwhelmed. Upset by the latest turn of events, I found it difficult to wrap my head round the fact that Cheteshwar was once again expected to shoulder the sole blame for India's defeat.

'Oh my god! It's happening again!' I thought. 'He'll have to put up with another round of senseless vilification. I can't bear it. The last time was bad enough. This entire process of getting dropped and picked is just too much!'

Aloud I said, 'I think you're not being given your due respect, and I don't think you should put with it.'

Cheteshwar was silent, realizing that I was deeply upset.

'Why should you put yourself through so much scrutiny,' I said, my voice rising.

He was still quiet and did not say a word. And then I broached the unthinkable—retirement.

'Why don't you call it quits? It's getting too much. Why should we put ourselves through this whole process of being selected and then not being selected. What do you have to prove to anyone? Let's just retire! —'

I suddenly stopped. I had not meant to bring up his retirement; the words had tripped out, unconsidered, but now that they had been said, I could not unsay them. I acknowledged to myself that the belief that Cheteshwar was not being treated well in the cricketing world had been festering inside me for a long time. I felt his humiliation as if it were my own and I did not want him to take it on the chin. I wanted him to rebel, retaliate—anything was preferable to this humble silence.

Cheteshwar finally spoke. 'According to me, my body and mind, my reflexes are at their peak. I am at peace, whether I'm selected or not selected. I don't think one game can define anyone's form. Besides, I'm happy to play the game whenever or wherever I get the opportunity, because it is something I love.'

'But this does not just concern you, Cheteshwar,' I protested. 'You're not the only one whose going through these highs and lows. We, as your family, are equally affected by it.'

'You all don't need to worry about me. Why don't you just focus on enjoying life,' he shot back. 'In any case, my cricketing career will end at some point. I think you should start detaching yourself from it from this moment on. Don't watch matches—there's no point in letting your blood boil every time I hit a low. I enjoy the game—it's my career—and I'm not affected by it as much as you are. Worry about yourself, not me. I don't like what this game is doing to you. Act as I have already retired—that I've already left the game—because the anxiety is yours, not mine. I'm okay if I'm not selected or if it is all over, because one day—let's face it—my career, like everything else in this life, will come to an end.'

I gazed at him vulnerably. 'After seeing you serve the nation for so many years, I just wanted a happy ending—'

Cheteshwar smiled at me gently. 'We are a loving family, we get along well, we have a child who gives us so much joy. Our families love us and we love them back. What more do you need, what more do you want?'

'I suppose you're right,' I agreed, though not completely. There was merit in what he had said. He was right. We did not need validation from anyone else. He had every right to choose his own path. It was not right for me to push him into a direction that made him uncomfortable.

The outcome of this conversation was almost immediate. We switched back to our tried-and-tested mantra of the past and started focusing on the things we could control, and stopped worrying about situations we could not.

But now and then, Cheteshwar would catch a glimmer of pain in my eyes. It moved him to expostulate. 'Stop worrying about me. I'm at peace.'

I nodded mutely. There was nothing to say.

A few days later, he came up with a suggestion. 'I have an idea,' he said abruptly.

I looked at him inquiringly.

'I've been thinking of those journals that you've been writing.'

I nodded, wondering what he was about to say.

'Why don't you convert them into a memoir?'

My eyes gleamed with interest. It was a brilliant idea, but would I be able to do it?

'I'm sure you will,' he said, correctly reading my thoughts. 'You can do anything you put your mind to.'

Intrigued with the possibility, I started rifling through my journals and realized that there was a memoir in the making in those pages. If I was not mistaken, my notes amounted to about a third of what my final offering would be and all I needed to do was flesh it out.

I started writing this book and soon became immersed in it. The long hours I put in helped to shut out the outside noise. It was a cathartic process and as the memoir approached completion, I realized that it had somehow helped me to purge my soul of the dust and grime called experience. I felt cleansed and happy. I had found my own peace.

Cheteshwar continued to enjoy his cricket. We both let go of our angst and stopped worrying whether he would be selected or not. He went back to domestic cricket and continued to play the counties, playing almost non-stop from August to March with hardly any breaks. I kept scribbling religiously.

Now when I think back of those times when we had felt so lost and helpless, it no longer touches me. Cheteshwar had hit rock bottom then, but he fought back. Written-off, derided, he had faced his worst-ever existential crisis and emerged out of it to claw his way back into the game he loved. Cheteshwar rediscovered his mojo and our struggles taught us a sobering truth—failure is never permanent and success is not a constant. But our most important learning came from the Bhagavad Gita: 'Be in the present as the present is the present of the Supreme Presence.'

Notes

4. A Whirlwind Betrothal, a Game of Cricket and Media Attention

1. J.K. Rowling, *Harry Potter and the Philosopher's Stone*, Bloomsbury, 1997, p. 145.

5. In the Beginning

1. John Drew, 'The Christmas the Kolis Took to Cricket', *Daily Star*, 6 December 2021.
2. Boria Majumdar, *Lost Histories of Indian Cricket: Battles Off the Pitch*, Routledge, 2006, chapter 1, p. 4
3. G. Vishwanath, 'The Pujara Saga in Saurashtra's Folklore', *The Hindu*, Rajkot, 2 October 2012.
4. ESPN Cricinfo, 'Arvind Pujara Profile', 5 July 2017.

6. In the Maidans of Mumbai

1. Ramchandra Guha, *A Corner of a Foreign Field: The Indian History of A British Sport*, Penguin, 2002, 2014, p. 26.

2. Ibid.
3. Sir D. E. Wacha, *Shells from the Sands of Bombay*, published by Syed Abdulla Brelvi, Bombay Chronicle Press and published by K.T. Anklesaria, The Indian Newspaper Co. Ltd, 1920, p. 85
4. Prashant Kidambi, *Cricket Country: An Indian Odyssey in the Age of Empire*, Oxford University Press, 2019, p. 6.
5. Ram Chandra Guha, *A Corner of a Foreign Field: The Indian History of A British Sport*, Penguin, 2002, 2014, p. 29.
6. Ibid, pp. 30-31.

About the Author

Puja Pujara is the wife of Indian cricketer Cheteshwar Pujara. She was born in Gujarat and studied at a private school in Mount Abu. She has an MBA in retail management and has worked in marketing and customer service as a manager in a multinational company.

About the Co-author

Namita Kala graduated from Isabella Thoburn College, Lucknow, and worked as a journalist for *The Indian Express*. She currently works with *The Weekly* and *The Pioneer*, writing on a wide range of subjects, with special interest in politics, the environment and the supernatural—an odd but eclectic combination. Namita has turned to editing and translation as well, having translated *Haidakhan Baba: My Years with a Himalayan Mystic*. She has also co-authored the biography *Just Transferred*.

HarperCollins *Publishers* India

At HarperCollins India, we believe in telling the best stories and finding the widest readership for our books in every format possible. We started publishing in 1992; a great deal has changed since then, but what has remained constant is the passion with which our authors write their books, the love with which readers receive them, and the sheer joy and excitement that we as publishers feel in being a part of the publishing process.

Over the years, we've had the pleasure of publishing some of the finest writing from the subcontinent and around the world, including several award-winning titles and some of the biggest bestsellers in India's publishing history. But nothing has meant more to us than the fact that millions of people have read the books we published, and that somewhere, a book of ours might have made a difference.

As we look to the future, we go back to that one word—a word which has been a driving force for us all these years.

Read.